D0272573

Jayo

BAINTE DEN STOC

WITHDRAWN FROM DLR LIBRARIES STOCK

Jayo

MY AUTOBIOGRAPHY

Jason Sherlock

with Damian Lawlor

**SIMON &
SCHUSTER**

London · New York · Sydney · Toronto · New Delhi

A CBS COMPANY

First published in Great Britain by Simon & Schuster UK Ltd, 2017
A CBS COMPANY

Copyright © Jason Sherlock, 2017

The right of Jason Sherlock to be identified as the author
of this work has been asserted in accordance with the
Copyright, Designs and Patents Act, 1988.

1 3 5 7 9 10 8 6 4 2

Simon & Schuster UK Ltd
1st Floor
222 Gray's Inn Road
London WC1X 8HB

www.simonandschuster.co.uk
www.simonandschuster.com.au
www.simonandschuster.co.in

Simon & Schuster Australia, Sydney
Simon & Schuster India, New Delhi

The author and publishers have made all reasonable efforts to contact
copyright-holders for permission, and apologise for any omissions or errors
in the form of credits given. Corrections may be made to future printings.

A CIP catalogue record for this book
is available from the British Library

Hardback ISBN: 978-1-47116-603-7
eBook ISBN: 978-1-47116-604-4

Typeset in Bembo by M Rules
Printed and bound by CPI Group (UK) Ltd, Croydon, CR0 4YY

Simon & Schuster UK Ltd are committed to sourcing paper that is made
from wood grown in sustainable forests and support the Forest Stewardship
Council, the leading international forest certification organisation. Our
books displaying the FSC logo are printed on FSC certified paper.

For Louise, Caoimhe and Joshua

CONTENTS

FOREWORD

Jim Gavin, manager of Dublin senior footballers

'It's got to be said for the little man, give him a sniff at goal – and he is deadly.'

Jimmy Magee spoke the above words when referring to Jason and the first-half goal he scored against Cork in the 1995 All-Ireland semi-final.

Two months previously, 30,000 supporters had packed into in Páirc Tailteann in Navan to watch us play Laois in the Leinster semi-final. With fourteen minutes remaining on the clock, Jason made a darting run across the 21-yard line and I duly delivered a cross-field ball to him. Jason spun, left the Laois defender in his wake, while losing his boot, and buried the ball in the top right-hand corner of the goal.

Deadly!

It's a privilege for me to be asked to write the foreword for Jason's first book. I've known Jason for half of my life and I have sailed through the ups and downs of the sporting ocean with him. We have also enjoyed some great family occasions together.

I first came to know Jason as a nineteen-year-old. He made an instant impact and was a major factor in our All-Ireland football final success of 1995. Right up to my exit from the

Dublin team at the end of the 2002 season, I had the honour of sharing the field with Jason and the good fortune of witnessing at close range one of the most consistently dangerous forwards in the game.

Since his playing days, Jason has dedicated himself to the Gaelic Athletic Association, working as a coach to Dublin GAA development squads, along with his demanding role as coach/ selector for the Dublin senior football team. His capacity for hard work, a trait he displayed early in his playing career, has never diminished.

Over our years on the pitch together, Jason became a close friend. He was always jovial and up for a good social night out too, with or without the girls.

When it came to sport, Jason displayed an in-depth knowledge of his craft, gained from his time on the GAA or soccer fields or the basketball court.

Jason is a deep thinker and student of the game. He's a problem-solver and has a great eye for detail. He thinks outside the box and is very articulate in getting his coaching point across to players. He's free-spirited, resilient and loyal – traits that I like in coaches. Jason's contribution to the performance of the Dublin senior football team has been immense.

In Dublin GAA we are lucky to have him and I a'm personally lucky to be able to call Jason, Louise and their family my friends. I wish Jason the very best with his book and future career. Like everything else he has focused on, they will be a success.

Jim Gavin, 2017

PROLOGUE

November 2014, Dublin

It was as if a part of my heart had started to beat again.

A few weeks after Dublin had been beaten by Donegal in the 2014 All-Ireland semi-final, a text came through from Jim Gavin asking could we meet for a cup of coffee.

I replied saying that I'd have the kettle on.

After he moved on from the team and our playing days together ended, I had always kept in touch with Jim. Without fail, for the next seven years or so, on the morning of a game he would text to wish me luck, signing off with a simple message: 'Super Blues'.

When he took over as manager I would return the gesture, finishing my text with the exact same message.

By the time Jim was appointed I had started to drift away from the Dublin squad. Pat Gilroy, the former manager, had cut me from his group in 2010, telling me initially that I wasn't the type of player he was looking for. I struggled to accept that.

*

On a Saturday morning, eight days before Dublin's 2010 All-Ireland semi-final with Cork, I got a text from Pat looking for us to meet the following Monday. My mind raced with possibilities. Logically, I could only assume that he wanted to ask me back into the squad to play some role should they beat Cork and reach the final, just as Tyrone had done with Stephen O'Neill in 2008 when they recalled him to the fold for the All-Ireland final win against Kerry. That was my mindset.

But the reason for the Monday meeting couldn't have been further removed from any such thoughts. During an uncomfortable conversation, Pat mentioned that he had been due to get back to me. He said that some of the players had spoken to Caroline Currid, the sports psychologist who was helping us, about whether I would or could come back and the upshot was that some of the players didn't want me around any more.

That shook me.

A while later we met again and Pat told me that if I put on 10 kilos of muscle it might be a different conversation.

I went off and, over three months, piled on the required bulk. But still the invitation didn't arrive.

*

So over the next three years the 'family' I had always longed to be a part of, the family I had more or less lived with for a decade and a half, gradually became strangers. I did stay in touch with a few, however, the likes of Alan and Bernard Brogan – and I think Jim knew that.

When he texted, just like when Pat had made contact, my mind raced once more. Someone from the Dublin camp getting in touch – I wondered what it could mean.

Jim arrived at the Louis Fitzgerald Hotel, where I worked, and came straight to the point: 'Jason, I want you to get involved with us, mainly on the offence side of things. You'll have free rein in what you do.'

Dublin were still licking their wounds after a devastating defeat to Donegal at the end of August. They had put up what would normally have been a winning score, but their defence had leaked pretty heavily in the end. Nonetheless, there was Jim asking me to get involved in coaching the attack, an area in which the team was already functioning well. He was also taking a punt on a guy with no real coaching record and who had left Dublin football in less than happy circumstances. It was a big call for him. And in making it he earned my boundless admiration.

My heart pounded. My first thoughts were to shake the hand off the man and look to start there and then. But I paused for a moment and resisted that temptation. Self-doubt kicked in.

How could I change the perception the players had of me, especially if there were lads still there who hadn't wanted me around the place in Pat's time?

Did I really want to be around fellas if I couldn't get them to trust or confide in me?

Why would I be needed? The attack had been faring well. What would I do on the training field?

There were other questions. For starters, what experience did I have of top-level coaching?

And then there was a certain stigma. One that bled me like a leech at times. When I looked back on my career, I saw stop lights for every season I spent with Dublin. It was impossible to avoid the lingering sense of disappointment.

Fourteen years of failure. That's how I saw my career.

Yeah, there was the 1995 All-Ireland win and all the insanity that came with it, but I had long since forgotten that. The trouble for me was everyone else had kept harping on about it, kept reminiscing, when all I had wanted to do was look forward.

From 1996 until 2009 I struggled to achieve what I wanted in sport and that weight of disappointment became a real burden.

In the long run I became haunted by self-doubt. Contrary to what casual observers might have assumed, I questioned my own worth.

Was there something deeper in that? Did it come from how I looked?

Growing up in Finglas South in the 1980s and 1990s I had mostly felt the same as all the other kids, but there was no escaping that I looked different. My father was Asian and I was picked on because of that. Nowadays it's called racial abuse. Back then it was slagging.

I also lacked the traditional background of a Gaelic footballer. I came from left of field – a soccer player and captain of Irish basketball teams. In North Cork, where I spent some of my summers as a kid, they knew me as a hurler.

Against that untypical backdrop I was picked for the Dublin minors in 1994 and from there I was thrust straight into the big time. Within a year I had won an All-Ireland senior title. Success hit and it hit hard. 'Jayomania' was born. I was handed contracts and crowned the GAA's first pop star. I landed newspaper columns and a job as a TV presenter. I opened cinemas with Richard Branson and Boyzone. The *New York Times* came to town to get my life story. By day I did photo shoots with fashion models and by night I partied hard. The whole country wanted to know me. Hill 16 had a song about me. I was living the dream – or so I thought.

As the success of 1995 dimmed, and the seasons ticked by, my form dipped. So did my confidence. I started to second-guess myself, wondering if I was on the Dublin team because of who I was or how I looked and not because of how I played.

For personal vindication, I desperately needed another All-Ireland medal but that second album never came. I laboured hard for it, going through a roller coaster of emotions along the way. On that journey I saw not only how a star profile could make people love you, but also how quickly things could change, and how the whole bandwagon thing could spit you out.

When I finally knuckled back down to sport, I went from not applying myself fully to becoming obsessive in the pursuit of winning again, probably going overboard at times. As Dublin managers came and went like buses at a depot, I adapted and changed my approach, going from a goal-hungry, shoot-on-sight forward who took on his man at every opportunity to becoming a more thoughtful playmaker. No matter who the manager was I kept trying to fit in.

In a sense, being a Dublin footballer was the only identity I ever had and I didn't want to lose it.

I wrung every inch of potential from myself and in the process went from being the most recognizable sportsman in the land, a marketing man's dream, to being a media recluse.

My personality changed.

Looking back now, I can see that I craved acceptance, just to walk into a dressing room and feel part of something. I grew hungrier for success, I desperately wanted more medals and, somewhere along the way, I became obsessive, angry and intolerant.

That was the backdrop to Pat culling me and, a few years later, Jim calling me back in.

A week after that initial meeting with Jim, I chatted to him again to flesh out the invitation further. Jim spoke about what he wanted to achieve, how he wanted to achieve it and my role in the set-up. He came back to me with specific examples of where I could fit in and how I could assist with the values and culture that he was instilling. I interpreted my role as being something of a middleman. Jim was the boss, and we were there to assist the players in their performance. In between, I would have autonomy on the offensive side of our game. I had to help influence the lads while also conforming my input to Jim's blueprint. That would be my challenge.

After we spoke again I was clear on what Jim wanted from me and felt reassured by the faith he placed in me.

I thought back to my former basketball coach Joey Boylan. I remembered how much I trusted him, how I loved playing for him. Instinctively, I knew the first thing I had to do was to mirror Joey and win the trust of the players. That's what I tried to do on my first night working with them, showing that I was there for them and that I cared. And that's what I'm still trying to do three years on.

As Dublin offensive coach and now selector, I'm dealing with some of the most talented players in Ireland and they might be forgiven for merely humouring me, or turning a blind eye to my input, but it's been completely the opposite. Despite their success the players have bought into things that I've suggested as we've worked together to eke out the small margins that in elite sport are so often the difference between winning and losing.

I'm still really only at the start of my coaching career curve. I'm just so lucky to be coaching at a level where the people I'm dealing with are the very cream of the game both on and off the field.

If I'd arrived to the job with ten All-Ireland medals of my own, would I be in as good a position to help?

I'm not so sure.

The failures of my own career will forever be in my head. When you've been there and lost more than you've won, you can draw on those encounters to help others. Winning all the time can breed a false reality, but the one thing I know is that things can change very quickly. After the track I've taken I know not to look too far ahead and my perspective will always be grounded in the defeats I had myself.

The whole experience has reignited something inside me. I no longer look back on my playing days with the Dubs as utter failure. Yeah, I never got to win that second All-Ireland, but there were good times in the trying.

For years people have been asking me about my roller-coaster ride of giddy highs and devastating lows. It's only now, in my forties, that I feel qualified to talk about them.

This is my story.

1

Different Strokes

Here are two stories embedded in memories of my childhood.

One day, as I headed out to join the kids from Carrigallen Park for yet another soccer marathon in the estate, a pal started off on me, singing a song called 'Japanese Boy' at the top of his voice. When I cast my mind back the tune still grates.

The rest of the lads found it hilarious and started doing this geisha-girl dance. But I was humiliated. Devastated. I picked up a rock, flung it at the window of my pal's house and waited for the sound of smashing glass. To my disgust I only cracked the pane.

I ran into my house and sat waiting in the sitting room for the investigative process to get underway. My uncle Brian was alerted to what happened, he arrived on the scene and went to inspect the broken window. When he came back there were no questions but I knew what was coming. Brian let me have it. There I was, in my own mind the injured party, punished and embarrassed, and because I made no effort to explain why I had thrown the rock, why I had reacted like I did, I compounded my own misery.

I was slagged off for how I looked but I wrapped it up inside.

Looking back, Brian probably defended me in public before chastising me in private, but I should have spoken up and told him the full story.

Trouble was, I never told any of the family about stuff like that.

Another memory.

In general, our little cul-de-sac, not a mile from the Tolka River, was a good place to grow up and most of the young lads I knew were big into sport. I remember one summer's day in particular, when all of my energy was devoted to kicking, hitting or chasing balls, regardless of size. Soccer was the most popular kid in the class and from morning to night I think we played a hundred games of three-and-in, boys and girls. Wimbledon was on TV too, so for a break we started swinging racquets. In those days TV channels were limited and it seemed that the BBC devoted their morning schedule to show this rather unusual sport called cricket. You would always get some lad coming back from his holidays in England with a cricket set that would then be assembled on the green. I spent hundreds of days like this. We were sport-mad. We were influenced by what we saw on TV. Improvisation was our strength. We used trees as goalposts, gates as nets. The evenings would be spent playing rounders at the end of Carrigallen Park, played by every boy and girl on the road that we could round up.

We had other games too, the usuals like bulldog, world cup, squares, paths (which was called kerbs if you were born on the Southside of Dublin!) and snatch the bacon.

*

When I flip back over the pages of my childhood, these memories nicely describe two key factors of my early years: a burning obsession with sport and the perpetual pursuit of normality.

*

Overall, mine was a happy upbringing, no doubt about that. Warm in so many ways. But it wasn't totally carefree. There were the usual growing pains of youth, but some more complex issues too. It was a different upbringing, more than likely, from yours.

It made me all the things I am today, though: resilient, determined, fiery, a fighter. The early road was potholed with conflicts and challenges and it took quite some time to understand that I was seen as different. It took even longer to fathom why that was so.

I arrived on 10 January 1976 into 7 Carrigallen Park in Finglas South. Home was a cosy, three-bedroom, semi-detached house shared with my mother, Alice; her two brothers, Eddie and Brian; and their mother, Kathleen, my nanny.

Mam and Nanny shared a double bed. Eddie must have drawn the golden ticket, being the eldest, because he had an island all to himself, his own room. Meanwhile, I shared a room with Uncle Brian.

That was my reality.

Was it an average Irish childhood? I thought it was normal enough – I was reared with the same values and beliefs as most other kids – but on a fundamental level my situation was highly unusual, even unique.

Carrigallen Park was probably much like hundreds of other streets in all the other Corporation-built housing estates that ring Dublin. It was full of decent, hard-working people, mostly minding their own business, but who were easy-going, friendly and always willing to help a neighbour in need.

Finglas could be rough and tough; there's no point denying that. There were plenty of negative vibes, a few bad areas and if you wanted the rumble of thunder you never had too far to travel – that route was well signposted. Sadly, the area would eventually become linked in the minds of many with robberies, drugs and gangland murders.

But on my road we had mainly a sense of togetherness. We were a little community. In the late 1980s and early 1990s street parties were in vogue. There are some great people living on our road and Brian still lives there with his wife Vanessa and his pride and joy, his daughter, Angela. It was totally safe and sound.

Our next-door neighbours on one side were the Geraghtys: Willie and Margaret and their three boys, Pat, William and Michael. They had two sisters, Brigid and Ann. They were originally from the country, so there was a bit of a culture clash, which led to a few run-ins between Michael and myself. It was only kids' stuff – they were great people. On the other side were the Cahills: Martin and Monica, and their kids Audrey, Adrian, Stephen, Gerard and Sharon. We became instant friends; I spent as much time in their house as in my own.

I was an only child and typically that meant that if I was in the house during the day it was with my nanny, driving her mad. With bags of energy to burn when I came home after school I needed an outlet and I always found a welcome mat at the Cahills' front door and a place at their dinner table. They were never too busy to bring me in and never once made me feel I had overstayed my welcome. Their house was my first drop-in point and my home from home in life.

Paul Butler and Pato McCarthy were two other close friends. The two boys shared the same love of sport that I had and the three of us were forever kicking a ball about the place. We were kindred spirits and we loved football and anything associated with it. Pato won a Senior Championship medal with Na Fianna and went on to play twice for the Dubs. Down the road were the Lalors. Eric was a few years older than our group but he played soccer and excelled at that too.

Another uncle of mine, Martin, moved out of Carrigallen Park to Cabra, where he married Esther and they raised their two children, Andrew and Christine. Andrew is a few years younger than me and played football for St Oliver Plunkett's. I spent many Sundays with them in Cabra. But as Eddie and Brian lived in Nanny's house they were my primary male guardians.

Brian played soccer for Great Western Rovers in the Dublin amateur leagues before switching to Kinvara Boys. He played at full-back and he was hardworking. As a player he was just as honest and diligent as he is as a man. I was his number-one fan. Because he didn't drive we would spin out, wherever the game, on his racing bike. No matter if it was boiling sunshine or spilling rain, I would be perched clumsily on the crossbar as he pedalled furiously to Ballymun or Castleknock for Sunday matches. That in itself would have been a good workout for Brian, but it probably wasn't always the ideal approach to a hard game of ninety minutes. Brian and Eddie had a great *grá* for the Dubs and instilled that passion in me when I was scarcely out of the babygro. I mean this literally, as you will discover.

Nanny Kathleen was a great woman. Her husband, Laurence, had died before I came on the scene and she was left to cope on her own. Through a scheme that encouraged inner-city people to move to the suburbs, she had transferred to Finglas from Great Western Villas in Phibsborough to start a new life.

And that life included me. As my mam, Alice, worked Monday to Friday as a civil servant, Nanny became another mother figure to me. She was a steely countrywoman, originally from Errill in Laois, a Cleary before she married Laurence Sherlock and, cheeky and all as I was, she never took any nonsense from me.

The Clearys were a noted sporting family. Páidir, a cousin of mine, played hurling for Laois in the 1980s and 1990s. My second cousin Micheál Webster, a Cleary on his mother's side – she was Breda Cleary – hurled at full-forward for Tipperary in the noughties. I met Micheál at various family functions through the years and followed his career on the pitch.

Much as I loved her, Nanny was firm with me as I began to find my feet and my voice. I too had a stubborn streak and so there was a bit of conflict there as I grew up. Not having my biological father in the picture brought its own issues. I was an only child, no father around and so I considered myself an independent republic – I could do as I pleased.

Nanny in her wisdom decreed otherwise. She saw possible consequences to my youthful rashness and always tried to paint the bigger picture for me. Born in 1911, she was made of stern stuff and in many ways had seen it all: the Easter Rising, the War of Independence, the Civil War – turbulent times. People had it hard back then and her generation didn't tend to speak much about what they'd been through. The few times she did reminisce you might hear talk of the old IRA and how and where they got and hid their guns, but you wouldn't get much more out of her. 'Say nothing and keep saying it' would have been a mantra for many of her generation and Nanny stuck to those principles.

When things started to take off in my sporting career she still kept a lid on things. She was about the only one! She wasn't entirely happy as the hype exploded around me post-1995. None of my family were. It was because she was humble and never liked to talk us up. I knew she was hugely proud of me but she just didn't advertise it.

There was a real single-minded determination to Nanny and that is one trait she passed on to me. I can so clearly trace my doggedness and combativeness back to her. For instance, in late 1997 her health declined suddenly and we thought she was gone from us, but she rallied fiercely and we were blessed with her presence for many years more. She lived until she was 101 and I'm very thankful that she saw me win an All-Ireland with Dublin. She was a great lady.

Mam always worked hard. She spent forty-three years with the civil service and it's only in hindsight that I've been able to fully appreciate all she did for me. I didn't realize it at the time but she made serious sacrifices. Being a single parent must have been so tough for her – and to be living with her mother and brothers as well – but she kept things as normal as possible in the circumstances. Every Friday she would come home from work with a bag of swag that included the *Roy of the Rovers* comic and a bar of chocolate. That was always the treat.

Mam depended a fair bit on my uncles to keep me occupied with sports and that suited me just fine, because when they weren't around I might be dragged off with her shopping or to the hairdresser's or to visit her friends and have to spend half a day there. In fairness to Mam, she was only going about her chores, but for me it was mental torture.

Even going on holidays was surely tough on her. Other families were there fully formed – a mother and father and two or more kids, and all of them hopping off each other. Normality. I sometimes hankered for that feeling and I'm sure Mam did too. My holidays were either spent with Mam and one of her friends, or Nanny. During the days I would try to befriend the local kids but at night, when I'm sure Mam wanted to enjoy a bit of the social side of things, she had to watch over me and that can't have been easy.

Until she married Bill Ingle in 1991 she possibly missed out on many things because of our family dynamic. Most of my friends had their two parents at home, and as I entered my teens I copped the various downsides to Mam's, and my own, situation.

There was something else that made me feel different and excluded: beyond my own turf I often sensed the inquisitive stares of strangers. The reason was obvious enough – I had Asian lineage and looks. I didn't like standing out and I remember vehemently telling people my dad was Irish because I didn't want to be perceived as different.

Looking back now, maybe if someone had just sat me down and said, 'Jason, you're a little different because of where your father came from, but sure we're all different in our own way' – it might have saved me so much grief and turmoil. Had it been explained to me why I was slightly different from others, and why some people might remark on that or even show hostility or prejudice, I might have understood and learned earlier how to deal with it. But that is all reflective.

I can fully understand why my family didn't do that – sure they had no preparation for anything like that. There was no manual to dip into for instructions. They did their best and they didn't want to accentuate any sense of alienation.

Without even realizing it, all I wanted was to be accepted and the search for acceptance defined my childhood. Along the way, I often felt isolated, however, and I could lash out pretty quickly if I was antagonized.

I went to school at St Oliver Plunkett NS in Finglas and later St Vincent's NS in Glasnevin and, kids being kids, some were slagging me from day one. I don't consider that it was racism, most of them didn't know the meaning of the word. There was no multicultural Ireland back then and people weren't educated as to what you could and could not say. Really, you could say anything. That was pure ignorance, not racism. In fairness, many others were just interested in my story and where I came from. But to me it felt like everyone was needlessly probing. And so my defence mechanisms were always to hand. In some ways they are still in place today.

Children can be cruel – they can slag each other for being overweight or skinny or wearing glasses – and I got loads of it.

When I got a bit of it around Carrigallen Park I really struggled with that. My own patch. Sure I was one of them, wasn't I? It wasn't always nasty or aggressive but I usually reacted by fighting fire with fire. As I grew up I understood, though, that once I strayed beyond my home turf, and Finglas being an area of multiple layers, there was a much darker edge to stuff that was shouted at me.

I was fair game for all sorts and I didn't know how to process it. In my mind I was the same as them. From Carrigallen Park. A Northside Dub. Irish. I decided that the only way to deal with what was becoming a daily nuisance was to confront it head on. Subconsciously, I would crave acceptance and normality. But on the ground and school-ground battlefields the defence mechanisms would be engaged and the fists would fly at the mere sound or sign of a taunt. I found myself fighting a lot and then ended up feeling degraded and belittled in front of pals who witnessed those battles.

I just didn't know how else to deal with it. I don't remember ever going to my uncles for support, either physical or moral – I just shouldered it myself. It was a big ask for a kid in school, primary or secondary. My friends? At that age you don't really go to war over something you hardly understand.

I was on Carrigallen Drive, walking to the local shop one day, when a lad from the other side of the estate approached. A tough guy, in front of four or five friends, with a firm message: 'Fuck off back to your paddy fields!'

Naturally, cue another tussle. When I got home, Mam saw the state I was in and went to seek out the lad's parents to sort it out. Once again I didn't plead my defence, I never relayed what had been shouted at me. Firstly, I didn't know why I was getting this abuse and secondly, I didn't even realize it was abuse. Maybe if I'd known what the nature of the abuse actually meant I might have told someone.

What I do know is that I definitely started to become more and more embarrassed. At how I appeared to the others. By how I looked.

That's just the way things were. There was hardly any taboo attached to racism. You could say what you wanted and there was little or no comeback. No one would pull you up on it. No right or wrong.

I certainly was no spokesperson for trying to shift people's mindsets, much less educate them. Why would I have been? The last thing I wanted to do was draw attention to something that was proving to be a massive negative point in my life.

Indeed throughout my youth and career in sport I largely shied away from speaking about the abuse; I suspected it would only make things worse for me.

Keeping quiet about it remained my default setting for a long time, but when Lee Chin of Wexford and Aaron Cunningham of Crossmaglen Rangers were racially abused in 2012, and both highlighted what was said to them, I finally found myself at a stage in life where I was in a position to speak out. The actions of those two lads were a catalyst for me and I felt they needed my support. They had done nothing wrong and they deserved help because they had been brave enough to shine a light on their experiences. I admired them for the fact that they spoke directly in the media after games, highlighting the racial abuse they had received.

In 1995 I won an All-Ireland with Dublin and found myself with a huge national profile but even at that stellar point in my career I chose to stay silent about what I had endured, and was still enduring. Why? Because I was almost the only one out there who looked different – around Finglas, in the GAA, in sport. The last thing I wanted to do was magnify the perceived differences at the root of the problem.

Now I can see that if speaking out or sharing something like the lads did can even help one person it is a worthwhile exercise.

As a kid I was so wrapped up trying to fit in I lost track of how bloody great it can be to be different. We're all different and we should be curious as to why we are different. We all have individual stories and should celebrate that. If you look different and feel different, well then that's okay. It would be a dull existence if we all looked and acted alike.

But nah, as a youngster I couldn't get my head around that. Aaron Cunningham could probably go and bounce his problems off his father, Joey, who was also a great sportsman. In my time dealing with it I had the support structure of my family but none of us knew how to deal with it and, because of my reputation of having a very short fuse, I received very little sympathy. Nowadays, when we see temperamental children, do we take enough time to consider the reasons why?

I was loved and I was safe and sound, I wanted for little or nothing – but I looked Chinese and I didn't have my father around. Those were two biggies for a boy growing up in Dublin in the 1980s and 1990s.

It wasn't all my dad's fault that he wasn't on the scene. I didn't exactly roll out the red carpet for him. His name was Denis Leung and his family had moved to Ireland from Hong Kong in the 1970s. He and Mam were not in a relationship when I was born but in my early years I saw him from time to time, although our meetings were few and far between. I didn't get to know him. He would work out of Ireland and sometimes pay us visits when he was back in the country. The clearest memory I have of him is the time he brought me to a funfair close by.

Denis had three brothers – Martin, Peter and Robert – and two sisters – Dearbhla and Jane. His parents ran a Chinese restaurant above a jeweller's just off Grafton Street, close to the Duke bar. Mam brought me in there a few times when she could over the years and Denis's family would always try to insist we ate. To me, eating Chinese food would be accepting that I was Chinese so it was always fish and chips, much to the amusement of all. It was only years later with my wife, Louise, when I could finally bring myself to have a Chinese meal with her family, that I felt I wasn't going to be associated with being Chinese because I was eating that type of food. I'm sure Louise's gang just thought I liked bland food when we went out, but avoiding Chinese food was the real reason. That was what was in my head. And only after that could I see that the food offered by Denis's family had been a matter of hospitality and not some statement about my ethnicity.

Denis's family were always warm and welcoming. They had this Chinese tradition where they would have their own red envelopes, they would pass them around and put a fiver or a tenner in them for good luck and give them to me. That, not surprisingly, was one part of their culture I had no problem with! That nudged me to go visit them on more than one occasion! I also remember another visit when Martin Leung brought me down to a sports shop at the end of Mary Street and bought me a Liverpool kit.

In terms of my own sporting life, 1995 proved a landmark, but the year ended in tragedy when I got a phone call from Martin and he was absolutely distraught.

'Jason, it's your dad. He's been murdered in South Africa.'

Denis had been living in South Africa and had his own family there. On the way home from work he was robbed and murdered. I remember the strange feeling that accompanied the news. I wasn't sure how it should affect me. I rang Louise, who was my girlfriend at the time, and I also rang my close friend and teammate Mick Galvin, who offered to call around. But I didn't really see the need because there was no massive sense of grief. Not for a man I didn't know. Not even for the man who was my father.

That night I had a soccer match for UCD against St Pat's and I didn't share the news with any of my other teammates. Instead I just went and played. So the news of Denis's death had nowhere near the significance it might have had and possibly should have had. It was a peculiar one to deal with. I don't know all the details of how he was killed, or who was responsible, because it was something I never explored. I am conscious, however, since Louise and I have had our own kids, that they know their grandfather was Chinese, from Hong Kong, and that they acknowledge it. Actually it was amazing to me to see the kids growing up, listening to them explain to their friends how one of their grandfathers was Chinese. That was that then. Done. All natural. Out in the open and dealt with.

Whereas in my early years most of what I recall is living with this nagging burden of denying that, coming from a Chinese heritage and hating it. Not fitting in. Being so embarrassed about it that it became a stigma.

Clearly, because of that I didn't want to know my father and had no urge to learn anything of his ancestry. Whenever Mam wanted to visit my dad or his family I would try to back out. Bad enough to look distinctive, I thought, the last thing I needed was to embrace that difference.

So it definitely was not all Denis's fault that we had no relationship. Nor his family's. They still live around Dublin but I've always felt that I shouldn't impose on them. They are not responsible for me and so should not have to make room for me. Why would they even want to know me? I've seen them over the years but I don't seek them out. I always feel like an outside addition when I do meet them.

When Denis died they invited me to the funeral. It was maybe half expected that I would go, as it is in their tradition to have a son leading the funeral rites, but I said no. I didn't feel going to South Africa to the funeral of a man that I didn't really know was something that I wanted to do.

They were lovely about it, but if I've seen them since a handful of times that's it. There was a time when I tried to meet up with Martin Leung, who lived in Castleknock with his family, but that petered out after a while. I was also invited to Robert's wedding reception and I went along, but I didn't see much of them afterwards.

I suppose it's sad in a way. Do they understand how I feel? Do they know what was inside me as a kid desperately trying to be Irish? I don't know. I must say, though, that they have always been receptive to me. Always. As a kid I was the only grandson on their side of the family and so there was a lot of affection towards me.

I remember Denis's mother, my other nanny, showing me off in their restaurant. She was adoring, like any proud nanny, inspecting and admiring my hands and nails, rubbing her hands all over my face. When I went to see her after hearing the news of Denis's death she jumped out of her seat, hugged me and kept pointing at me, saying, 'Football, football!' Her English wasn't great but that was her way of communicating with me.

I do feel bad at how things have worked out. It is a part of my life that I haven't yet come to terms with or addressed as I should.

2

Part of a Team

When I was seven, Uncle Eddie brought me to Croke Park for Dublin's 1983 All-Ireland semi-final with Cork. We were members of the Dublin Supporters' Club from the early 1980s and we travelled the length and breadth of the country following the team.

There were two rows of seats in front of the Hogan Stand that were literally at pitch level and that's where we were for the Cork game. I always loved sitting there. I can still see Ray Hazley going down the wing and crossing the ball to Barney Rock who got the equalizing goal.

I missed the replay, which was fixed for Cork, because Nanny had booked a holiday for us in Mosney. I was truly devastated. On the day after the game I rang home and burst into tears as, over the phone, Brian and Eddie recalled vividly and with great enthusiasm the events of the day. I got a detailed report on how they travelled down from Dublin on the bus, how the locals waved them through all the villages and towns en route to Cork. The novelty of the Dubs on tour. The supporters at the back of the Blackrock End christened the terrace Hill 17! The lads described all the bunting and flags on the way out to

Páirc Uí Chaoimh and how Dublin scored four goals. Missing all of that took the gloss off my holiday to Butlin's. I was only in Meath, but it felt like a gulf of a thousand miles.

Tracking the Dubs home and away became my obsession. On one outing I remember sitting beside Mick Holden in a waiting room before we boarded the train for home after an away game. On another occasion Davy Foran came into the carriage I was in and invited me along to get team autographs from the rest of the lads.

I scoured programmes to see who was who and what clubs they came from. I went into huge detail with every snippet of information that I scavenged. I was a geek when it came to Dublin football.

I got to go to the 1983 All-Ireland final win over Galway and this time the only tickets Eddie could get were for Hill 16, the Dubs' spiritual home. I can still remember the excitement as Eddie hoisted me on his shoulders so I could give him a running commentary. He wasn't the tallest so he needed regular updates! He was delighted to get an offer from a man beside us to take me on his shoulders for the second half and I relayed the action to Eddie, who was crouched over in agony, recovering from having me on his shoulders. I suggested to Eddie several times that Pat Canavan was having a brilliant game and Canavan was duly voted man of the match on *The Sunday Game* that night.

As I moved through childhood into adolescence I became increasingly self-conscious but thankfully there was always a place I could go to where I would fit in and feel normal – and that was wherever the Dubs were.

Despite all the fights – and we had loads in Carrigallen Park even before we started squabbling with kids from other roads – the thread to unite us all was soccer or football on the street. It was there I found an outlet for all the energy and frustration I had built up. When I was feeling down I would get out on the road and kick the leather off a ball.

I was always out on the road, wearing down another pair of runners or ripping the knees out of another pair of tracksuit bottoms. I broke Mam's heart as well as the bank on that front too, she was always buying new runners and tracksuits. But the knee patches killed me – you know those leather ones that attracted so much attention, and in a bad way? I was going all out to keep my head down and I used to beg Mam to sew my ripped tracksuit bottoms together rather than stick on those rotten patches!

When I wasn't playing sport, I was looking to go to games. Brian took me to a few matches in Lansdowne to watch Jack Charlton's Ireland side and we went to Dalymount Park to see Bohemians. Brian had been to Euro 88 and had season tickets block-booked for the Italia 90 qualifiers at Lansdowne Road. They were serious tickets and we had great seats high up in what was then the new stand, just above the scoreboard. Back then you could ring the FAI, book your tickets, they would come back to you with specific seat rows and numbers and those were your seats for an entire qualifying campaign. It was so easy.

One February night in 1985, the Republic of Ireland played Italy at Dalyer, with the crowds hanging from the rafters. We couldn't even get in. We were pondering our next move when President Patrick Hillery swung by in his chauffeur-driven state limousine, with the window down, and Brian cheekily asked, 'Any chance you can get us in, Paddy?' In fairness to Hillery he saw the joke and shared the laugh.

In March 1986 we went to Jack Charlton's first game as Ireland manager against Wales and I remember Neville Southall doing all these skills in the warm-up before breaking his leg in the actual game. We were there, too, in May 1987 when Liam Brady scored and we beat Brazil 1–0.

Between those games and supporting the Dubs I was busy. We would head off on the 40C bus to Croke Park or the Supporters' Club bus for farther afield games in the National League. What I remember vividly from those away trips was snuff, the old fashioned tobacco, being passed around, the smell of the bus and lads eating chicken sandwiches.

After games, the two boys, Brian and Eddie, would go back to Hedigan's Pub – The Brian Boru – at Cross Guns Bridge for a few pints. It was a handy stop-off point as it was near the bus stop on the way to Croker and easy to head for Finglas afterwards. They would be on their high stools having a chat and I would sit down between them on the footrest. I got away with murder listening to the stories and the craic, hiding away there under a table or a counter ledge long after other kids would have been expelled. After I had listened to all the great pub talk I was apparently allowed to perform my own party piece: the Irish-language poem 'Lámh, lámh eile, a haon, a dó'.

Before Hedigan's became a haunt, the uncles used to bring me to Bermingham's on Dorset Street. I was only a toddler at that stage but the two lads still get a great kick telling stories of them bringing a bottle for me, getting the barman to warm it up, with the barman then checking the temperature on his arm to see if it was okay for me to drink.

To this day Eddie still claims to have brought me to the 1977 All-Ireland semi-final between Dublin and Kerry, one of the greatest games of all time. I wasn't even two years old and have my doubts about being at that one, but Eddie insists I was there and Brian backs him up on it.

On Sundays I would head to league matches, come home and that evening tip back out on to the road to replicate what I had seen earlier in the day. My heart was very much with the Dubs. They were my first love and there was a warm feeling of acceptance when I was with them. I felt part of something when I took off for the day. I was a Dub.

As with so many other kids my age, my heroes were Kieran Duff, John O'Leary, Anton O'Toole and Barney Rock. Shortly after the team had won the 1983 All-Ireland final, I was taken to the Green Isle Hotel to meet the team at a Dublin Supporters' Club function. The Wolfe Tones were playing the same night. I politely hounded lads like Tommy Drumm, Kevin Moran, Barney Rock, Mick Holden and John O'Leary until they gave me an autograph. And a photo, too.

When we won the All-Ireland in 1995 I was able to show John the picture of the two of us taken in 1983. It was weird to think that the next time Dublin won, the 7-year-old in the photo would be playing with him!

I was certainly easy to spot that night in 1983 because I was wearing my Communion suit – a blue jacket and white pants that Eddie had bought for me in Spain! But I still felt part of a big family, a supporter like all the others when I followed the Dubs. Unlike other boys and girls, I might not have had my dad there, but I had my uncles and I was one of the gang. Acceptance!

Everywhere I went I sought autographs and pictures and photos. I was an anorak. My love affair with Dublin football and my interest in soccer and other sports kept me within the right environment and that was important because that danger of going down the wrong road was always there. It wasn't always easy staying on the straight and narrow.

One Saturday night I went to a local chipper on my own and was met by a group standing outside the door, blocking me and slagging me over my looks. The abuse had long since ceased to be funny, so I went and hit one of them. Next thing your man's older brother appeared, gave me a dig and busted my nose. I went home to Mam and she was distraught. So was I. Brian says I came back with my bag of chips but didn't go near them. Instead I cried for a full hour. He says they were heartbroken for me. But that was how close you were to trouble should you happen to be in the wrong place at the wrong time.

Around Finglas it was more petty crime than drugs back then. You had people robbing cars and stuff but apart from the odd one that sped up the road that ran parallel to the back of our house – and the odd horse and bareback jockey that might trot down your road – I was sheltered from all that. I was spoilt – no doubt about it. Being an only child, maybe that's inevitable, but my shared love of sport with my uncles meant they were more like pals, so that was a stroke of luck.

There were times when I sat back and wondered how it must feel to look the same as everyone else, to have a brother or sister, to have a father, and to go on holidays with them. I won't say I obsessed about those things, but I did often think of that ideal scenario and how it might have been.

I wonder, though, if the grass is greener on the other side, because I had plenty of love. Mam would go through the ceiling for me, Nanny helped rear me too and Brian and Eddie brought me everywhere. In Cabra, Martin and Esther treated me like a son and Andrew and Christine were like my little brother and sister. When I was ten Brian brought me on holidays to Salthill for the Galway Races and I remember one day in particular very warmly. A few sets of tennis in the morning, then a bit of lunch and off to the pitch-and-putt course. To the races next, with Brian too wrecked to put on his few bets so he got me to do all the running over and back to the Tote.

A horse called Pinch Hitter was our banker at that time. He always seemed to win. In 1982 he won the Galway Hurdle with Jonjo O'Neill up and won again in 1983. A few years later there was an event at the Phoenix Park, sponsored by Horgan Meats, Uncle Eddie's employers. We went into a tent where I met Jonjo, the comedian Brendan Grace and the Manchester United and England captain Bryan Robson.

I told Jonjo how Pinch Hitter had never let us down and then asked all three for their autograph. All three obliged but Jonjo personalized his message: 'To Jason, best wishes, Jonjo O'Neill.' Bryan gave me a simple 'Best wishes', while Brendan just signed his name. In later years I always remembered how much it meant to see my own name on an autograph and, when time allowed, I tried to show the same courtesy whenever I was asked.

They were great days. While poor Brian was exhausted every time we went to Galway, I always dragged him along for more. After one day's racing, we headed for Terryland Park to watch Galway United take on Celtic in a friendly. Brian wanted a pint on the way home so we stopped off at a pub and he went to the bar to order his drink and a glass of orange for me. By the time he got back to the snug with the drinks I was fast asleep. And when he had taken a few swigs of his pint he too nodded off. Both of us were shattered.

I have some difficult memories from growing up – being called a chink, not having a dad, getting aggravation for looking different. But I have so many memories to treasure. Truth is, because I had no brothers and sisters I was the centre of attention when it came to Mam, Nanny, Brian and Eddie. And that had its own benefits!

3

Shooting Star

When playing on the road or in the schoolyard I could draw on a bottomless well of energy and run all day long.

Even before I developed real skills, I was endlessly willing and fiercely competitive. But in my teens I became aware I was also handy at a number of codes, mainly soccer, and in the third year of secondary school, basketball. Some of my teachers in St Vincent's used to refer to me as the Pied Piper for the way I went around rallying the troops to play games.

The classroom itself appealed to me about as much as a tooth extraction with rusty pliers. I wasn't lacking in the brains department – when I first went to St Vincent's we were all ranked on our academic ability and I was placed first out of the thirty-two in my class. I could hit the books when the humour took me but more often than not when the body was in the classroom the mind and heart were elsewhere.

During my primary-school years Mam switched me from St Oliver Plunkett's NS to St Vincent's NS and my first priority in St Vincent's was to keep a low profile in the corridors and around the yard. I wanted to merge into the background, but when it came to slagging it was open season at times.

There were plenty of bright moments and they were mostly to do with sport. When the American basketballer Michael Tait was in Dublin to play with the St Vincent's senior team he visited the school and strode into our class, a towering giant about to take over Lilliput, his chosen sport something exotic, from a different culture. He was brought around by a coach from the St Vincent's team, Joey Boylan, to help recruit new players. I was in fifth class at the time and I was ready to sign up there and then.

Seeing Michael was the reason I started playing basketball. Immediately he had my attention and I was intrigued enough to take in a Super League game a few weeks later between St Vincent's and Killester. Every other Sunday I would go to watch St Vincent's home games. There I saw other American imports, including Kelvin Troy, Terry Strickland, Kenny Perkins and Deora Marsh. And even though I didn't get to see Mario Elie, I was fascinated that a guy who played on our small island could go on to play in the NBA with the Houston Rockets, win three NBA Championships and have a street named after him in Houston. I was in awe of these lads – there was something superhuman about them.

I loved reading up about the game of basketball and discovered there were several hotbeds for the sport around the country: Castlebar, Kerry, Cork, up North and, of course, Dublin. I learned how big an event the Irish Cup final in Neptune Stadium was – a weekend when the game got to show off its wares on national TV. I got to experience all of these places first-hand through playing with St Vincent's.

As I lay in bed at night and stared at the walls, I pictured Michael Tait standing there and imagined his head must almost be touching the ceiling. I thought of how he commanded everyone's attention the moment he walked into our classroom. As I look back, though, I think what I loved most was that no one cared about the colour of his skin. He had star appeal, an aura. We saw him as a celebrity and that was all that counted. I identified with that and maybe deep down wondered if I could achieve something similar. Jesus, maybe some day people might see me and remark how good I was at sport rather than how 'foreign' I looked.

I got Mam to buy me a basketball and out I went playing on the road every night. I had to improvise back then as there were no basketball nets around Finglas South so I targeted numbers stuck on to the lamp posts, 10 feet above the ground. To begin with I used the one closest to me, with a number five sticker on it. When that sticker had faded from the ball rebounding off it I moved on to the next. It wasn't long before every sticker on every lamp post had faded. Then Brian got a net, attached it to the shed at the back of the house and that's where I practised my shooting. I went along to my first formal training session with St Vincent's and there I met Joey Boylan in person, a man who would have a significant impact on my life and sporting career, and not just in basketball.

Joey greeted me warmly with a big toothy grin that shone through a jungle of a beard that hadn't seen a pair of scissors in ages and after quenching a cigarette butt he shook hands and got straight down to the business at hand.

The first thing I noticed about Joey was his unrelenting dedication. He was at St Vincent's for every session with every team. He not only organized and coached, he also mopped and swept the courts and helped take down the seating after his own games. He was some man. A hoop-dreamer grounded in the reality of Irish basketball. A grassroots disciple who spread the gospel wherever he went. He had me converted straight away.

Joey was unique in that he had played in the Irish Super League across four decades and had captained Jameson St Vincent's as they were known at the time. The bonus was that his brother Pat, another international basketballer, had played football for Dublin in the 1980s and I was delighted to be able to tell Joey that I had Pat's autograph in my collection. Pat was known as a more talented basketballer but Joey had serious heart and spirit and he worked even harder because he knew he had to. He brought that work ethic to his coaching career too.

As for the game itself, I became fascinated by it, though I wasn't entirely sure why. Maybe the fact it was global and open to everyone, or that many of those I played alongside became good friends. Or was it the charisma of larger-than-life figures like Elie, Troy and Tait? Whatever it was, once I hit the boards I went at it full throttle and I had to be around a gym every chance I got.

Basketball and soccer became the two core elements of my school life. With basketball I had embarked on a magnificent adventure and I had to try and fit it around soccer because I was also starting to make inroads there.

While I marked time in the classroom I saw myself making tangible progress under the hoops. I looked at guys I knew, the likes of the Donnelly brothers – Karl, David and Emmett. Karl and David were both a couple of years older than me and fabulous athletes. Karl was one of the most talented players Ireland has produced. They were representing Leinster and Ireland at under-15, and I started wondering if I could get there too.

Seeing the Donnellys come home from tournaments with their Ireland tops, God, had they returned as decorated war heroes I couldn't have been more impressed! Gareth Winders, one of my best friends, was equally stirred. His brother, David, had played with the Irish team too and Gar and I both pledged we would make the Ireland under-15s within two years. That was our goal. It was not that we hoped to get there – we *would* get there.

There was a slight problem though – I was small for my age and was never going to be a beanpole. Besides which, I wasn't particularly skilful. Not to be deterred, I was determined and listened to every word that Joey said. I watched all the top players from our teams to see what they did. Meanwhile, Joey was always there to help and soon we were training up to four times a week.

Joey's genius as a coach was in explaining the fundamentals, from elementary stuff like travelling to double dribbling. Joey mixed all his sessions with technical, tactical and gameplay. We would do shooting practice and lay-ups. I was a *ciotóg* in school but decided to shoot right-handed. After early blocks of training I progressed rapidly to playing for Vincent's in the under-13 and under-15 leagues. There I began to understand the philosophy of the game.

I played point guard. Given my height disadvantage it was one of only two realistic options available to me, shooting guard being the other. Point guards have probably the most specific role in the sport; they are expected to run the offence by controlling the ball and making sure it gets to the right players at the right time. Above all, the point guard must totally understand and accept the coach's game plan. Think a rugby scrum half, an American-football quarterback or a midfield general in soccer.

The primary job is to engineer scoring opportunities. I just revelled in that challenge and the pressure of being aware of times on the shot clock and the game clock and the score. There was a lot to take in but getting five players to move in sync and sing off the same hymn sheet was deeply satisfying when it happened. I wasn't the most gifted physically, but if I could succeed in my job of making the rest of the guys on the team look and play better that was no small contribution. I knew I wasn't the most talented guy on the team when it came to the offence but

I came into my own in defence. Mentally, I was totally focused on the job of wearing down the opposition's strongest man. I loved the anticipation of what would happen next and getting steals. There was no better feeling.

Teamwork is the real beauty of basketball – five people gelling and moving as one. The collective takes precedence over the individual and the individual becomes selfless. Something about that appealed to me too.

My biggest role was on defence where I used my quickness and anticipation to good effect. I was generally used by Joey to mark the opposition's best player no matter what size he was. I revelled in this role and sacrificed my own game fully to meet these challenges, knowing the job I was doing for our team. I loved the task of marking these talented players, maybe I was taking out all my own inhibitions on them and proving to myself that I was as good as them in some way.

Every Saturday night, for reinforcement, I would flick on the BBC to watch NBA highlights after *Match of the Day*. In the late 1980s the Lakers were top dogs but it was their fiercest rivals, the Celtics, who were my heroes. Larry Bird was a legend but I loved the rising star Michael Jordan more than anyone else. I had his *Come Fly With Me* video on non-stop in the living room. I just wanted to be like him. Indeed to this day when I concentrate I still notice that I stick my tongue out just a little – one of Michael Jordan's traits on the court. As we got older, Gareth and I wanted to be a duo like the Golden State Warriors duo Tim Hardaway and Chris Mullin.

Like Mario Elie, the possibilities that basketball offered were also made real to me by a guy called Muggsy Bogues, who became a useful reference point. Muggsy was a squirt at only five-foot-three inches, the shortest man ever to play in the NBA, a dwarf in a land of giants. But he had ferocious drive to succeed and he lasted fourteen seasons in the NBA, including ten with the Charlotte Hornets. I loved his motto: 'Try to improve the team every time you go on court.' Muggsy was pulling the strings. I could relate to that.

Spud Webb caught my eye too. In 1986 he won a slam-dunk contest despite being, at five-foot-seven, one of the shortest players in NBA history. I would eventually make it to five-eight, bigger than both Spud and Muggsy, and while I didn't have their 'ups' I did have boundless enthusiasm, an exceptional coach, a strong work ethic and a great circle of friends in the likes of Gareth, Peter Donnelly and Gerry Noone.

The game had me lock, stock and barrel – and that was even before I copped on that basketball was played by girls as well as boys. Could a sport get any better? For a teenager like myself, finding his way, there was nothing more exciting than going to a basketball camp with 400 kids, boys and girls, strutting my stuff and trying to impress. There were camps in places like Dungarvan and they were a mighty buzz.

As soon as Mam, Nanny and the uncles saw that I was happy, safe and getting on well, they were okay with me spending evenings on the courts, although Mam will say she worried about me wherever I went in life. They did urge me not to neglect the studies and so I did the bare minimum just to keep them off my case. And as things started to happen for me with basketball and I got my name in the sports pages, they must have been quietly pleased, because they didn't make a big deal about the books and I got away with lots of stuff.

As I turned fifteen I knew that the goal of making the interpros was within reach and right on cue an envelope dropped in the door from the Leinster Schools Basketball Association.

24 October 1990

Dear Parents,

Congratulations on the selection of your son, Jason, for the
Leinster under-15 basketball team. I enclose a fixture list with
the times and dates of Leinster's games. The only expense is
the price of the Leinster sweatshirt, which amounts to £12.
I hope your son will benefit from the experience.
  Yours in sport,
  Denise Brett (Manager)

I punched the air with delight and phoned Gareth, and sure
enough he too had been picked. Gareth's joy was less complicated than mine, however, because not for the last time in
my life I found myself in a sporting tug-of-love. On the same
weekend I was rostered to play for Leinster, I was also named
on an under-15 Dublin North soccer squad against Wales. I had
gone for trials for this Dublin representative team at the King's
Hospital in Palmerstown and Gareth Farrelly and Tony Scully
were both also picked and went on to play in the top flight in
English football. I did well at the trial but then found out the
actual fixture was the same weekend as the under-15 basketball
interprovincials. It was always going to be basketball first as this
had been the dream for the previous couple of years.
  Cue the mayhem. The soccer lads said I would be mad to
miss the Wales fixture because there would be scouts present.
More on that later! They couldn't get their heads around me
missing it. But I was only ever going to opt for basketball. So
off I went and played for Leinster. We won and I did well.
The national team was picked on the basis of this tournament
and on 2 January 1991, the dreamed-of letter from the Irish
Schoolboys Basketball Association dropped into the hall:

a summons from the under-15 management for the Four Nations Championship against Scotland, England and Wales. I was to become an international player.

As I counted down the days, Mam, Bill, Brian and Eddie made arrangements to attend my breakthrough match.

First up were England in Castlebar and it was like those American movies where a college team runs into the gym and the whole place erupts. God, we loved those nights. Having been well sequestered in the dressing room, unaware of the din and unsure even how many had turned up to watch, we sprinted on to the floor and not only was I blinded by the lights but I was deafened by an incredible wave of sound, like the noisy thud you get when you enter a packed arena. I looked down the court and couldn't see the sidelines for the numbers thronged there. Upstairs was heaving too. The atmosphere was so intense, like nothing I had ever known. If you had a weak disposition this was no place for you. Still, I felt I could handle all of that. In fact, I revelled in this atmosphere.

I stole the first ball and it was then I knew I was good enough. I belonged. That was a marker laid down and it upset the English who were taller and more skilful than we were. The crowd rose to cheer that steal and that rattled the English too.

We won by nine points on an electric night for Irish basketball. I walked into that gym a young boy, a kid who had been picked on for being different, treading carefully with shivers of excitement and trepidation. I emerged fuelled by the sweet scent of success, knowing for sure that hard work really does pay off. I felt a new resilience and strength. I was going somewhere. I was someone. Those are feelings you don't get every day of your life.

We were heroes. Joey gave us sweets and teddies to hand out to the crowd and back we went to soak up the acclaim and adulation. Amid all the madness I gave Mam, Bill, Brian and Eddie a massive hug.

As I headed back to the changing room, knackered but happier than I'd ever been, I thought back to the day Michael Tait came into the classroom and about the aura he'd exuded. Not black. Not speaking with a different accent. Not freakishly tall. Just a sports star. I loved that whole weekend, staying in the Traveller's Friend Hotel, wearing our Irish uniforms, the notoriety around the town before and after the game and obviously the win. From the day Joey brought Michael Tait into my class I had dreamed of playing the game and it was everything I hoped for.

For a change I was being highlighted for a positive thing, the right reason. I was also part of a team, a family.

I was small, yep, but I was also the best point guard of my age in Ireland.

It just showed what hard work and dreaming big could achieve.

4

Blending In But Standing Out

In 1992, I was named captain of the Ireland under-17 team for a four-nations tournament in Athlone but on the morning of our first game, against Wales, I came down with a fever. It hit me hard and Joey was advised to leave me off. But he knew me better than most. He came over and asked: 'Jason, are you okay?' I was weak and shivering, but I told him I would be good to go. No way was I missing this one. I forced myself onto the court and played in a game that would go down in the annals. We won 106–102. At half-time it was 66–66, an interval scoreline that is simply unheard of. We just kept the scoreboard working overtime to win a famous clash.

In the final we were beaten by England and there's a photo out there of the England captain and myself being presented with our winners' and runners'-up medals by Kelvin Troy. I look absolutely traumatized. The English boy is ecstatic. But I was gaining experience and picking up lessons all the time, learning more about myself along the way.

The under-15 four-nations tournament in Castlebar had been my first exposure to the higher pressures of elite sport and it was a fantastic experience to get at such a young age. As I developed, so did my self-belief and appetite for battle. Trying to make the right calls and plays, making decisions on the hoof and always under pressure, you get to know yourself pretty well.

Some years later, during my debut season with the Dublin footballers, people wondered how this small, skinny kid coped with all the pressure and scrutiny. For the answers they need not have looked beyond Castlebar 1990; or Strabane, where I played an All-Ireland under-16 final against the hosts. We also beat St Malachy's Belfast on their home court in an under-19 All-Ireland final. I had played in venues like the Neptune Stadium in various national finals. By 1995 I had grown well used to sporting pressure.

On the basketball court, even with the adrenaline racing and the body in overdrive, I was encouraged to slow down and analyse on my feet and they were great tools to be given. It was priceless schooling on the road to playing before sellout crowds at Croker.

More success was to follow those Irish caps and first piece of silverware. After that under-15 tournament, I won nine All-Ireland titles at various ages with my club and school. And with one of those came the honour of representing Ireland at a European Schools Championship in Turkey. Right from the opening ceremony the 5,000-capacity stadium was full to the rafters. We didn't win – there were some brilliant teams out there – but again I was getting the education I valued most.

In my last year of secondary school I had one final target. I badly wanted to win the Irish Schools Cup again, as the winner would once more represent Ireland in the European Championships. I had actually repeated fifth year and the main reason for this was to win this competition. This would be my last hurrah at schools level. But we were beaten by Coláiste Éanna in the semi-final and I remember being devastated by the loss.

Joey stayed with me in the dressing room for thirty minutes afterwards, saying nothing, but helping me compose myself before I headed for home. He was always there for me.

Again, though, with the wisdom of hindsight, I can see that my reaction to that Coláiste Éanna defeat was over the top.

Why did I lose all perspective? I suppose I had invested so much in the pursuit of sporting achievement, to the exclusion of almost everything else, that I took defeat as utter failure.

Time was becoming precious and the diary was jam-packed. I was also doing well with St Kevin's Boys, the soccer club I had joined in 1989, and soccer scouts were turning up weekends to check out if this unpolished diamond was worth investment. Almost by accident I was making some headway in Gaelic football too, playing for the St Vincent's school senior team amid rumours of a trial with the Dublin minors. I reflect fondly on that period of my life because all I see is a lovely madness.

Midway through 1994, a newspaper reporter penned a piece about me, the gist being how remarkable it was that I could be starring at basketball despite also playing football and soccer to a decent standard. I hadn't even told him about my summers spent hurling competitively in Ballyhea, County Cork. I didn't want to confuse the poor fella.

One quote I gave him stands out: 'Obviously school comes first in this my Leaving Cert year.' Complete rubbish of course. And then this contradictory, and more accurate, gem: 'My mother has talked to the people in charge of the basketball and the people in charge of the Dublin minors and my studying won't affect anything there.'

In short, nothing was going to interfere with my sporting endeavours. And sure how bad? Having not excelled at anything as a kid and been the butt of name-calling and slagging, I was now, in a heartbeat, an athlete, and a decent one at that.

Newspapers published articles about me and shortly after

one appeared I was walking to class when a fella came against me, his eyes dancing with devilment. He stopped and dropped his schoolbag. I had been down this road many times before and so I winced, preparing myself for what was coming next. This time, a welcome change. The lad dropped to his knees and started bowing, lowering his hands in an exaggerated but good-humoured gesture of homage. 'Here comes the king!' he shouted. 'All hail the king!'

This guy was only taking the mickey, but it was a hell of a lot better than the other bile I had endured. The downside was that in the following months he would bow to me every time we met and very soon the warm feeling of being a 'royal' cooled off.

Clearly, sport had started to smooth my path in school. Competitive sport had become my response to, and escape from, the ethnic jibes and taunts. Through basketball I got to travel the country and made some great pals. I got to know and play with and against lads from all four provinces.

At home we had some great games at Vincent's, especially when Ballina came to town and the McHale brothers, Sean, Anthony and Liam, assumed the role of pantomime villains. Oblate Hall at Inchicore was another hotspot, and I loved playing there. The Roy Curtis tournament threw up epic games over the years. When we'd go down to play North Mon we made loads of friends, lads like Eddie Cooke, whom I would often host when he came to Dublin to play. And I loved the Neptune Stadium as well. It was the basketball Mecca and I got to play there in the last National Cup final weekend.

It was thanks to Joey and the other coaches that I continued to push myself hard, always trying to learn more at the coalface. Training sessions were brutally intense. Scores were recorded for contrast and comparison, and Joey was a coach on a mission. In a cabinet at his house he kept files with all our career stats. Joey used to meet us for one-on-one sessions to go through our stats sheets from training and mine had data on every free throw, every lay-up, every plus and minus – there was no hiding place.

Joey would run through our play and what I loved was how he would spend fifteen minutes walking us forensically through each move so that come match day there would be no confusion. We might have a game, do some more shooting and log all our final stats, but the most impressive thing for me was that everything we did had a reason and a rhythm. Every scenario was planned for – 'This is what we will do if we are four points down and there are only sixty seconds left. If we are five ahead with ninety seconds we will run this play.' The detail of turning defence into offence with the flick of a wrist and getting your four teammates on message was all accounted for.

I was known for my defence and so come match day Joey would ask me to shackle the opposition's best player and grind down his resolve. I loved the challenge of that.

That soon led to my next major representative honour – playing for the Ireland Juniors (under-19s) in a championship in Estonia in 1993.

Later that year we played another tournament in France against a French team whose smallest guy was six-ten. There I was at five-eight up against those monsters, but I wasn't fazed. I actually loved the role of underdog, battling the odds. One newspaper photograph showed me with a teammate, Colm Moran from Castlebar, Colm at six-foot-nine towering more than a foot above me! It didn't bother me, nor the rest of the lads. The teams I played on all latched on to the underdog spirit that Irish teams and athletes are famous for. We definitely tapped into that and it worked.

There came a time, however – and I would say it was during that tournament in France late in 1993 – when I realized the effort of juggling several codes might be too much. I was struggling to keep all the balls in the air. Since the age of fifteen I had been continually attending basketball camps, but I was being invited to plenty of soccer trials as well, and that became a big issue. I didn't get selected for the Ireland under-17 basketball team in my first year because I was on trial at West Ham. It was hard to be in two places simultaneously.

By then I had four different sports on the go. To this day people ask why I didn't pick one and stick with it. Mind you, Joey always doubted that one code would have been enough for me! Sure I was only a kid, I would have played anything.

I flirted with the idea of heading out full-time to the USA and seeing if I could make it there on a basketball scholarship. Getting into a Division II college was a certainty if I wanted it, but there was also a chance of making a Division I. Those DI colleges are seen as feeder units for the NBA, but to even get to DI, I would have had to go to high school over there or get into some pre-scholarship programme, so it wouldn't have been straightforward.

Every year Joey brought five or six players to the Pocono Invitational Basketball Camp in New York. I had seen Karl Donnelly and Aidan Nutley return with most-valuable-player (MVP) awards from stints there and I wanted one of those MVP T-shirts. In 1993 I had been voted Irish Schoolboy Basketball Player of the Year and so I hit the States brimming with confidence for the four-week camp.

Coaches from the US colleges make it their business to go to these camps and I was the only one of the St Vincent's crew ever to win the weekly MVP award for two of the four weeks I was there. I won it one week when our team was made up of all Irish players, but it was even more satisfying to win it when playing with American kids that I didn't know.

Again I attracted attention out there because I didn't look Irish. One coach invited me to the Bronx to play in a pick-up game with some kids he knew. With the way I looked and the way I played he thought the brothers in the Bronx would love me. Joey wouldn't have any of it. While he was easy-going in some regards he wasn't that easy-going. He was probably right!

A couple of high-school coaches wanted to bring me over for a year or two and when I returned home I got a few letters offering me places. But while I was obsessed with the sport, several factors worked against me making the move. Leaving Ireland would have been a massive wrench. Besides which I doubted I would do well enough in their SAT exams to get into high-school or college programmes. And to make the NBA is to make the best league in world team sport. It's as close and as insanely competitive as a player like Johnny Sexton making it and Ronan O'Gara not, or vice versa.

During my school years I had always been more passionate about basketball than soccer, so I stayed with it. It offered more scope for self-expression and creativity and I especially loved the challenge not only of reading an opposition defence but also of anticipating their attack and trying to counter that. I had only started off playing because I was impressionable and thought the American lads were supercool. In my bedroom I had posters of Tim Hardaway and Michael Jordan and I'd drifted off to sleep looking at those idols.

In May 1994 I played for the Ireland Juniors and we won the Four Nations Championship, beating Wales at the National Arena, having easily defeated England and Scotland and it was my last time representing my country in the sport.

I hadn't done too badly. We were the most successful school and club in Dublin in that period, jousting numerous times with Coláiste Éanna and we had a cabinet full of Dublin leagues and cups. I got to play for and captain my country and travelled the world doing it.

What I remember most, though, is the craic and the

friendships and the fact that Joey used to bring us to McDonald's in Phibsborough after a final – if we won. That was a serious part of the motivation! Sometimes the school would foot the bill but more often than not Joey paid out of his own pocket. That those memories stand out above all the medals all these years later shows you what a good coach Joey is and how a coach should be remembered.

But as I looked forward to finishing school I saw my time on court coming to an end, certainly at the elite level. Soccer was giving me more options and offers and it seemed I might be good at Gaelic football if I ever gave it a shot. Much as I loved basketball I had lots of other stuff going on. To play at senior level in the Irish Super League would mean having to give all of those things up. I was only seventeen, in no rush and up for every challenge.

Looking back, I think the US trip had somehow scratched a certain itch, playing against DI guys and coping just fine in their company. But after deciding not to follow my hoop dreams to the States full-time, I turned my attention to soccer and GAA.

I played basketball socially for a couple of seasons when my Dublin career finished and for the last couple of years I've been playing in an over-40s competition, renewing old acquaintances from my basketball world of over twenty years ago. I love being back playing.

But there is no doubt that basketball helped me during the rest of my playing career and I would again look to the sport when it came to establishing my own coaching philosophies.

5

The Boys of Summer

In 1985, Uncle Eddie left behind the economic gloom of Dublin and went off to work at Horgan Meats in Charleville, County Cork. It was a big move for a true-blue Dub like Eddie and the joke at home was that he would need to show his passport and employ an interpreter once he got to Charleville. But to everyone's surprise he made the transition seamlessly and quickly settled in.

He came back to visit on his days off and at Christmas arrived up with posters and pictures of the local hurling team. They wore magpie-coloured jerseys and were called Ballyhea. Eddie hadn't been involved with teams in Dublin, but now he was some sort of managerial guru on his new turf. My guess was that in Ballyhea he was dragged into the club, an outsider co-opted to the fabric of the parish. He had been given a job he couldn't very well refuse – had he declined he might have remained an outsider. You know the way it is.

At first Eddie lodged in a guesthouse owned by the Gleesons outside Ballyhea but he later rented a house in nearby Charleville town. He grew to love Ballyhea and once I started secondary school, and he was up and running in Cork, the call came for me to venture down there on summer holidays. It was a win-win situation: Nanny would have more space in the house, Brian would have a room to himself and Mam would know I was safe, which was all she wanted. It didn't stop her from worrying all the time, though. She would also have a break from constantly shopping for knee patches! But more than anything her mind would be somewhat at ease. Eddie would have a bit of family company and Ballyhea would be a safe haven for me to roam wild in.

Swapping the hubbub of Finglas, population 31,000 and rising, for a rural townland of a 1,000 souls seemed to me no bad exchange. And so, age thirteen, I headed off full of anticipation. I wasn't disappointed. I loved it so much that for the next three years I would head south with the first call of the cuckoo for four months of sweet freedom. Brian says the downside was that on returning to Dublin in August I would have knots in my stomach and would spend days moping about the house and pining for my home from home and my country pals. This is probably the compulsive side of me, I tend to throw myself into things 100 per cent and when I'm invested in something all of me is fully engaged.

My time in Ballyhea proved idyllic. I thrived in the ease and innocence of it all: the fields of cowslips, the hedges loaded with blossom in summer and berries in autumn. It was a far cry from the gritty suburban sprawl of Finglas and Glasnevin.

Down south sport greeted me like a long-lost brother and helped draw me into the heart of that rural parish. At the start I went down for the odd weekend but as I got older I spent entire summers there.

On one December weekend in 1985, with Mam and the uncles all around, big Niall Quinn made his senior debut for Arsenal, grabbing a goal against Liverpool. In 1983 Niall had played hurling for Dublin and because he was a young Irish lad whose father, Billy, had hurled for Tipperary against Cork, the Ballyhea folk could probably relate to him. As we played pool in the local pub, The Lodge, and gathered around the TV to watch the match on *Sports Stadium*, I already felt part of their group.

Ballyhea lies peacefully on either side of the main Cork–Limerick road, two miles south of Charleville. The local currency is hurling and the GAA pitch is the central bank, with a tidy fence guarding it. I had no ties to any club in Dublin so I decided that while playing away from home I would chase any ball rolled in my direction – and it was nearly always the small ball. I began to realize how passionate they were about it and how the tradition had been lovingly handed down from generation to generation till it grew into obsession. It would consume me too.

I wasn't there a dry week in my first summer there when a group of lads invited me to join them for a knockabout. This wasn't hurling but soccer – the usual stuff, headers and volleys – and I didn't need a second invitation to get stuck in. I had a bit about me from the street-style football of Carrigallen and when I tried a back-heel flick one of the lads, Christy Broderick, laughed, 'Ah will ye look at Pelé!'

Immediately my defence shot up. I rushed at him and hit him a dig, 'Don't you fucking slag me off!' Poor Christy was more surprised than injured. He had meant it as a compliment, but of course he couldn't know the taunts I had endured in Finglas and how my defences were on permanent alert – sometimes to the point of paranoia.

But Ballyhea and Finglas seemed a million miles apart and I knew straight away I had overreacted. I also began to recognize that I could maybe relax a bit in this new environment. I can say hand on heart that in all my time there not one unkind word was ever uttered to me by any of those Ballyhea lads. They were lovely fellas and once I got a few hurling matches under my belt I was part of the clan.

I was proud of them. Proud to be of them. I wasn't blessed with a majestic touch on the sliotar, or the sweetest *camán* skills, but with my aggression and athleticism I could offer my services as stopper or sweeper-upper, and just as in basketball I was often placed on the opposition's best man with orders to wear him down. But the longer my stay in Ballyhea, the better stickman I became, the softer my touch and the sharper my strike.

As Eddie's new house was up the road in Charleville, to avoid constant toing and froing I ended up moving in with the O'Riordans in Ballyhea. There was no formal arrangement, I just kept turning up at their house and not a second glance was cast in my direction. They had a gang of boys and they were all my friends. They told me to make myself at home and I gladly did. What a lovely family! Diarmuid was my best pal and he had a battered old Honda 50 that we would ride around the byroads. He let me take the reins a few times too as we popped down country lanes – where the only traffic you might meet was a tractor – and off to the Morrisseys just a few miles away.

Along with Ollie, Padraig and Eamon Morrissey, Chuck O'Connor, the Mortells – Mick and Dinny, and the Ronan cousins – Ian, Darren and Neilly, all lived nearby. We had a ball. Eamon Morrissey would go on to play hurling for the Cork seniors and Neilly Ronan started all of Cork's games at full-forward in their 1999 All-Ireland success. It was a simple life, carefree and chilled, and that suited me just fine. We rose in the morning with the sole aim of hurling from breakfast to sundown with the odd game of soccer thrown in. What more could you ask?

Naturally, I was expected to muck in – and sometimes to muck out – with the other O'Riordan boys on the family farm.

I was glad to help. None of the tasks were back-breaking and the only time my city breeding let me down badly was when I tried to milk a cow. I might as well have been pulling thistles for all the milk I got out of poor old Daisy.

Another time we went piking bales. On the way home, near Charleville Golf Club, with Diarmuid and I on top of the load, the bales split and I went crashing though the middle of them. I fell off the trailer but I was lucky that Maurice (Diarmuid's father, who was driving the vehicle) had seen what had happened and had braked. For when I opened my eyes I was staring at the rear tyres!

Dinnertime at the O'Riordans' was a daily feast – huge spreads of meat, spuds and veg, good country food. Diarmuid was my age and we got on famously. There was also Sheila, Donal, Máiréad, Tomás, Liam, Niall and Áine. Tomás would go on to win a Dr Harty Cup medal with St Flannan's Ennis. Even with that great big household, Mr and Mrs O'Riordan – Maurice and Ann – had no bother putting me on the roster for the summer months and treating me as one of their own. Some of the time they had one or two of the girls away in college so there was room. It was a wonderful act of generosity and hospitality.

Hurling dictated the parish mood and I wanted to help keep the spirits up. With all the practice morning, noon and evening, my touch improved, the wristwork got slicker and I soon made my debut for the Ballyhea under-14s. I loved going to Hennessy's shop with the petrol pump outside, across the road from the church, and seeing the club notes pinned to the window detailing who and where we were playing next. You'd look forward to that because you knew the whole parish would come out to support you. It reminded me of those American movies where there would be a convoy of vehicles going to high-school games to offer support.

When I started with Ballyhea I was a bit of a gouger, still on red alert for any abuse and not wanting to be seen as weak. Sure enough the abuse came, mostly when we played away from Ballyhea. It was savage, even more basic than what I was used to in Dublin. I was called a black fucker and a nigger.

I brought some of the trouble on myself. I was overly defensive and overly aggressive and at the least provocation I would pre-empt the insults by getting my digs in first, making myself even more of a target. But in one game against Freemount the slagging was just relentless. The opposition weren't too bothered about geography – I heard every racial slur from China to Japan to the jungles of Borneo and back again. I eventually lost the head entirely and tore into my nearest tormentor with fists, feet and hurley flying.

Eddie hauled me off straight away and when he met me on the sideline and clobbered me I burst out crying in frustration and anger: 'Why am I getting all this? Why do I have to put up with it? Why can't I be the same as everyone else? Who even cares?'

It was a watershed moment.

Turns out very few were there to help me, not because people didn't care, but because no one – not players or teammates or coaches or referees – knew how to tackle racial abuse at the time. There were no codes of practice, no established norms. There was no moral compass to navigate your way around racism. There may have been some vague sense that the abuse sounded ugly and wrong, but no one knew what to do, or if they should do anything at all. There were no repercussions, social or sporting. Back then it was a much different Ireland from the one we have now, where lines have been drawn and all reasonable people respect them.

But the events of that day helped change my mindset. The abuse wouldn't stop for many years to come, but as time passed, the events of that afternoon made me realize that I had to blot it out as best I could while on the field. I had to stay focused on the game, because I was becoming one of the better players. If I didn't stay calm I was useless to the team.

Right there and then, however, in the heat of it all, Eddie lost patience and, probably embarrassed at how his nephew had shown him up in front of all the travelling supporters, issued me with an ultimatum: cop yourself on or go back to Dublin. He had an entire team to look after and, as he has since told me, he was harder on me because we were family. Stubborn and in tears, and taking him at his word, I went back to the O'Riordans' and started to pack for the journey. Diarmuid came into the room, saw I was preparing to leave and he started crying too and pleaded with me to stay. Straight away my outlook changed. It meant an awful lot to see someone upset for me. To see someone who cared enough for me that he was actually crying.

After thinking about it some more I unpacked the bag and pledged to fight my battles in a different way. Outward shows of emotion, especially among boys, were rare enough at that time but Diarmuid's tears showed me that someone cared, that I was wanted, that I belonged in Ballyhea.

In the middle of the 1991 season I was put forward for a Cork under-16 hurling trial. I didn't make much of an impression but no big deal, I was happy that it was another adventure. The gas thing was I played hardly any Gaelic football for the first two summers I was down there because hurling was really the only show in town. Most of us were busy playing one or two levels above our age group anyway so the schedule was always full.

Eventually, I got to play a few football games too. I enjoyed it and after a while we heard that a Cork minor football selector was coming to one of our games to run the rule over me. It was mid-season, Cork had just won the 1993 Munster Minor final and were en route to winning the All-Ireland title, so I doubted there would be much demand for my services. But I played away and it went fairly well. Years later, I met a former teammate who had played alongside me for Avondhu, the divisional side. 'God, Jason,' he said, 'I thought Cork would pick you. You scored 2–10 that day with the selectors looking on!' I just smiled and joked that it was actually 2–11 I scored!

But this was B-level football so I don't blame Toddy Cuthbert, the Cork manager at the time, for not bringing me in. The Cork management had their panel picked and Toddy's son Brian, who later managed the Cork senior team, actually went on to captain the county to the All-Ireland Minor title that year. They managed just fine without me!

Had it gone another way could I have played for Cork? It's a good question. I had no burning ambition to play for them, I was just happy playing for Ballyhea without a care in the world. The hurling trial and speculation about the minor footballers just happened and I went with it. Who knows, maybe it could have been an interesting dilemma for the family, but I never went out of my way to make it happen.

We did win a fair few trophies with Ballyhea. In my time there we won numerous North Cork titles and a County Championship. One season that stands out was when we beat Youghal and Ballincollig at under-16 level. I have great memories of that campaign. In the North Cork under-16 final we played Mallow and I was given the job of marking their main man, big Fergal McCormack. Fergal was huge both in body and reputation and my sole brief was to stop him at any cost. I took my orders literally and as soon as the sliotar was thrown in I began by tripping him with my hurley. I tried to cover him like a rash for the rest of the game, trying not to let him hurl because I knew if he did he would kill us. More often than not, that was my job on match days. Basic enough, but fine by me!

By then I was taking my 'enforcer' reputation a little too seriously. We were drawn against Charleville in an under-14 league game and I was to start at midfield against their latest star, a lad who by all accounts was not only destined for the big time but was also something of a crowd-pleaser and a pop idol. 'Jason, this lad is a bit of a showboater but he's bloody good too,' my teammates said, no doubt rising me. 'Name of Dominic Foley. He's a snazzy dresser, wears polo necks and jewellery – a typical townie.'

'I don't like him already,' I grunted.

By now the Ballyhea lads had taught me some of the darker arts! The first 'skill' was how, at throw-ins, to chop down on your marker's hands, not his hurley. The second skill was not getting caught. I mastered those two quickly. Game on, and I whipped the hurley down on poor Dom's hands. Did it make any difference? I don't know, but we won.

I got to know Dom better a few years later when I played soccer against him for St Kevin's Boys against Charleville in the under-17 All-Ireland Schools final, which we won 6–0. He was sound and to his great credit that chop-down never came up in conversation. Dom went on to play soccer for Watford, played at most levels underage for Ireland, won six senior caps as well and had a great career in Belgium. But back then, in that town-versus-country showdown, he was in my cross hairs.

When I was sixteen I played on the Ballyhea under-21 team that reached a North Cork final. I carried an injured ankle going into the game and after fifteen minutes I gestured to Tom Gleeson, one of the mentors, that I needed some spray on the ankle because it was hurting me. Tom and the lads thought I was struggling badly with the injury, though, and they took me off. I was fuming. I sat on the sideline, tears coming down my face and I told them that I was only looking for a bit of spray.

They threw me back on for the final twenty minutes and I got the winning goal in the last minute. We won by a point!

They were the perfect summers.

*

Back in Eddie's house in Charleville I would sit in front of his TV when he was at work. As a treat I could head down to the local video shop and pick out two movies. Eddie Murphy was all the rage at the time and thank feck because my uncle only had one video – that of the Cork Tony Forristal squad he was involved with. I had so much spare time I ended up watching it over and over, and one name stood out in the footage and on the old-fashioned, clumsy subtitles: BRIAN COR-COR-AN.

Jeez, this lad was different gravy altogether. He was then at under-14, but the next year he was picked for the Cork minors and soon after graced the senior squad. I remember watching that video repeatedly and marvelling at how good he was. From then on, while I obviously supported Dublin in Gaelic football, I always kept an eye out for Cork – and for Brian Cor-cor-an – in the hurling. I ended up playing an All-Ireland senior football semi-final against him in 1995.

I immersed myself in the culture of Cork hurling. Eddie and I went to a stack of Munster finals and we admired marquee players like Teddy McCarthy, Pat Buckley, Ger Fitzgerald, Tony O'Sullivan and big Kevin Hennessy. For those matches, Eddie would collect a gang of lads and we'd all head off. Everyone loved the craic. We were blood brothers.

Did I miss Dublin at the time? Not really. I felt huge pride playing for Ballyhea and I think they felt proud too when I later got going with Dublin. It was a strong link even after the summers ended because I would go back down some weekends. That would mean leaving school in St Vincent's on a Friday at lunchtime, heading to Heuston Station and fretting all the way from The Curragh onwards that I would miss my stop at Charleville. Come evening time I would be with the Ballyhea lads playing football and hurling matches.

On Monday mornings I'd hop on the 6 a.m. train from Charleville back to Dublin and be in school that afternoon for the all-important Religion–PE double-header. I could manage it all. Just don't ask me what classes they had scheduled on Monday mornings!

But this part of my life was also nearing an end. One September weekend in my sixth year I was training with the Irish junior basketball team – a comprehensive all-day session on Saturday in Malahide. The next day we were training at Coláiste Íde, Finglas, from ten till noon. I finished up at half-twelve and there was Tom Gleeson from Ballyhea waiting to ferry me down to play one last match for them. No problem. I hopped into his Caddy van and we spun down the N7 for an under-21 County Championship hurling game, which turned out to be my final game for them. I was only sixteen but I had scored the winning goal in the North Cork final and as Tom's van sped southwards, I sat in the back, bumping up and down, thinking how cool it was to be able to mix sports and lead this double life.

I was so happy that I was wanted by the people of Ballyhea and valued by the basketball family too. That was a huge thing. As we eased out of Limerick City towards Charleville, I felt once more the warm glow that came from being part of the parish.

When I got my first Dublin Senior Championship jersey after we played Louth I had it framed, drove down to Ballyhea and presented it to the club. That same year, 1995, they reached the county senior hurling final. I might have been with them had things not exploded for me with the Dubs.

I attended both the county semi-final and final and went into their dressing room each time. They asked me to join them on the subs' bench outside and when they lost that county final to Seán Óg Ó hAilpín's Na Piarsaigh I suffered with them. I loved the Dubs and supported them from the cradle, but without Ballyhea and those wonderful summers down south I would have struggled to identify with the parish ethos for which the GAA is famous.

Dublin is a great hotbed of Gaelic games but the approach is a lot different from what you get down the country. It's a lot harder to get that same cultural identity as you have in small rural clubs, where the life of the parish revolves around what happens inside four white lines.

I still remember one of my first under-14 matches; it was against Fermoy. I went for a ball and pulled so hard against my marker's hurley that timber cracked and splinters flew. I emerged from the melee, looked to the line, held up my shattered stick and roared 'Hurley!' at the top of my voice. Mick Copps, a selector, came sprinting over, thrust the replacement into my hand and whacked me a fierce slap on the back. As he grabbed the broken stick and gathered up the offcuts, Mick shot me a look full of meaning and roared, 'Now you're hurling, Jason!'

I can still feel the shiver down my spine from that comradely thump and those words of validation. It was like I had arrived in the parish. I was one of them. There and then I wanted to bleed for Ballyhea.

They tell me I scored three goals that day but I don't recall any of them. All I can remember is tearing upfield in pursuit of my next victim and glancing over to see the diehard fans of Ballyhea rise to their feet in the stands and roar my name. In a small field in Shanballymore, they were reacting to a stick being splintered by a rookie blow-in, who looked a bit foreign, from the Northside of Dublin. There was something fiercely tribal about their welcome for me and something beautiful to it too. It's still a memory I treasure and a sign of the glorious madness that's special to hurling.

Yeah, I had the racist stuff down in Cork, just as I had everywhere I played in Ireland, and yeah, I got abused in most games. But in Ballyhea I belonged. In a childhood full of contradictions and complexities, I had found some longed-for normality 150 miles down the road from Finglas.

6

The Beautiful Game?

It was 4 January 1992, and the normality of Ballyhea was a world away. A chill wind lashed the suburbs of East London, rattling rooftops, scattering debris and shaking street lamps.

I stood shivering on the sideline of Upton Park, a few yards away from the West Ham manager. Billy Bonds was under pressure – you could tell that just by looking at him – and I'd say he was perplexed to see this youngster standing near him by the tunnel.

I was fifteen and had been invited with my Carrigallen friend Pato McCarthy from St Kevin's Boys FC for trials with the Hammers. Shay Noonan, a well-known player for Drumcondra during their glory days in the 1960s and 1970s, was a scout for West Ham and had arranged our trip over. Jimmy Neighbour, West Ham's youth development officer, looked after us during our stay and on this particularly unforgiving Saturday afternoon he had brought us to Upton Park for an FA Cup third-round match against the non-leaguers Farnborough Town.

Before the game Jimmy gave us the itinerary, which seemed pretty straightforward, just like the game itself was supposed to be: 'Fellas, in the eighty-fifth minute head for the exit gate and I'll meet you in the car park.'

Couldn't go wrong. And so with time ebbing away and West Ham only 1–0 up, Pat and I made for the exits and the car. We had just fastened our seat belts when the stadium erupted in a roar from the visiting supporters' end of Upton Park.

'Fellas, follow me!' Jimmy shouted, as he rushed to the scene of the action.

We raced after him, through the players' entrance and straight down the tunnel, guided by the shaft of light. As we burst from the bowels of the stadium into the arena the cause of the commotion was clear: West Ham had just conceded a penalty to the minnows. As the referee delayed the taking of the penalty while an injured player was attended to, Billy looked visibly rattled, his cheeks blowing bright red and you could see his breath.

That part of East London gives off a vibrant sense of community, from the bustling shops to the noisy, friendly market stalls, but at that moment all you could sense was frustration in the air, because the Hammers' league campaign was floundering too. The terraces were restless and Billy bore the brunt of the fury.

His side were struggling at the bottom of Division One and the FA Cup was realistically their only chance of silverware. That night twenty coachloads of Farnborough fans had paid a bargain £5 per head to travel to Upton Park and flying their yellow-and-blue balloons they were making plenty of noise and colour. In a crowded house of 24,000, about 6,000 had sworn undying loyalty to Farnborough and it almost felt like a home game for the visitors.

A guy called Dean Coney stepped up to take the penalty kick that he himself had won. I can still see his shot – it was hard and low and it squeezed home to clinch a famous draw.

Back then the FA Cup still commanded respect and passion.

Its essence had yet to be diluted and that day, as the little-known goalscorer whirled away in celebration, his legend assured for life, I witnessed at close quarters the magic of the competition.

As the stadium emptied and the unhappy locals streamed away into the early evening, Jimmy whisked Pat and myself back to the car and away from the seething, cranky chaos. There wasn't much conversation between us on the journey back to our digs!

That match is the most vivid memory from my first soccer trial across the water.

My relationship with the 'beautiful game' is a peculiar one. Despite a lot of talk and fuss about getting trials here and there, I only ever had two try-outs in England and both of those were at West Ham. I never harboured any raging passion for the game but like most kids growing up in Carrigallen Park, I kicked a ball happily around the roads and parks of Finglas and every Saturday lunchtime we would flick on ITV to catch *Saint and Greavsie*. I followed Spurs for a while and celebrated like mad when Ricky Villa got that wonder goal in the 1981 FA Cup final, but I soon got sense and switched colours to the red of Liverpool.

When I was eight I joined Rivermount Boys and because the youngest team they fielded was at under-11 I was thrown straight in with the big boys. I was small, the Mitre ball was heavy, and so the coaches put me on the wing because I looked like I might be fast. But it didn't matter how quick I was, the ball was too heavy for me and most of the time I couldn't even get it off the muddy ground of the Tolka Valley pitch. The odd time I did get a bit of purchase on it, I might kick it too far and it would roll down the bank into the River Tolka and I would be dispatched to go off after the ball.

Our pitch beside the river was shared with St Helena's,

whose youth and senior teams when they played there used to rehydrate on flagons of cider at half-time! We took it a bit more seriously at Rivermount, where Jackie Kenny ran the show. Our coach, Joe Bennett, was so passionate he would inspire you to play to your maximum. Tony Flanagan and Mick Grogan took teams I played on too and Paddy Fenlon was another leading light, the father of Pat, or 'Nutsy' as he was known. Pat was our first local hero; he was headhunted by Chelsea and was always over for trials. He was the guy you wanted to be.

That under-11 team was my introduction to structured competition. At that stage there was no GAA in my life so I played away with Rivermount until I was fourteen.

Meanwhile, some of my friends made their way on to the radar of English clubs. Darren Grogan was tracked by Spurs and he had all the Hummel gear at the time as they sponsored the club. Darren spent a lot of time there before going on to play League of Ireland with Sligo Rovers. Alan Moore eventually signed for Middlesbrough and played for the Republic of Ireland. The three of us hung around together and it was great to see them do so well.

The club was a breeding ground for heroes but Nutsy Fenlon intrigued me most. When he was over with Chelsea he had the perm that was then in fashion and when he'd arrive home with all the Chelsea gear he was the bee's knees.

I was a bit of a rebel at times, which possibly didn't help the cause. I was fiery and didn't always see eye to eye with the management, but a coach called Joe Fox changed my outlook and application in many ways.

Joe had once been for trials at Manchester United and was another local hero in Finglas. At Rivermount, he took over my team, the under-12 seconds, and straight away he was one of those guys you wanted to do well for. It wasn't so much what he said, but more how he made you feel. Like Joey Boylan, those are the coaches you want – the fellas you can connect with.

You'll scarcely remember what a coach says, but you'll always remember how he makes you feel, and Joe's approach was excellent. It's a trust thing. Do they have faith in you? I trusted Joe and so did the rest of the boys. In fact, our second string turned out to be better than Rivermount's first team!

In 1990, the St Kevin's Boys Club came looking for me to play with their under-15s. They were seen as the better team. We were decent at Rivermount but maybe there was a feeling that a change would be no bad thing. The main point of contact there was Jimmy McMullan, a relative of Ronnie Whelan. Jimmy was from Cabra and a larger-than-life character who also had faith in me.

Success soon followed at St Kevin's. We beat Carrigaline in the under-15 SFAI Cup final in my first season. That game was played in Tolka Rovers' ground not far from St Vincent's and my basketball buddies came to watch the game. At half-time they shot a few hoops in the basketball court and, when I saw them, I asked Jimmy if I could go over to them! Jimmy obliged. We won 3–1, I scored one, made one and was given the man-of-the-match award.

I played as a winger when I was younger, and sometimes when I played with older teams the coaches would play me at full-back, where I could read a game pretty well. The coaches were always at me to improve my speed and then they would see about getting me over to England for trials. That was the Holy Grail for any decent young soccer player in Dublin – going for trials across the water – and all of that came on my radar at thirteen or fourteen.

So what did they see in me? Well, from the age of thirteen I played up front and usually got a few goals. I could see a pass,

I was energetic and brave and enjoyed getting stuck in. If I was being extremely generous to myself, I'd like to think I was a Luis Suárez type – by that I mean being very busy around the opposition and never giving a defender an easy ride.

I was athletic and decent in the air and not shy about getting my retaliation in first either. I played up to a hardman image and more than once went into tackles with studs up. I remember going in hard in games against players from big teams like Belvedere, Cherry Orchard and Home Farm. It was only when someone went in on me with their studs up that I recognized the real dangers of a tackle like that. In general, though, I had no problem living up to my reputation, just as when Eddie told the lads in Ballyhea that some lunatic from the flats in Finglas was on his way down to join them.

There was a hard edge I felt I had to keep sharpened.

Now my days were split between soccer, Gaelic football, basketball and hurling. I was in my mid-teens, playing 24/7. Rushing from team to team, sport to sport, session to session – this was being a kid in its essence. To me it was the norm. My old schoolteacher, John Horan, says he will always remember seeing me cycling frantically in the school gate from a basketball game, dropping the bike, running over to him to collect a jersey for the school's Gaelic football team and then sprinting straight on to the pitch for the match.

Yeah, there was pressure to choose just one sport, but you had to be totally sure before you made a call like that and deep down I wasn't so certain how I felt about soccer.

In 1992, there was a clash of dates between the Dublin under-17 soccer squad playing in Germany and the basketball camp in the Poconos. Again, because I chose basketball I remained on the bold list.

'He's just not committed' was the complaint I heard on repeat. But it wasn't that simple. I actually felt I was very committed. I did enjoy soccer and when I was much younger I would wait with some excitement for the *Evening Herald* schoolboys' football pullout every Tuesday to see when, where and who we were playing at the weekend. But I didn't really know if I could go further, or why I was even playing soccer! I just kept playing games. It was down my list of priorities for a long time.

Still, there were some soccer competitions I did attend. We travelled with Kevin's to a highly regarded tournament at the Keele University, where we were up against teams from all over Europe as well as the USA. I did quite well in that tournament and attracted a bit of comment. It seems coaches and scouts were talking about me. Just before the end of the tournament our assistant manager, looking quite excited, took me to one side and said, 'Jason, there was an Everton scout at that last game and he said you're going to be a million-pound player!'

I kind of shrugged the shoulders. Maybe the way things were going that might actually happen but I never dwelled too long to consider what more I needed to do to make sure it did. At one stage there was something of a summit of all my coaches – basketball, soccer and Gaelic football – at my mam's new house on the Navan Road as they tried to figure out which direction I was going in.

I left it to the adults to sort. I just wanted to keep playing; there was never any master plan.

The speculation continued and the rumour mill kept on turning. One Christmas Eve there was a knock on the door from a guy who introduced himself as Noel McCabe, a scout for Nottingham Forest, the same man who, apparently, brought Roy Keane to the City Ground. He came into our house, pro-duced his credentials – all those guys had a letter with a club stamp to show they were legit – and talked the talk. Noel said he would get me to Forest and I sat back beside Brian and listened as he painted a rosy picture of how it might all pan out. I never heard from him again.

Did that put a damper, even subconsciously, on my already lukewarm affection for soccer? It possibly did. Jesus, how could you call to a youngster's home on Christmas Eve, promise the sun, moon and stars, and then make no attempt to deliver on it? Deep down, I think that always stuck with me and sowed the seeds of suspicion about the 'beautiful game'. It wasn't that feckin' beautiful.

I did go to West Ham, however, for the first time in 1992. I was nursing a groin injury from basketball and actually sought physio while over there. Not the best first impression! I walked into the physio room with my studs clanking on the floor and saw that big Frank McAvennie was on the bed getting treated. I had just left the dressing room, where Stuart Slater was getting slagged for being linked with a £2-million move to Celtic, but here was an even bigger name.

'Son,' Frank said with a big smile but all the time eyeing my boots, 'you cannae come in here with those on.'

Another great impression!

Otherwise I did okay at that trial, but on my return visit a year later I did myself no justice at all. Basketball commitments had kept me away from soccer for ages and I was rustier than an old gate. Maybe if my true goal at the time had been to play in England I would have been more focused – and maybe my mentors would have recognized the fact and prepped me better – but sure there was no strategy.

A few years later I was down in Wexford at a wedding and got chatting to a lad, one of several guests over from Britain.

'Who do you support?' I enquired.

'West Ham, mate.'

'Ah, I was over there years ago for trials,' I said, smiling at the memory. 'They played Farnborough Town in the FA Cup while I was there. I was actually out on the sideline beside Billy Bonds when Farnborough got a penalty. Some lad called Dean, I think, stepped up and scored it.'

With that, the guy offered his hand, laughing heartily. 'Dean Coney is my name, mate – I'm the lad who scored that penalty!'

Small world!

7

Dublin Calling

The gas thing is that while I idolized the Dubs almost from the cradle, I still didn't have a Dublin GAA club I could call my own. When I did play in St Vincent's secondary school it was mostly to dodge the books.

I cut my teeth in Gaelic football at primary school and was picked to play in goal when in third class at St Vincent's NS. Two of my favourite teachers, Mr Molumby and Mr McKeever, were in charge – they were most likely my favourites because they looked after the teams.

By fifth class I was at corner-forward, a position that seemed more suitable. We got to Croke Park and played Scoil Mhuire Marino in the Cumann na mBunscol Sweet Afton Cup final, or the Corn Afton as we called it. Imagine a schools competition being sponsored by a tobacco company these days! Anyway, our build-up was hectic, fuelled by a welter of nervous energy, and when match day arrived we were running on empty. Sucking air almost from the throw–in, I was soon taken off as we slumped to defeat.

We got a chance to exact revenge the following year when we met the same opposition in the final.

Once more I was put in at corner-forward. And once more I was taken off! We sank under the weight of anticipation and anxiety and I graduated from primary school with a bare trophy cabinet on the Gaelic front. Back-to-back final defeats and taken off twice in a row – not the best of memories. It's a story I share with kids of that age now when I explain to them that they, too, can play for Dublin. I wouldn't have thought it was possible after those two final defeats!

But it was class to play in Croke Park. I loved the novelty of that – the school preparing for the final with cheesy rhymes, sing-songs and supporter meetings. Flags and posters were dotted around the corridors in the weeks leading up to those finals and there was great support from the student body in terms of where they sat during the game and what they sang – all choreographed for maximum effect.

I remember the day of the second final. Off we headed in the direction of Croker in a roomy Hiace bus humming our tune, 'Capitaine Furillo', the theme from the TV show *Hill Street Blues*. I sat beside Derek Brennan, brother of the former Dublin footballer, Ger, and Darren Ducie. While I vaguely remember running on to the pitch I cannot recall touching the ball much. Marino just seemed to have the better of us and that was that.

Primary school ended without me being attached to any GAA club in the city. I had played with Ballyhea and before that I had the odd game here and there for Erin's Isle GAA Club, which was only over the road from where I lived. But I played only if the likes of Peter Williams – whose brother Paul played for Dublin – knocked at the door and said they were stuck.

It was much the same with Na Fianna. In school, Fiachra Leahy asked me to play the odd game with them because of my connections with St Vincent's, which is a nursery for the club. I would have played a few mini-leagues around that time but it was only ever a casual thing. I was in the catchment area of both clubs but I never officially joined or signed forms with either.

John Horan helped change that. He was a science teacher in the secondary school before he became principal there and now he is also the incoming GAA president! John saw something in me and he played me on sixth-year teams in both Gaelic football and soccer when I was only in second year, which was a fair leap of faith. Not only was I raw, but I was much smaller than the giants I would play alongside and against.

In my first year at secondary I loved being in one particular classroom that was perched strategically above the canteen and overlooked the school playing fields. Gazing out on to those lush, green lawns, watching Dessie Farrell and the St Vincent's seniors playing, while a teacher droned on about maths or grammar or science, well, a young man could be forgiven for daydreaming. And I certainly let my imagination run free. Dessie was the rising star of Dublin GAA at the time and a huge figure to me.

It helped that my basketball buddies Dave Donnelly and John Kelleher were on the Vincent's football teams I played on. With every passing year I improved a bit at the sport. One game when I was in sixth year stands out: I scored 1–4 against St David's Artane, and our art teacher, Mr Whelan, sought me out and shook my hand. That felt strange, to be singled out for having played well, but it was a nice strange and the handshake stuck with me all the same.

Brian Talty, the former Galway player who lives and teaches in Dublin, was at that game. He later linked up with Alan Larkin – the former All-Ireland-winning Dublin centre-back – and they took over the county minor team and invited me for trials.

I didn't know it but after the Artane match Brian went straight to John Horan to enquire about getting me on the Dublin squad. To be honest, I was only having a bit of fun that day – they were an A team and we certainly weren't. Three of my other basketball mates played for us that afternoon, lads who by their own admission wouldn't be footballers at all. At one stage Gar (Gareth Winders) threw his left foot at the ball and hit fresh air – we fell around laughing.

I was called for Dublin minor trials. I agreed to pop along but without any great expectation. On the eve of the trials I found myself with a free gaff so I sent out word to my basketball pals. A few friends came over and we watched videos well into the small hours. It was a late night and the next morning I rubbed the sleep from my eyes, threw on a tracksuit and went out the door to play football.

Arriving in Westmanstown I recognized very few of the other lads on show. I was handed a bib and thrown into the fray – and for the first ten minutes I didn't get a look at the ball. For a while nothing would stick and as the errors multiplied so did the realization that I was blowing my chance.

That's when the referee, Joe Woods, came to the rescue. Joe was deep into a fifteen-year inter-county refereeing career and had taken charge of All-Ireland minor finals, so he knew a thing or two about the game. During a break in play he tapped me on the shoulder: 'Young fella, just relax! Settle down and keep it simple.'

Desperate to make an impression, I had become anxious and Joe brought me down a few gears. His words of wisdom had a calming effect, I began to find the pace of the game and made an impact. The group of triallists was culled and filleted over the following month but at the end of that process I was still there, part of the official panel.

I hadn't played much Gaelic football but I knew I wasn't out of place at this level. Once I got to grips with the movement and positioning and got the ball in my hands, I was well able to take on a defence.

Alan Larkin, our manager, was an interesting character. He had retired with two All-Ireland senior medals and later managed Dublin to an All-Ireland minor title. He was different and did things his way. We had to wear shin pads, for instance, which few of us would ever have bothered with. He also made gumshields obligatory. Alan was just making sure we were safe and I loved training under him.

I gave it a right good go. I don't recall missing many basketball games but I didn't miss much Dublin training either and as the season developed Gaelic actually became a priority. That was a huge shift in attitude.

Cossy (Ray Cosgrove), Whelo (Ciarán Whelan), Robbo (Ian Robertson) and Eamon McLoughlin were star names on our panel and seemed destined for the big time. Eamon looked like he could be first to reach the top. He was playing soccer at a high level with Cherry Orchard and was frequently over to England for trials. In Gaelic football, he was a great free-taker; with minimum fuss he could tap over frees with either foot.

For me, with my size, getting the ball was the biggest battle. Once I had my hands on it, I had the ability to take my man on, turn him and get a score.

There was another problem, however, and it concerned paperwork. I couldn't play with the Dubs while registered with a Cork team and the time normally needed to transfer would rule me out of playing Dublin minor. The adult troubleshooters were dispatched to the scene and there followed intense dialogue between Uncle Eddie down in Ballyhea and members of the Dublin set-up.

I left them to it, totally comfortable that they had my best interests at heart. They concluded that I should declare myself illegal in Cork and take a rap on the knuckles. My last game for Ballyhea had been in the under-21 county championship against Watergrasshill a couple of years earlier, when I was still under-16.

In fairness, I hadn't a clue what was going on. To me, playing for Ballyhea had been entirely legal and wholly acceptable, as I had no club in Dublin. They were my people down there. But now I was told that the quickest way to get me in a Dublin shirt was to declare my illegality in Cork and take a one-year ban before I could play for the Dubs.

That's what happened.

The case went to the GAA at central level and I was hit with a retrospective ban but the suspension was then lifted by the GAA mercy committee. I was effectively freed to play immediately with Dublin.

The reality was that I couldn't commute to Cork forever, but looking back, that red-tape thing still rankles a small bit. It just left the door open for cynics from neighbouring parishes down there to tell my former clubmates, 'Ah yeah, ye did win a lot but sure he was a banger. He was illegal.'

Fair enough I was the one who stated to the GAA that I was illegal, but I was a genuine Ballyhea player every time I put on the jersey. What I did in the summer of 1994 was simply what I had to do to play minor with my native county. My time with Ballyhea is something I am proud of.

Anyway, I joined Na Fianna on Mobhi Road, having gone to school in the parish, having admired Dessie Farrell and having played with so many Na Fianna lads at St Vincent's. Erin's Isle were closer to my home in Finglas and had nurtured football immortals like the Deegans, the Barrs and Charlie Redmond and they were also way more successful than Na Fianna at the time. But Na Fianna have always welcomed players from St Vincent's and, with the paperwork complete, I was picked to play corner-forward in the Dublin minors' opening game of the 1994 Leinster Championship, away to Kilkenny.

The opposition were hardly giants of the game but there was a lot of excitement and a lot of nerves for me – and it showed on the scoreboard. I drew a blank that day, which annoyed me a little.

Mick Mortell, a friend, had driven up from Ballyhea with Uncle Eddie for the Leinster quarter-final against Kildare and I was delighted to do well in front of them, winning five frees that Eamon McLoughlin converted. I also grabbed a point; a confidence booster because back then a young forward was judged solely by what he scored, though that has changed now. Eamon and myself were the only Dublin players to score on the day.

In the semi-final we played Carlow at Croke Park in front of a small-enough crowd. A few of my basketball pals were down the Canal End. During a lull in the play one of the boys, Cameron Day, found his voice and it echoed all around that end of the hallowed stadium: 'Sherlock, you sheepshagger!' There was a ripple of laughter among the crowd and I couldn't do anything but have a chuckle too.

Soon after, I got a goal. Eamon took possession from a quick free, won the ball around centre-forward and played it low and hard in to me, a real daisy-cutter. I had made a diagonal run to greet it and, soccer-style, took a touch and met it with the side of my foot, slotting it into the far corner. The next day Con Houlihan highlighted the score in his *Evening Press* column, describing it as an effort any striker at USA 94 might have been proud of.

We made the final. Twice a week we trained ahead of it and there was no doubt that I improved with every session and flourished within the whole set-up. Shane Herity from Ballyboden was on the team and his dad knew someone that owned Club Sarah in Rathfarnham, which was handy because some of the lads were only seventeen and, unlike their 18-year-old teammates, couldn't get into nightclubs. But at Club Sarah we all found a home. Just going in there with the lads made me feel part of the family.

There was another perk to being a Dub. In the build-up to the Leinster final we were given an Arnotts T-shirt and, as I was fascinated with the three-castles crest and all it stood for, I took great pride in wearing it. All the gear thrown at fellas nowadays is taken for granted but to get even one polo shirt back then was massive. It was a big deal to represent Dublin.

Another spin-off to playing so many sports was getting half-days off. Some teachers resented that I didn't work harder on their watch and got to skip so many classes. One or two gave me a hard time. Mind you, I could be bolshy enough myself at times.

Dessie Farrell and Kenny Cunningham had just passed through the school and given St Vincent's a great profile. I just assumed I was going to continue that tradition and that's why I scarcely bothered with the books. It is a regret to this day.

Years later, through a Gaelic Players Association (GPA) scholarship, I would go to college to study for an MBA, but it's unfortunate it took me so long to see there could be a good balance – and lots more opportunities if I was disciplined with my time – between education and sport.

Along the way there was also a chance to join the civil service. I went for their exams in the RDS at Simmonscourt along with hundreds of others, with the top 300 getting through for interviews. I was one of those selected and it was something Nanny would have loved because she always wanted me to join the civil service – a safe and secure job! I did go for an interview and it went well. As I had just broken through to the Dublin senior team, Róisín Deasy, wife of my teammate, Dermot, worked in the Department of Health and followed up with contact on my behalf but I declined to go any further in the process. We discussed the possibility of deferring my involvement and Róisín urged me to come back to them but I never did. It was a good, pensionable job but I didn't see any real way that it could help me with sport!

All through Leaving Cert classes I had passed the time perfecting my autograph in anticipation of great things to come. That was really all that was in my head around that time.

An important milestone on my life journey came years later when I eventually grasped that while sport is important and sporting dreams are there to be chased it is equally important to have other dreams, like academic goals.

When Dublin won the All-Ireland in 2013 against Mayo, at least twenty of the panel were in college and it was roughly the same for Mayo. That statistic offers a great message to impressionable youngsters: you have a better chance of playing football for your county if you go to college. Had I received that message as a kid I would have studied like a surgeon. Instead I put all my eggs into the hoops basket and, later, the football kitbag. Ahead of the 1993 All-Ireland schools basketball semi-final I picked up a dead leg and actually took three weeks out of school in sixth year to get right for the final. Well, that was my excuse anyway. Madness!

I knew that my Leaving Certificate exams would clash with USA 94, so I wore it as a badge of pride that the exams wouldn't interrupt my viewing of the World Cup. I chose my subjects based on how soon I could finish – so biology got the nod over art – and I picked my subjects on the basis of exam scheduling. The upshot was that I managed to get all my exams out of the way in just six days, which left me with ample time to watch all the games. That's where school stood in my list of priorities and such were the crazy decisions that followed.

While some teachers frowned, others aided and abetted my wander years – they would get me out of class on errands! One of my regular duties was to visit the launderette in Phibsborough to get the school soccer jerseys washed.

I ducked and dodged shamelessly. Having worked out when the career-guidance teacher took half-days, I would excuse myself from maths or English on the grounds I had a meeting with the same career-guidance teacher – who by then had left the building.

It was easy to get away with it but it all ended on a pretty low note. I did the Leaving and did okay, scraped a D3 in higher-level English and a few honours at pass level. I switched to pass maths a week before the exam. Just imagine what I could have achieved had I opened a book. When the CAO offers came out, I was given the option of meat marketing in some college somewhere but I didn't take up the offer!

It illustrates, I suppose, the moral of the story about education: you can't make sport – whether football, rugby or swimming – the be-all and end-all. You need a plan outside of it too and some kids might need assistance in seeing that.

Still, I have fond memories of my school years. I went from being a kid who was harassed and abused because of the way he looked to being a kid who stood out because he excelled in sport.

8

Minor to Major

On the day after we beat Wexford in the 1994 Leinster minor final we headed out to Malahide to celebrate in the St Sylvester's clubhouse where a few of the Dublin senior team – Ger Regan, Shay Keogh and Paul Clarke – were inside. After a while they beckoned us to join them and it was an easy sell because those lads were heroes to us. We were sheepish because we were in awe of them and we couldn't believe that they wanted us to join them.

But in that clubhouse we shared stories. We were all Dublin footballers.

We had dealt with Wexford handily enough, 2–12 to 2–6. I managed to get a goal after Whelo hacked at a ball out the field – though he later claimed he passed it – and sent it whizzing towards my patch. Whatever it was I should have appreciated it because I didn't get many more off him! Out to the corner I tore, turned my man, cut back in and finished it off. That's what I was about – get the ball and go for goal. I had a real hunger for goals.

With Dublin playing Meath in the 1994 senior final on the same day we got a much bigger crowd than for the minor semi-final against Carlow. The game was tight and the ground was pretty full and fairly buzzing at the end. I got a nice feel for the place and as the ball shivered the net, despite being down at the Canal End I wheeled around to gesture back to Hill 16. Just like that night playing basketball in Castlebar, the rush I felt was something I will never forget.

Eamon McLoughlin was another who wasn't bound by GAA convention. He decided that after the game we should run to the Hill, crawl on the ground and pay homage to the supporters. We did just that and ended up all over the back page of the papers the next day.

Two weeks before we played Galway in the All-Ireland semi-final I damaged knee ligaments and that badly curtailed me. They had players in Richie Fahey, Declan Meehan, Pádraic Joyce and Mikey Donnellan, who would go on to be superstars. The 1994 season would prove a golden one for minor football, with a hugely talented Kerry team coursing through Munster, Galway were up there with the best and we were a good side ourselves.

I got the first point of the semi-final when I fisted the ball over the bar, but maybe I should have gone for the jugular when the chance arose because we were going to need all the goals we could get. I still get cheesed off thinking of that match. The Leaving Cert results were out that week and we played like a team that had been out on the town celebrating. It really pissed me off, because we just didn't perform. They beat us by three points and, to be honest, the margin flattered us.

They had a guy called John Concannon who gave our full-back, Tom Flaherty, a big man from Kilmacud Crokes, a tough time. Concannon was unmarkable the same day and got a great goal, slicing us open at the back with a jink before hammering the ball into the top corner of the net from 20 yards.

At the other end all the ball was heading into the wrong

corner of the field – for me, at least. Teammates at the other side of the attack feasted on possession while I scrambled for crumbs. Tactically, back then, there were no crossfield balls, the ball was just pumped in. The annoying thing was I felt I had the beating of my man but received no supply. Alan switched me to the 40 and out to centre-forward in the second half and it helped. Frenzied, I went to make up for lost time. We got back into the match after being six points down. That's when my frustration boiled over. I went up for the ball, won it and got taken down by a marker who had been dishing out the verbals. I reacted, as I sometimes did, with fury, passing the ball into my marker's face.

On RTÉ's *Sports Stadium* in the week leading up to the game, Joe Lennon, the Down legend who at that time was considered the foremost expert on the rules of Gaelic football, highlighted my goal in the Leinster final and showered praise on me. But after that All-Ireland semi-final Joe replayed footage of my fit of anger and deplored my lack of discipline. It would be a good while before I learned to control the impulse to retaliate.

Worse still, the first time I met my future father-in-law and was introduced to him as a Dublin minor footballer, he asked me who was the little gurrier on the team that threw the ball at people! I feigned deafness and changed the subject.

There was devastation after that semi-final loss. On the following Monday we took off to St Sylvester's GAA club and then headed for a place close by called The Buttery. As the evening warmed up, Shane Herity spoke: 'Lads, I don't know about ye but I gave up everything for this year for this team.'

A few of us started giggling but Shane spoke away and after a few minutes lads started crying. Joe Woods dropped his son in to meet us and he saw the state of us, lads bawling everywhere at seven o'clock in the evening. It was going to be a long night!

I was back at Mam's house when the phone rang later that week. Mam had met her future husband, Bill Ingle, and had moved from Carrigallen Park out to the Navan Road to live. I went with her. Bill also had a huge interest in sport, he was a cousin of the Irish former boxer Jimmy Ingle. Like myself, Bill would watch anything on TV – horse racing, golf, boxing, GAA. He loved fishing, and he brought me for my first game of golf on a course in Deer Park, before then it was on fields at the back of the house in Finglas. Bill came to some of my basketball games and an awful lot of my soccer and football matches, he drove me around to quite a few of those matches too and followed my career right through until he passed away in December 2014. He loved when my friends called around so he could talk sport to them and Mam always said that he was very proud of what I achieved.

Anyway, when Mam passed the phone to me, I didn't realize that another chapter of my sporting journey was about to unfold.

'Jason? Paul Smith here from Na Fianna,' said the voice on the line. 'The county board were in touch and want you to play a challenge match for the Dublin seniors at the weekend. It's in Nobber against Meath.'

This was three weeks out from the Dubs' 1994 All-Ireland final date with Down and Dr Pat O'Neill, the Dublin manager, was sending out what was essentially a B team against Meath. To me it was an unbelievable invitation. Robbo got the nod too and on match day we sat in the team bus and listened enthralled as Dessie Farrell, Paul Curran, Mick Galvin and Keith Barr exchanged shot-by-slice accounts of their most recent golf rounds. We hit every drive and nine-iron with them on the road to Nobber.

I put in a busy twenty-minute shift near the end of the game, running the legs off myself as usual while all the time observing

Tommy Carr, who was now playing in the forwards and up against a young defender just starting out, Cormac 'Spud' Murphy. They were locked in hand-to-hand combat; two tough boys, going at it from start to finish.

It was great just to hang around in the senior dressing room. Bealo (Paul Bealin) christened me Little Bullet and for the next two weeks Robbo and I were asked to stay on and help boost numbers at training. I saw it as a pretty cool thing to be training with the Dubs in the lead-up to an All-Ireland final and it was brilliant to be in and around the senior players.

We trained at Parnell Park for the fortnight before the final. Pat didn't talk much to us fledglings but we were still part of it. It was great craic. Johnny Barr, Wayne Daly and Shay Keogh would start a sing-song after training in the showers, your well-known Irish ballads with a few Wolfe Tones numbers thrown in. We got a Mars bar afterwards and went our separate ways. As I look back now, it was proper old school.

At training they threw me in at corner-forward. There were a couple of injuries and suspensions for the manager to contend with and Paul Curran was only returning to the team at corner-back, having missed the All-Ireland semi-final with a broken jaw. Rusty and obviously looking after himself in the lead-up to the big game, Curraner spent those couple of weeks literally hanging out of me, holding me back and chuckling away to himself.

The thing was that when he got to Croker he couldn't just pull and drag Mickey Linden as he had done with me. Curraner had a tough day in the corner and maybe that's because he hadn't challenged himself as much as he might have in training. But I was only a kid – I was hardly going to speak up and complain that one of my heroes was tracking me so closely.

I got two tickets and one pass for the post-match celebration from the county board for my efforts and the minor panel met at Maher's Bar beforehand. It was a dirty, drizzly day and we wanted to see who would win the minor final. We watched that game from the Hill, looking on as Kerry beat Galway. I kept my eye on Concannon and saw the robust welcome he received from the Kerry full-back. He wasn't as effective that day! As for our seniors, well everyone knows that we missed a penalty (again) and lost by two points. With the rain lashing down and the reality of another loss dawning for Dublin, the day was nicely summed up by one supporter during one break of play. As the lull of silence descended on the Hill the supporter cried out: 'Fuckin' Jaysus. Fuck.'

We all nodded in agreement.

After we left Maher's we moved out to Na Fianna before I headed across the city to commiserate with the senior team at the Burlington Hotel. Any of them I saw came over to say hello and told me I would be with them next year. That was very nice of them considering how low they would have been after that defeat. Their encouragement was music to my ears. One guy told me, 'Jason, we need new blood and you'll be part of it.'

As much as there were a few drinks oiling the conversation, it was nice to see that kind of genuine warmth. Later in the evening, I spotted Páidí Ó Sé. Being a GAA anorak I was in awe of him and all he stood for. The prince of them all. Páidí walked past me, turning heads as he did so, but then did a double take. 'Ah, the man they brought out to the forty,' he quipped, referring to my switch to centre-forward in the minor semi-final against Galway. It showed the depth of Páidí's knowledge that he remembered me!

Uncle Eddie felt I should even have been named as a sub for the final against Down but there was no chance of that happening.

With winter approaching, my minor teammates Eamon and Mick O'Keefe went to open soccer trials with UCD and

I tagged along, although after a few weeks I decided there was no point in continuing the trek across the city and out the N11 because I wouldn't have had the necessary points to get into any course at the college. I saw no mention of meat marketing anywhere on the Belfield curriculum! I rang The Doc – Dr Tony O'Neill, UCD head of sport – to explain why I would be dropping out of trials, but he told me not to worry, to keep going and see what transpired.

Thanks to The Doc, I ended up on a UCD scholarship, studying part-time for a diploma in health, safety and welfare, the first course of its kind. I remember The Doc bringing me to the door of the lecture theatre, like a proud parent dropping off a child for the first day at school and then leaving me to it. That's as far as he could take me and only as he dropped me off did the reality of what I had signed up for strike home. I had little interest in doing that course and didn't really want to be there.

Luckily for me, Ken Hogan, the former Tipperary hurling goalie, was doing the course too, as without him I would have been lost. I was just eighteen in a group of much more mature classmates who were all in outside employment and unlike them I was there not so much to study as to play soccer. I made a beeline to sit beside Ken. He knew my background, so we had things in common.

The course entailed lectures two nights a week and as I lived on the Northside the logistics proved a real pain. I had to take the number 10 bus over and back, sometimes sitting in traffic for two hours as we crawled across a crowded city in rush hour. It was a massive bore and it didn't help that I had little interest in the course material. But it was all just a means to an end.

Many former teammates and friends were moving on with their lives and carving careers but, from my point of view, there was no panic at all. I was in college, playing soccer, getting a few bob for it and about to become a full-blown Dublin footballer. I had options in a few sports and I reckoned I was doing okay. I was my own man and liked the variety and breezy independence of it all. I don't recall ever sitting down with a frown, worrying about the path that lay ahead. I was too busy getting on with life.

In the winter of 1994 I was officially called into the Dublin squad for the 1994–95 Church & General National Football League and I had just signed a soccer contract with UCD and would be paid £60 a week for the duration of the season in the League of Ireland First Division. The most coveted perk was a £10 win bonus per match. It turned out we had a great team and won seventeen league games that season. Every three or four weeks we would cash in that win bonus to get our hands on a few extra bob. I started off that campaign in the reserves and played against Ken DeMange who was with Bohemians. Ken had been with Liverpool before that and he told me to keep working hard and that I had a good chance of making it. I heeded his advice, put my head down and after a couple of weeks broke into the starting eleven and stayed there for the season.

I was having a whale of a time, with few overheads to worry about and I was playing sport for a bit of pocket money. The UCD team was sponsored by Budweiser and let's just say we appreciated their backing and the few pints after games in the Sports Bar in the Montrose Hotel!

In between my Dublin football commitments I managed to play weekly for UCD. We went on to win the 1994–95 First Division title and I was voted PFAI Player of the Year for that tier. I reckon I barely pipped my strike partner Mick O'Byrne to it, because Micko had been locked and loaded all season and scored fourteen goals. He would hit another fourteen in the next campaign. The newspapers had us down as Irish soccer's most lethal pairing and every day there were new reports of UK scouts coming to look at us.

Nice to read, but little substance to them.

Still, that season gave me a taste of what life as a full-time soccer professional would have been like because, at the end of March, Micko and I were named as two League of Ireland players called up to feature in the Republic of Ireland under-21 squad against England in Dalymount Park, a game that was live on Sky Sports. We were handed numbers 19 and 20 but didn't get on against an English team that included Ray Parlour, Gary Neville, Nicky Butt and Trevor Sinclair.

I got no game time, but didn't feel at all out of place at training and Micko and I were then invited to spend the following week with the Irish senior side. The FAI had a PR initiative of inviting League of Ireland players to train with the seniors and the two of us were sent forward ahead of the team's Euro 96 qualifier with Northern Ireland (which would end 1–1). We joined the squad at the Forte Crest Hotel in Dublin Airport, trained with them for three days, ate with them and took our place on the team bus and later in the dressing room on match day. The day before the game we trained at Lansdowne Road and I remember Roy Keane and Jason McAteer whipping in balls for Niall Quinn, John Aldridge, Micko and I. Was this what I was destined for?

Being in a full Ireland squad was fairly surreal but they were all normal lads – Roy Keane, Niall Quinn and the rest of that team. Alan McLoughlin stood out, a good guy, and we chatted quite a bit. They were household names who enjoyed the perks of celebrity when they came to Dublin. One afternoon we were given two hours free time and Jason McAteer got the bus back from town weighed down with armfuls of stuff, including boxer shorts that normally cost £20 a pop – all gifts from admiring manufacturers and shopkeepers. Roy was always about the lobby, just one of the lads at that stage. I asked him to sign a shirt for a relative and it was no problem to him.

One night we all went to the cinema in Santry and as soon as the squad walked in it was carte blanche – we could have whatever we wanted. I ended up sitting beside Tony Cascarino watching *Dumb and Dumber*. Tony was cracking up all the way through and again it was unreal to be there beside him.

Travelling with the team on match day was an experience too. Mick Byrne was the masseur but he was much more than that; he was largely responsible for the camaraderie in the camp and looked out for everyone. Going to the stadium on the team bus with Irish songs blaring was part of the experience I really loved! I remember Jack giving the team talk with his back to me. I was sitting in between Ronnie Whelan and Andy Townsend, Ronnie was telling a joke and Jack heard the fuss. He turned around to see who the culprit was but Ronnie denied everything! It was obvious he wasn't flavour of the month with Jack at that stage. I did all I could to keep a straight face on me or it definitely would be my last time in an Irish dressing room!

I felt no great sadness when the squad broke up and I went back to normality. Maybe I just assumed I would get back there again and took it for granted all that would fall into place. And sure if it didn't, I had dreams to play with the Dublin footballers to fall back on.

In later years, I met many of the Ireland soccer team through my TV work and they would always approach me and shake hands. But on the afternoon we drew with Northern Ireland they flew back to their clubs and millionaire lifestyles and I felt no great let-down heading home.

Truth be told, Micko and I found the whole 'stay in your room' thing a bit boring. We were closed up in our bedrooms for ten hours a day at times. As for Big Jack Charlton, well, he hadn't a clue who I was – but from what I heard I wasn't the only one in that boat!

There was a bit of added sparkle to UCD's season when, thanks to The Doc's connections, we got to play a friendly against Liverpool in May 1995 to celebrate the club's centenary. They had played Blackburn Rovers on the Sunday – the day Blackburn, managed by Kenny Dalglish, clinched the title in Anfield. They landed in Dublin and played us the following Tuesday, 16 May, and on a rain-drizzled night over 20,000 turned up at Lansdowne Road.

All the big names were there: Steve McManaman, David James, Robbie Fowler, Jamie Redknapp, Phil Babb, Nigel Clough and Michael Thomas. We didn't have much of the ball but I held my own and early in the game I won a couple of frees off Steve Harkness, who wasn't too pleased and accused me of diving.

Phil Babb, whom I knew a little from training with Ireland, came over to me and offered friendly advice: 'Jason, stay on your feet or you'll get done here.' I protested to Phil that I hadn't gone to ground intentionally at all and just then a ball came down between us. I let it slip through my legs – and Babbsy's – and he was less than impressed at being nutmegged.

Packie Lynch scored from the free. I had a few goal chances myself but David James, one of the biggest men I had ever seen on a playing field, had gloves like shovels and saved everything. We lost 3–1 but acquitted ourselves well.

Back at the Burlington the Liverpool manager, Roy Evans, stopped me in the lobby: 'Listen, well done tonight,' he said. 'We'd love to have a look at you in Anfield. Would you like to come over and train with us?'

'Yeah,' I replied, 'that'd be great.'

The next day I was splashed all over the back pages. Newcastle and Everton were reportedly after me. This time there seemed more substance to the reports. The *Irish Press* had Everton's chief scout in Ireland, Jim Emery, saying they wanted to strengthen their Irish connection. The *Evening Press* reported that Newcastle's Dublin scout, Frank O'Neill, was compiling research on me.

I never heard anything concrete but in the following weeks, months and even years the media raved about me going to any number of clubs, until I eventually started to wonder if I was being set up for a fall.

But in 1995 there was little time to stop and think about that because there was another game looming. The Republic of Ireland under-21s were playing Austria and I was determined to make my mark and get a game. Mark Kennedy had just moved from Millwall to Liverpool for £1.5 million, a British transfer record for a teenager at the time. He was Ireland's main man at under-21 and he called all the shots. Ahead of the game in Inchicore, on 10 June, we were sent out training under Maurice Setters. I put myself about in that session, but some of the players, including Mark, didn't appreciate my intensity and told me to ease off as that wasn't how they did it in England on the day before a game.

I got stuck in even harder.

With twenty minutes left in the Austria game at Richmond Park, I warmed up hoping that I would get a call. Maurice turned to me and gave me the nod. I was called off the bench and handed my only cap. I have no doubt it was on the back of the impact I had made in training and Maurice was acknowledging the effort I put in.

While on the field against Austria, I created a goal for a fella called Declan Perkins, an English-born lad, and we won 3–0. Near the end, and maybe this is unrealistic thinking on my part, Perkins could have returned the favour by putting me through on goal, but he went for his hat-trick and I missed out on what would have been a great moment to score on my debut. That turned out to be my last game of soccer for the year.

The Leinster Football Championship was only days away and my life was about to change.

Forever.

9

Boom Boom Boom

A snapshot of how things used to be.

On a Saturday night in December 1994 I headed up north to play soccer for UCD against Finn Harps and, to his credit, Dr Tony arranged and paid for a taxi to bring me from Donegal to Dublin afterwards, as I was playing football for Dublin the next day.

I was starving on the journey home and asked the driver to stop off in Sligo for a bag of chips, but it was a quick stop-off. The following afternoon's game threw in at two o'clock and I needed rest.

On the Sunday, I lined out for Dublin against Donegal at Croker and grabbed a goal and a point. I scored the goal after snaffling the ball from the Donegal goalkeeper Gary Walsh and as it hit the net I turned to the Hill, waving and milking the applause. I was in soccer mode!

My teammate Sean Cahill came steaming toward me: 'Jason, we don't do that! Get back in position!'

But I was happy. Happy going from week to week, sometimes day to day, serving two masters – or doctors, as it happened.

Dr Tony wasted no time springing me into the UCD first

eleven and Dr Pat pitched me right into the cauldron with the Dublin seniors during the 1994–95 league campaign.

I had put my name to a contract with UCD but the crucial part of that deal was being freed up to play for the Dubs whenever possible. It was no big deal, the GAA wasn't anywhere near as demanding as it is now and Dr Tony knew that me playing for the county footballers would help UCD's profile.

I got into both first-team squads around the same time and it also helped that the college played their home games on Thursday nights, mainly to attract student support, so I was usually free for weekends of Gaelic football.

Not long after Dublin lost to Down in the 1994 All-Ireland final, I was given my full Dublin debut, away to Kerry in the first round of the NFL. There was no hoopla about it. In those days the league started before Christmas and even though it was Dublin and Kerry, there was little hype. I was allowed to get on with things.

Dublin were still in semi-mourning after that All-Ireland final loss and the first stage of dealing with the grief involved bringing in some new blood in the hope of reviving the patient. Enda Sheehy, Martin Doran and myself were identified as hopes for the future but the main thing for me was that I had trained with the lads for two weeks before the All-Ireland. They knew me and I knew them. The fortnight's training had reassured me I wasn't out of my depth.

That said, my first game more or less passed me by. We took the morning train to Killarney and I remember we were served with a full Irish breakfast. It's a far cry from the pre-match meals nowadays!

Late in the game, Dessie Farrell helped me make my mark. Dessie was starting to own the centre-forward slot and he made a great run that drew my marker as well as his own. Suddenly I had space, Dessie played me in and while most players might have popped it over the bar, my instinct was always to see if a goal was on. It was. I let fly from 20 yards and the green flag shot up. It looked like we would leave Kerry with a draw, no small result, until they raced up the other end and fired the winning point.

They beat us 1–12 to 1–11 on the last Sunday in October and that was a foretaste of how the league would pan out for us. We slipped into a relegation battle but I had survived my first test at that level and was going to get more opportunities.

To this day, league football can be like an audition on *The X Factor*. Play well, get through to the next round of auditions and go from there. I remember doing well against Laois in Portlaoise in front of 6,000 people in November and a few months later I hit five points in the annual Dubs Stars challenge which took place at Ballyboden St Enda's. That day I met Jim Stynes, an inspirational, larger-than-life figure who left Dublin to play in the Australian Football League for years, impacting on many lives during his short time on this earth.

There was plenty of excitement brewing through my hectic double life and the endless possibilities opening up. In January 1995, Jimmy Magee highlighted that dual life while commentating on an FAI Cup first-round tie between UCD and Cork City. Jimmy suggested it was easy to see why I was in demand and that was really the first time at national level that people from outside the GAA could see what Pat O'Neill saw in me.

The tie against Cork turned into a marathon series. We were a First Division team and they were top of the Premier Division, the best team in Ireland. I scored in the first game, at Belfield, but an injury-time equalizer by Billy Woods brought us all down to Turners Cross for the replay, which also ended in a draw. They had John Caulfield, Patsy Freyne, Declan Daly, Dave Hill, Johnny Glynn and Pat Morley and while they could play a bit they could kick lumps out of you too.

The flip of a coin determined the venue for the third match. Packie Lynch, our captain, took some serious slagging when he lost the toss and it was back down to Cork again for a midweek game with an afternoon kick-off – there were no floodlights there at the time. On a horrible January afternoon of snow and sleet, we were beaten a 1–0 in extra time. But it just showed the level we were playing at, it took them three games to see us off.

UCD beat Longford Town to win the First Division title on a Saturday night in Strokestown. It was a huge deal but I declined to go on the lash with the lads because the Dubs were out the next day, 29 March, against Derry at Croker.

For most of that game against Derry, a relegation clash for us, we trailed, and I was still warming the subs' bench with twenty minutes to go, frustrated because all I ever wanted to do was play. 'Are they going to bring me on or what?' I grumbled to no one in particular.

Next thing I heard a rumble from the selectors: 'Jay, you're on!'

I hopped up and ran to the sideline only to get a puzzled look from a selector: 'No! I said Shay [Keogh], not Jay.' I was livid because I wanted to be part of the action, especially after my abstinence from UCD's celebrations on the previous night!

Eventually, with seven minutes left, they brought me on. I went in and around the Derry full-back line, won two frees, both converted, and we drew 1–9 apiece. That afternoon I left Croke Park with the complete hump

After missing a night celebrating with my UCD mates, after going straight home on the night we won the league title, to come back with the Dubs and get only seven minutes? I wasn't happy. That might come across as cheeky for an upstart only in the squad a wet week, but I had belief. And I loved playing. I was also strong-minded, determined and impatient. It would be the first of many challenges with Dublin management teams.

*

The anger simmered and spring arrived, the ground hard-ened, temperatures rose and Dublin played a challenge with Westmeath less than a month out from the 1995 Leinster Championship. Mick Galvin and Dessie Farrell arranged to give me a lift down to the game and we met at Hanlon's Corner. We hammered them, scoring seven goals in the process and immediately afterwards I headed off to join my UCD teammate Shay Kelly at his house in Offaly to celebrate his twenty-first birthday. We spent a second night celebrating with Shay, a brother of long-time Offaly goalkeeper Padraig, and his family in Mucklagh, where they owned Kelly's Roadhouse. From there it was back to Dublin for UCD training before I made for Portugal on a week's holiday with Uncle Brian to get some rest before the GAA season really took off.

Dr Pat was happy enough and didn't put any real pressure on me to commit 100 per cent. Pat was quite aloof with his players; I think he felt familiarity with any of us might weaken his authority.

Throwing a guy like myself, with no real background in elite football, into that pressure cooker was a gamble but Dublin had been so close so many times – losing the iconic games against Meath in 1991, the All-Ireland semi-final against Derry in 1993 and two All-Ireland final defeats against Donegal in 1992 and Down in 1994. I think Dr Pat was brave and he backed me. He recognized I brought certain qualities that could help: an ability to take defenders on and shoot.

For the first time in years, our half-backs wouldn't make those lung-bursting late runs into the opposition half for which they had become famous. The half-backs had long been known as a marauding, attacking unit, but in 1995 they were told to hold their shape, that defending was the priority. The forwards were trusted to do the job up front. At training, cones were placed just in front of the halfway line and they were told not to pass those marks. Instead they had to feed their forwards quicker. It made sense. We had great lads up top – Clarkey, Dessie and Charlie Redmond – and I had broken into the side too, eager and hungry to find space and take my man on.

But I was given a reality check at the start of the summer. In the build-up to the first game, against Louth in Navan, I thought I was flying it after coming back nice and fresh from Portugal two-and-a-half weeks before the championship started. I horsed into the first session, intending to pick up from where I had left off, but by the end of it I was on my knees with lungs burning. I hadn't even taken a drink on the holiday, nor had I overeaten, but obviously I had lost a bit aerobically.

On the morning of the game I was home alone on the Navan Road. Mam and Bill were away on holidays and I had the run of the house that week. I was never the most domesticated – Mam and Nanny had always looked after me in that area – and so I had let the food supplies run low. I found some pasta twirls in the press and, after reading the instructions of how to cook them, I put a pot on the boil, then went to grab a tin of beans. There were none left so I reached for a tin of peas instead and stuck them in the microwave and mixed the whole mess together. It wasn't a very appealing concoction but I knew I had to eat something. Then I grabbed the gearbag and headed for the team bus.

On the way into Navan the travelling Dubs were out in force to welcome us. They formed what looked like a guard of honour to let the bus pass through the town and they shouted their encouragement to us as we went by. I realized just what being a Dublin player meant. It was rare enough we got out of the city in those days – it still is, I suppose – but you could see even the senior players were taken aback by the enthusiasm of the fans. It was a real buzz.

The welcome was great but there remained a problem: I was still ravenous. We headed for the dressing room, the players keeping their heads down, avoiding eye contact with supporters for fear of losing focus. But my eyes were wide open, my ears cocked. And then I heard the cry I'd been waiting for, as sweet sounding as the last school bell of the day: 'Any three bars for a pound! Get three bars for a pound!'

I dropped the gearbag, ran to the stall and handed the woman my punt. I gobbled two bars in the dressing room and saved the third for after the game. A delightful menu ahead of my first senior championship match: pasta, mushed peas and two lovely chocolate bars.

Inside the dressing room another problem awaited – I couldn't reach the clothes pegs without hopping up on the bench. Up stepped Clarkey, chuckling away to himself as he hooked my tracksuit on the wall, hardly able to believe his luck, the mileage he was getting out of me! It was a bit of fun before the serious stuff began.

I reckon that game against Louth was one of those where it was just predetermined that, unlike against Derry, no matter how the game would go, I was going to get a run. It happened sooner than I thought. I got on after twenty-one minutes when Sean Cahill was taken off. I was impatient to get stuck in and even more anxious to get the oversized tracksuit off me because I looked like the team mascot for the day. The call came and I sprinted on to the pitch with my precious slip of paper for Brian White, the referee. Just a minute later I made a run down the wing, stretching the Louth defence. I laid off the ball, took a return pass and won a penalty with my second touch of the ball after being tackled in the penalty area. As I fell in the tackle, the knobbly knees of another Louth player caught me on the head. 'Welcome to senior championship football, Jason!' I thought to myself.

Over comes Charlie: 'Jason, get up! Never let them see that you're hurting.'

I wasn't hurt, just dazed, so I got up and ran back out the field. Mick Galvin came over to check on me – something he would continue to do long after that day. I assured him I was grand and we waved the medics away.

Charlie's advice was simple but it stayed with me for the rest of my career. 'Never let them see you're hurting!'

Clarkey had taken over the penalty duties from Charlie and, wouldn't you know, he missed, his shot saved well by Niall O'Donnell. It was one of those things back then, no one on the Dublin team could score a penalty. It was just a phase we went through.

Anyway, I was tackled again soon after, this time by another Louth defender. I went down, but Charlie was over like a flash again: 'Get up, you're taking this, Jay!'

'I am in my shite, Charlie,' I replied. I had never before hit a competitive free, nor was I exactly known for my classical kicking style at that stage of my career.

'You are!' he roared. 'Just put it over the bar. That's the only way to respond.'

I was 21 yards out, the free was to the right of the goal and instead of placing my left shoulder to the posts and kicking with my instep, I just punt-kicked it straight on, all the time terrified that I would miss. I met it with the bootlaces and followed through. It was a shocking kick but it staggered over the bar and I proudly retired with a 100 per cent record as free-taker which I would later remind teammates of. As a coach nowadays, however, let's just say that I'm glad no footage of that effort has surfaced!

That was Charlie. He knew that nailing an easy free – easy by his standards – would help me. I reckon he wanted me to prove that I belonged at this level. The other side was that, if I missed the free, it would nearly have been the end of me because the jury was still out on whether the novelty of having me involved, and the attention I received, would offer any substantial benefit to the team.

The likes of Charlie and Mick also gave advice if a marker was giving me gyp. The moment my marker started to get physical with me I was to head towards the umpires with my arms raised. In those days a forward got mauled all the time, especially a fast forward, and being so young, small and light I was a magnet for all sorts of treatment. So that's what I did – every time my marker wanted to tangle I'd rush over to the umpires with my arms raised. This would lead to an air of bemusement for both the umpires and my marker who had never encountered anything like this before. That day in Navan the Dublin supporters behind the town-end goal looked out for me too; they were like a pantomime audience howling at the villain.

In a tight enough tussle we got over Louth 0–19 to 2–5 and I was up and running. Coming off the field with my first Dublin senior shirt on my back, I knew instinctively where it was going – to be framed and then down to the lads in Ballyhea.

There was huge amusement down south at the size of the jersey; one that I had swam in. I was just a kid in a man's world but I loved every second of it. I didn't dominate possession in our games in 1995, but I think I did make an impact in deciding the outcome of each game.

We prepared for Laois in the Leinster semi-final and come 1 July, with three more weeks' training under my belt, I was gearing up to make the starting fifteen. Getting my first championship start against Laois held much significance for me because it was where Nanny came from and where her people still live. They all came to see the game so it was a big one for them too. Laois were a quality outfit and we struggled for a long time to put them away. In fact, it was only when Jim Gavin came off the bench and put me through with a lovely diagonal ball that we put daylight between us. Collecting the ball, I turned my man, got in on goal and lost my boot in the process. But I lashed at the ball with my right sock and it flew past the goalie.

Usually, whenever I did get one on one, I was composed enough and my preference was finishing with the outside of my right boot, sliding it past the oncoming keeper. That's what I had done in the first half when Mick put me through on goal. But that shot hit the inside of the post, rolled across the goal line and then hit the other post. Technically, I had ticked the box but still it stayed out.

This time I fell to my knees after scoring. I was having a great time until Charlie came in, patted me on the head and told me to 'Get the fuck up'. I got up quickly, grabbed my boot and ran back to my position before putting the boot on.

The scrutiny definitely tightened from then. We beat Laois 1–13 to 0–9 and I was asked to do a post-match interview. No problem. I had a Reebok shirt on, but as I went out someone asked me to put on a Dublin polo shirt sponsored by Arnotts.

'Sure why would I do that?' I asked.

Through basketball contacts I had worn Reebok boots and gear. I had no deal with them but they were always sound so I stuck with them. But it caused a right stir when I refused the Arnotts shirt. I couldn't understand the fuss.

In the next week I was asked to do loads of media and PR stuff. Jimmy Grey, the former Dublin hurling trainer, put me in touch with Kevin Moran, who was an agent for sports athletes in the UK. Kevin was also working as an analyst for RTÉ soccer and Jimmy and I went out to Donnybrook to meet him one night and he said he'd help me out.

I knew the landscape and that I was now in demand. Kevin

just started to look after all enquiries so I didn't have to worry about them.

All of that was far from my mind as Leinster final day arrived. At some stage during the first half Colm Coyle sidled over to me, him tough as teak and me light as a jockey. Physically and verbally, Colm did everything he could to run me out of town and shadowed me everywhere but it didn't work. We were dominant in the first half but then they got a goal before Graham Geraghty put them a point ahead with twenty minutes left. But after Clarkey's goal they finally ran out of steam and we ended up winning handsomely by ten points.

After one stray elbow from Colm, I went down and the Hill howled in unison. The referee, Pat Casserly, ran over and awarded a free-in. As I lay on the ground, the TV cameras caught me giving Pat Duggan, our team doctor, a wink. I soon clipped over my first point, dragged myself off the floor and sauntered over to Colm.

'Is that your best?'

'I'm only getting started,' he replied, which led to me parking myself in front of the umpires and thousands of my new best friends up in the Hill.

We were both just competing as hard as we could and at the end I looked him in the eye and we shook hands. In later years he would have his revenge.

As I tried to make an impact that season, I was probably a bit rash and anxious when it came to shooting points. Sometimes I would snatch at shots and against Meath that resulted in me kicking two 'garryowens'.

For the first, I lobbed it high, it came back down and was recycled back out to me before I put it over the bar. For the second, I again went for the posts but I snatched at it again and the ball came off my boot all wrong and hung in the air for an age. When it eventually dropped Clarkey got a fist to it and directed it to the net. I did try to claim that I made an assist! The game turned there and then, and when with time running out Casserly penalized Colm for another foul on me, I leaned over and gave Pat a grateful peck on the cheek. It happened so quickly he was lost for a reaction.

After the game Seán Boylan came to our dressing room and spoke quietly: 'I have personal friends in here. I still went out to do my damnedest to beat ye. But Jesus, lads, I'm not doing a great job of it these last few years.'

It only took Seán a year to rectify things from a Meath perspective. It would be another seven years before we beat them again!

The following night, *The Game on Monday* editors ran a sequence to the tune of 'Mad About the Boy' showing my kiss for the referee, the 'sock goal' against Laois, the wink to Pat Duggan and a couple of other things. This wasn't the normal level of attention a kid in their debut season would receive. Meanwhile, the papers started giving me two-page spreads and, apparently, I was the GAA's 'first pop star'. But I also got my first inkling that not everything was going to run smoothly.

Nanny answered a knock to the front door and was met by a reporter and photographer who said they were from the local paper in Finglas, *The Forum*. They asked if they could come in, have a chat and take a few pictures. Nanny, being a little daunted but reassured that they were genuine, allowed them inside.

A few days later, and just before the All-Ireland semi-final, I picked up the *Evening Herald* and there was a four-page 'Jayo' special with a whole lot of family history and personal detail. My media profile aside, my mam, nanny and uncles were extremely private people and they didn't ask for or deserve any of that. I was raging.

We asked them not to run the second part of the feature but

they followed up with another four pages on me the next day! What upset me was they had loads of pictures of me as a kid, which they had obtained from our house and of course they hadn't cleared it with me. In my opinion, they took advantage of Nanny, no doubt about it. It was a disgrace – an invasion of Nanny's home and our privacy.

There was no apology or remorse from the *Evening Herald* when I spoke to them about what they had done. They had their story. Move on to the next one. I have never met the journalist whose by-line appeared on the story and have no desire to, but if he or his photographer colleague or his editor, or all three, are still around and happen to read this I hope they recognize even at this late stage how underhand and unprofessional they were.

I decided enough was enough. There would be no more taking advantage. I phoned Kevin Moran's agency – Proactive Sports Management – again and spoke to Jesper Olsen, his business partner and former Manchester United teammate. Jesper listened as I told him about the articles and other mounting demands on my time. That intrusion by the *Herald* was the first sour note in what would become a turbulent relationship with the media for some years afterwards.

Later in my career I would be written off for a few below-par seasons and that was actually fine by me. I was struggling and deserved criticism. As long as it referred to my on-field performance I was fair game. It was the intrusion into private and family matters that got me.

Reporters began ringing the house and Mam had to pull down the blinds a few times to keep prying eyes out. Journalists even rang her at work saying they would come to her office for an interview, but we are a private family and I wasn't going to be their performing seal. I wasn't going to do things for nothing either, so when they phoned looking to compile their specials,

I would enquire about the fee. There was never a fee, so more often than not I declined.

Still, there was no staying off the sports pages. As we prepared for the All-Ireland semi-final against Cork my name was splashed all over – but not for anything I had said or done. This time I was in the cross hairs because my direct opponent, Mark O'Connor, had told reporters he looked forward to our meeting and was confident he could tame me, since I had been subdued against Meath.

Mark gave that quote to the *Evening Echo* and it was probably just a throwaway line. But the *Evening Herald*, again, got hold of it and ran the quote as a roaring banner headline: 'I'll tame Jason.' With a subhead on how I had hardly touched the ball against Meath.

Billy Morgan had worked for RTÉ as an analyst for the Leinster final and was asked that night how, as Cork boss, he would stop me. Billy gave a diplomatic answer but Michael Lyster was having none of it and joked that it would be hard for me trying to sprint around with defenders dragging my shirt and tearing lumps out of me. Billy was clearly uncomfortable with the line of questioning and I was the focus all over again.

On the night before the game, I went to see *Riverdance* at the Point Theatre. I had first seen it on TV during the Eurovision the previous year when on the way back from Kilkenny with the Dublin minors we pulled into a bar in Carlow for post-match grub. When *Riverdance* came on it was clear straight away that we were witnessing something special. The place was riveted. If not for the clatter of dancing feet you could have heard a pin drop.

A year later in the Point, the dancers took my breath away all over again. The audience reaction was ecstatic, a standing ovation that lasted for ages, and as I left the theatre I was in awe of how those dancers and musicians were able to get such emotion out of people. I wondered would I be able to do something similar the next day at Croke Park. I wanted to give the crowd something to get excited about, feed off that same sort of buzz.

But all I did for the first ten minutes was to chase after Mark O'Connor's heels. I was completely out of it. I couldn't even catch my breath. We were all chasing shadows and out on our feet. It looked like Mark would be proved right – he was taming me. He pipped me to every ball and at the other end Mark O'Sullivan was destroying us.

For a while it seemed we were never going to match Cork's intensity. Then we got a free, which Keith Barr took quickly. Playing higher upfield – in that central role up top – I watched the ball seemingly head into the corner towards Mick Galvin. But I copped that Mick was gone. Mick was two steps ahead of everyone and he had vacated the corner to leave space for me.

I got to the ball before Mark. We were one on one. Mark was probably not the most natural full-back. He was powerful but not exceptionally mobile, so I squared him up, basketball style, and when I swivelled and turned he slipped. Off I went, bouncing the ball and almost missing the resultant hop. I saw nothing only space.

Kevin O'Dwyer, the Cork goalie, came off his line to narrow the angle, leaving what I saw as a massive gap on his left. As he advanced I pulled the trigger and the shot stayed low all the way to that corner of the net. Away to the Canal End I turned, adrenaline pulsing and electricity coursing.

In the 1992 NBA play-offs, Michael Jordan stitched together the most memorable three-point shooting sequence of all time. Rat-a-tat-tat they came, six three-pointers on the trot against the Trail Blazers. This led to what became known as 'the shrug' – after scoring the last of that incredible six-in-a-row in the final quarter, MJ turned to camera and threw his arms wide as if to say, 'I don't know why this is happening.'

After scoring the goal against Cork, I thought of that celebration and did my own version of 'the shrug'. I really didn't know why it was happening to me. And then I raced back on to the field before Charlie could get to me and deliver a good clattering!

There was a definite change of mood following that goal, both on the pitch and among the 63,000 in the crowd. The score liberated our team but sucked the life out of Cork. We gained oxygen and they lost it. The belief they had brimmed with drained away. Goals win games and Cork went back into their shell.

It was as if their game plan was in tatters.

As a team, we had shown maturity too. Against Meath in the four games in 1991, Dublin had been naive in the closing moments of some of those games, especially when allowing Kevin Foley through for his famous goal. A few lads from that Dublin team were still around but this time, with another All-Ireland final looming, they were more professional. Barrsy stifled Larry Tompkins any time he got near the danger zone – giving away a 21-yard free was a lot better than conceding a goal. We were more streetwise and got through 1–12 to 0–12.

I had just about enough time to shake Mark's hand, a great guy whom I've met several times since. Then a couple of stewards grabbed me and ushered me towards the tunnel. 'Off the field for your own protection!' one of them told me. But as the crowd poured on I was gobbled up, hoisted high on the shoulders of the blue horde and carried in triumph wearing Mark's Cork jersey and a huge grin.

The crowd struck up a version of the summer tune they had adopted from the Outhere Brothers. They adjusted the lyrics to: 'Boom boom boom, let me hear you say Jayo!' And to that chorus I was eventually led off, with three stewards riding shotgun and everyone wanting to shake my hand.

There I was, a 19-year-old kid from Finglas, with just a year of Gaelic football behind me, seventy minutes away from winning an All-Ireland title. It felt as if the whole world wanted to know me.

Mad when you think about it.

10

Blue Flag on the Summit

On St Patrick's night, 1995, hours after Kilamcud Crokes had won the All-Ireland club title, myself and two friends were on our way from Quinn's pub in Drumcondra to a house party on Jones's Road when we passed Croke Park.

Someone decided it would be great to go in and have a look at the hallowed turf. It was one of those good ideas people tend to get after a few beverages. In those days all we had to conquer was a 10-foot wall with some barbed wire on top near the Hill 16 end of Jones's Road. Our bravery was no doubt fuelled by our time in Quinn's so we went for it. We were young and nimble – it would be no bother to us. Well two of us! We couldn't pull the third fella up so he stood down and agreed to wait outside for our return and keep watch.

As we scaled the wall my pal gashed his hand on the rusty wire but it wasn't enough to prevent us from getting into Croker and walking up the steps into the lower Hogan Stand.

Once inside we just stood there looking out on to the pitch. It was very dark and the only visible signs of Kilmacud's victory earlier in the day was some purple and gold flags. I thought about how cool it would have been for those lads to play there and for them to walk up the steps of the Hogan to collect the cup.

After a few minutes we decided to head to the party but when we got back out on to Jones's Road we inspected my pal's hand under the light of a lamp post and knew he would have to pay a visit to the Mater Hospital accident and emergency department.

We were carrying a bag of cans for the house party and, reckoning we should leave them outside the hospital, we looked around for a hiding spot. There was a newsagent's across the road from the hospital and outside was a rectangular box where all the next day's newspapers were stashed. We decided to leave our cans there behind it.

Our injured pal received stitches in his hand, we retrieved the cans and headed down the road, hoping the party would still be in full flow. We hadn't gone far when a squad car pulled up alongside. Our first instinct was that we had been rumbled for breaking into Croker.

'Where are ye going lads?'

'Ah just here and there, guard. Heading to a house party now.'

'What happened to the hand?' the garda asked.

'Just ripped it off an old gate. I'll be fine.'

They weren't convinced.

'Come in here, get in the car lads and we'll go back to the station and have a chat.'

We were put into the squad car for the short trip back up to Mountjoy Station. I had never been in trouble with the guards and now our great idea of going into Croker didn't seem so clever.

Our interrogation started and it was soon evident that our trip down Jones's Road wasn't even on the agenda. Instead it turned out that a neighbour of the newsagent owner had seen us skulking by the wall and collecting our cans. The neighbour thought we were robbing newspapers and phoned the guards.

We were left to wait a while before the superintendent summoned me into his office. Luckily he recognized me. 'Are you the Dublin footballer they are all talking about?' he asked. I said I was and, copping that we were no great threat to public order, he told us to be on our way. I thanked him and headed for the door but the lad with the sore paw wanted to make a point.

'Lads, I know ye have a tough job, but wouldn't ye be better off out there picking up the fellas that are doing drugs and stealing stuff than taking the likes of us away in a squad car?'

I winced as the super looked at me and said, 'If I were you, I'd get your friend out of here very quickly.'

I didn't need a second invitation. We left the station and went back to Jones's Road and the house party, arriving there hours later than scheduled with everyone wondering how it had taken us three hours to get from Quinn's to Jones's Road. We decided it was best not to share our story!

As for our friend with the damaged hand, turns out he missed a club championship match for Na Fianna but could never say why!

I passed Croke Park again that night and imagined myself being back there in September – this time not as a gatecrasher but as part of a winning Dublin team. Now I was only one step away from that becoming a reality but we still had another river to cross and everything we wanted was on the other side.

*

Every Saturday, two weeks before games, we had a fifteen versus fifteen training match, As v Bs, at St Vincent's, as their pitch has the same dimensions as Croke Park. Robbie Boyle had been on the bench for most of the year but in the run-up to the final he was on fire. Every night at training he marked Dermot Deasy and there was no stopping him. Dermot had been struggling all year with injury, he had a back problem, and coming back from a complaint like that is not easily done. Meanwhile Robbie had been red-hot since the semi-final and was making more of an impact than any of the other forwards in the panel.

At half-time in the trial game, I decided to make a move to try and see if he should get a run on the A team. I ambled over to Pat full of purpose and asked if he wanted to try Robbie at full-forward on that first fifteen.

Pat looked at me as if I had just landed from another planet. 'What?' he barked, half irritated at the idea of being offered advice.

'Do you want to try Robbie full-forward instead of me? He's on fire.'

'We pick the team!' he snapped, as he turned on his heels, indicating that any such call would lie with the management and not a young greenhorn.

Pat was right, of course, but if I felt strongly about something I spoke my mind. That has always been, and still is, the way with me. John Horan recalls a day in school when I stood up for a classmate against a teacher. I landed myself in trouble for that, but I failed to see what I had done wrong. That's who I am. I speak up when it's needed, when I feel it's warranted, and just because someone is put in charge of me – or my group – I don't automatically feel I have to bow to authority in every situation.

That was why I felt free to offer my two cents' worth to Pat. I realize now that this is something you would not expect from a player preparing to start in his first All-Ireland final and maybe I was a little impetuous. No doubt his abruptness towards me was borne out of surprise at what I had said to him but I was annoyed at his response and so began a stand-off with the Dublin management that lasted right up until half-time of the All-Ireland final.

For the remainder of the build-up to the final there were

very few words uttered between us. I was stubborn at the best of times and I'm sure they were questioning whether I was ready for the challenge ahead if I was asking for another player to take my place.

There had been a little bit of tension anyway. Earlier in the year at one session I had felt too sick to train but the management insisted I take a full part in the session and even declared I was well capable of a 95 per cent effort. How they arrived at that figure was beyond me, but that's what they told me.

'Grand so,' I thought to myself, 'if that's what ye think, I'll train to exactly ninety-five per cent of my capacity and no more.' And as the speed tests started I would hare off, sprinting at full throttle until the last couple of yards and then suddenly apply the brakes. Pure thickness, I know. I suppose this was just an example of what they were dealing with.

Some of the lads on the team were asked by the manager to check in on me before the final so on the Monday before the match Mam and I returned home to find a car parked across the road occupied by three Dublin blue bloods: John O'Leary, Keith Barr and Mick Galvin. I was told to hop into the car, that we were going for a drive – it reminded me of the Paddy's night episode all over again! They brought me to the Hole in the Wall pub on Blackhorse Avenue, put a drink in front of me, a soft one on this occasion, and asked if everything was okay.

'What do you mean?' I enquired.

'The manager was just wondering if you're alright. They're worried the whole thing is getting to you.'

'No, it's not getting to me,' I answered emphatically. 'I'm just pissed off they dismissed me because I made a suggestion to try and help the team.'

The boys listened. Friendship with men of their calibre was a huge part of my 1995 season and I respected them. I would always go training with Mick, and Keith would join us later in the Shamrock Lodge in Finglas, which was owned by Shay Cassells. It was literally part of our regime that having sweated buckets on the training field we stopped in for a few sociables on the way home. It was part of the recovery protocol in those days! The boys would have a couple of pints of Guinness, but for me it was mostly Coke or Fanta. I often sat with them for hours just listening to their stories. Don't get me wrong, these boys were serious athletes, the training was as intense as anything I had ever experienced and they were well able for it. It was an era, though, when there was still a social side to inter-county football.

Back then GAA players all over the country might have a few pints after training and matches. Even on the Thursday before the All-Ireland final we were back in Shay's for drinks and the chat. And Shay was the perfect host. Rather than serve us in the public bar in the run-up to big games he would bring us to the privacy of an upstairs room.

Not that we would have minded chatting to supporters. That was how it worked at the time. Some current managers would read the riot act if you were seen anywhere near a pub in the weeks before a game – but back then you could train hard and still be sociable.

While Pat and I had our issues that year, I still don't blame him for anything. Very few guys would have known how to handle the situation we both found ourselves in, especially in light of what was about to happen at the All-Ireland final press night. That was another circus, absolute carnage. And once again I felt I was left on my own to deal with what was going on.

Shortly before the final, Mick Galvin collected me for training. We arrived out in St Vincent's GAA Club in Marino and you could see it was going to be nuts. The press night was due to take place upstairs after training and the fans were there too with autograph books and cameras.

All part of the gig, I thought to myself. I was spotted coming into the ground in Mick's car and we were both mobbed as we tried to make our way to the dressing room as a crowd of youngsters intercepted me. I signed as many autographs, jerseys and caps as I could and then sprinted for the safe heaven of the dressing room to get togged for training. No sooner had I run out the door than another group of kids came charging over. Teammates laughed as I was ambushed again and scribbled away frantically before making another break for the training field.

It was no use. It was like a David Attenborough documentary – I was the prey and the kids were the predators waiting patiently in the long grass before pouncing. They tracked me all the way on to the pitch. Hundreds of them. No area had been cordoned off for autographs, the supporters had 'access all areas'. No one knew how to react, especially not me. In fact most of the rest of the boys were already on the field, training away and highly amused at what was happening.

Eventually I reached Pat O'Neill. Well, myself and my new acquaintances!

'What's the story, Pat? Are we training?'

'Well you can't really, can you?' Pat said, looking bemused.

'Thanks for the help, Pat,' I thought to myself and decided to herd my entourage off the pitch and back to the dressing room so the other players could at least train without interference.

I went back to the dressing room and brought the posse with me. For the next ninety-odd minutes I signed autographs while my teammates trained outside. This was the 'Jayomania' people had been on about.

I would say Pat was perplexed. He had been involved with the Dublin management team in 1992 and had lost an All-Ireland final as manager in 1994. He was under pressure, because on top of managing the team he was now dealing with this youngster who had arrived on the scene with mayhem in tow. As a coach myself now I can empathize with the challenge he faced in dealing with this unique situation. He surely had enough on his plate trying to recapture Sam Maguire!

Dealing with authority figures wasn't an obvious strength of mine. I had grown up without my father and maybe that's why only a few people could get through to me, usually quality individuals or coaches like Joey who could harness the energy I possessed in a positive way. Once I was on board with them I would do anything for them.

But the consensus among the squad was that my involvement with Dublin had taken the heat off everyone else and that was great. The boys could work on their game largely undisturbed while I dealt with all the chaos. It was no bad scenario; most of the time I was able to deal with the glare of the spotlight and they were free to prepare for an All-Ireland final almost in the shadows. It was a lot of pressure to bestow on a 19-year-old rookie who had been playing football at a high standard for only eighteen months.

I loved the attention, though, and all those schooldays spent practising my autograph were starting to pay off. That evening I stayed there until every man, woman and child had got an autograph. Ironically, besieged by fans downstairs, I didn't even make it to the press event upstairs, which suited me just fine. Yet the sports pages that followed were devoted mostly to one man. Every paper you picked up had my face on it, the headlines screaming with startling authority:

PHENOMENON WAITING TO HAPPEN

RYAN GIGGS OF THE GAA HAS WORLD AT HIS FEET

VULNERABLE KID WITH GIFT FOR MAYHEM

Back then none of the family had cars and I used to take the number 40 bus – A, B or C – to and from Finglas. And when I joined UCD I took the number 10 across the city to Belfield. On all of those bus journeys I had never attracted as much as a second glance, but now when I boarded a bus there was every chance my mush would be plastered all over the ad space on the back. In a period of just six months I had become public property, recognized the length and breadth of the country.

*

As match day drew closer there was an obvious backstory and that was our poor success ratio against Ulster teams in the preceding few years. We had been favourites for the 1992 final against Donegal and the 1993 semi-final against Derry. As for the 1994 final against Down, many people felt we would be up against it but there was still a feeling that Dublin would have enough to cope with them. We lost each game.

The whole country seemed to think we had an issue playing Ulster teams but none of that cost me a thought, to be honest. I just focused on the season at hand. We had played really well against Meath and done enough to get over Cork, and while our poor record against northern teams and in finals might have been a factor with some of our more senior players, it didn't bother me. It was cool to be playing in an All-Ireland final. I had no baggage.

Mind you, on the Friday before the game I wondered if the whole thing was going to come apart. Often that summer I would head into town and meet Mick Galvin, who worked for Dublin City Council on O'Connell Street, for a few games of pool. That Friday we were in Ned Kellys when Mick asked if I had heard the news – Charlie was kicking frees the night before and had pulled his quad. He was nursing a thigh injury and thought he would be out for Sunday! I, for one, certainly wasn't going to be putting my 100 per cent free-taking record on the line by volunteering for the job!

Just then Dermot Deasy walked gingerly in to join us. He had come straight from the Rotunda Hospital around the corner after having an epidural for back pain. It is better known as a maternity hospital so we got great slagging out of that. Dermot was keen to play a few games of pool and each time he bent over to line up a shot he would grimace with pain and go 'Ohhhh'. That had us in convulsions. We wondered how he could play on Sunday either!

The following evening I travelled out to the semi-privacy of Belfield, where UCD were playing. On the way I stopped off at the Sarah Curran bar to give the owner two tickets and found all the staff there wearing 'Jayo' T-shirts.

From there I moved out the road to watch the game in relative anonymity until our PA announcer – the much missed Michael Higgins – greeted me over the tannoy and wished me luck the next day. The game passed the time. I went home, got some sleep and All-Ireland final day dawned quickly.

*

In those days, when we arrived in Croke Park Keith Galvin and I would drop our bags in the old dressing rooms down the Canal End of Jones's Road and take the steps up towards the upper Hogan. There we would stand for a few minutes to watch the minor games. In some ways we were still scratching our heads that we would soon be out there playing for the Dubs ourselves.

We went back to the dressing room, togged out and were soon parading around by the Canal End. As we marched by I looked up at the newly developed Cusack Stand and was struck by its dizzying height. Supporters seemed to be clinging to their seats for fear of falling over the edge. When I turned to Mick both of us burst out laughing and I stayed smiling and relaxed all the way to the team photograph. It's gas to look back on that picture now, because other teammates appear gaunt and drained whereas I look totally carefree. Maybe it was the innocence of youth!

We went out, threatened to blow them off the park and by the interval had built a healthy five-point lead. The selectors singled me out for praise at the interval. Pat too. That was our first exchange of words in weeks. All was forgiven!

One of my other abiding memories from that final is the half-time dressing room, when I sat beside Pat Gilroy. We togged out beside each other back then and we always got on well – even if that relationship would be tested down the line!

The summer had been one of blazing sunshine and the room was boiling hot. A guy from the county board entered to enquire if anyone needed to change jerseys. 'The only problem,' he said, 'is that the new ones are long-sleeved.'

I badly wanted a second All-Ireland jersey for keeps and my hand shot up.

Pat followed suit. He hadn't played in the first half but again demonstrated his shrewd business acumen sensing this was a great opportunity.

'Yeah, I'll definitely take one,' we chorused.

I had no intention of going out with long sleeves into that searing heat, so while Pat and his selectors tried to settle the team down and homed in on how we might kill off a Peter Canavan inspired Tyrone, I was trying to stuff the spare jersey into my gearbag without anyone realizing I had pulled a fast one.

I didn't score that day but I doubt I contributed more at any point that year. Before the break, with the game in the balance, Bealo got the ball in midfield and, from watching him day in and day out, I knew it was coming off the outside of his right boot and diagonally.

Like most of Bealo's passes it was overcooked and a Tyrone defender tried to clear it. Instinctively, I blocked it with my leg and the ball rolled invitingly towards the Tyrone goal.

As I raced to meet the ball, I saw big Finbarr McConnell, six-foot-five in his socks, tearing out. Technically, I knew I had to connect with my instep and try to divert the ball low to McConnell's left. I got to the tackle before him and side-footed the ball where I wanted it to go. As the ball broke away from McConnell's left-hand side I was hit hard by Séamus McCallan from Carrickmore.

The tackle made me tumble and lose my bearings and all I could see was a Dublin sock kicking the ball over the line. I didn't actually learn until after the game who had scored the goal that came from the breaking ball. In the heel of the hunt, Cliona Foley of the *Irish Independent* informed me it was Charlie. I had assumed it was Dessie.

Anyway, that goal gave us a cushion. We were on our way. People said it was brave to go in for a ball like that but Séamus came from my blindside and while I sensed he was coming, I didn't see him. I was just focused on getting to the ball first and sliding it under the big man. For years I had thrown myself around basketball courts trying to prevent balls from going out of bounds and that's just how I played games. The difference was there was less profile to basketball whereas this was the big time. An All-Ireland final.

Like the first half, the second was seriously intense. The players were nervous and the match itself bubbled over with drama. We didn't have the obligatory missed Dublin penalty this time but we did have one of the most bizarre occurrences in All-Ireland final history when Charlie Redmond was sent off after an incident with Fergal Logan, the Tyrone midfielder, in the forty-sixth minute.

There were no red cards or yellow cards back in those days. If you got dismissed the referee would just point to the line and that's what he did to Charlie. But Charlie thought he had only got a warning and didn't know he was being sent off, so stayed on the field for the next few minutes. Soon after, the ball broke in Charlie's direction and he got possession and kicked the ball to the far corner to Paul Clarke. At that stage the ref Paddy Russell came over to him again and said, 'I told you to go off.'

There was no time to think. Paddy reissued marching orders – this time for good – and we had to adapt. Charlie didn't have much luck in finals, having missed penalties in two, but he had brought us this far and had scored the goal for us. When he went off, I think that's when the rest of us really stepped up. In many ways we went into survival mode.

There was no point in looking around wondering what to do next. So maybe with my point-guard hat on, I was equipped to tactically adjust on the hoof and see what we needed to do with fourteen men rather than dwelling on Charlie's absence. In those days tactics were not a big thing. We hadn't trained to pre-pare for the situation of being a man down, and now Tyrone had big Mattie McGleenan on the field. We hadn't planned for him either. In fact, I remember the look of shock on Stynesy's face when he was told to go to corner-back and mark McGleenan. It was new territory for Stynesy.

It made sense to me to move out towards the half-forward line and leave the extra man in their full-back line to com-pensate for the loss of our man in attack. I told Mick Galvin where I was going, that I needed to be farther outfield to help us cope, and I just remember giving every ounce of energy I had. Desperation stakes. But I did what I thought was right for the team.

When I look back at the video, I have to admit that some of my shooting, and my obsession with going for goals, was bizarre. It was in my DNA to go for goal, but a calmer, wiser head would have ended up with a few points that day.

Together we slowed the play down, took our time when we had the ball and won lots of possession. They got 0–6 in the second half, and just the one point from play. After Charlie departed, it was more about perspiration but Clarkey gave us some inspiration with a point from near the 45-metre line against the breeze. A ball dropped into McConnell's hands, I went in to shoulder him but just bounced off the big man and he smiled at me. The same thing happened soon after and Finbarr was waiting for me to do the same again. This time, though, I stopped short of colliding with him and when he laid the ball off I caught him with a flick of my boot into, let's say the midriff area, and he went down to rapturous applause from the Hill! I thought I had got away with it but an umpire summoned Paddy Russell in and I was booked. There was going to be no kiss for Paddy after he booked me!

The other yarn that stands out from that final happened late in the game when we were hanging on with the fourteen men. Off the bench and into the fray sauntered Vinnie Murphy. He made his entrance like he was lord of all he surveyed, moved into my sector and beckoned to me: 'Jay, out to midfield!' he ordered in a tone that brooked no questioning.

I did what I was told, sprinted out the field and ran around like a spring lamb in a meadow, oblivious to the sideline committee that had gathered in front of the Hogan Stand, trying to get my attention. Eventually I glanced towards the line and there were Mick, Dessie and Charlie, all off the field and gesturing at me: 'Jay, what are you doing? Get the fuck back in!'

I gestured back, confused. I thought I was just following instructions. Vinnie had just told me to move out, surely he was carrying that message from management? Then I saw Pat O'Neill practically tearing his hair out and roaring at me, and

I decided to head back towards their goal not having time to dwell on the miscommunication. It was only after the game, on reflection, that the penny dropped. Maybe Vinnie had pulled a managerial stroke of his own! Perhaps he fancied grabbing the match-winning score! The fecker had me tearing around like a headless chicken in an All-Ireland final for five minutes, not knowing who to chase or where to turn!

Paul Clarke hit a point that would prove to be the winner. It was a crucial score because we hadn't scored for a long time. Then more drama – there was a disallowed point for Sean McLaughlin and Tyrone right at the very end when Canavan was adjudged to have handled the ball on the ground before offloading to McLaughlin. That was another huge talking point. Canavan was on fire, it was probably one of our least impressive displays all that season and we were barely hanging on. But we were still ahead!

Then the sweet sound of the final whistle. After so many years trying to break the door down the boys had finally burst through, and myself with them. It was all novel to me but those lads laid the ghosts of the past that afternoon. For the likes of John O'Leary, Paddy Moran, Keith Barr, Charlie and Mick Galvin, their long struggles in a Dublin shirt had been made worthwhile.

I fell into the embrace of Chris Lawn, a bear of a Tyrone man. It felt like there was an instant bond between us from the seventy minutes we had just shared in each other's company. The big man took lumps out of me but I felt there was serious mutual respect. I was privileged to mark him because he was old school, tough as northern granite. We just looked at each other and embraced again before the heaving masses pulled me away. After that year, whenever we were beaten, I hoped that Tyrone would win and Chris would get his All-Ireland medal. I was delighted for him when he eventually did in 2003.

I had Chris's shirt in my hands and as the crowd pressed against me I felt a persistent tug on it. I thought I was imagining it with all the bedlam but when it was nearly yanked out of my grip I decided to pull it towards me and there I saw a little artful dodger in front of me, trying to steal the prized memento. In the heat of the moment I kind of rabbit-punched the lad in the face and said, 'Hey, don't be stealing me jersey!' At which point he scarpered.

So somewhere out there is a lad who got a smack in the madness after the final whistle of the 1995 All-Ireland. I'd like to apologize for that. But I hope he learned the lesson that crime doesn't pay!

I saw Canavan and he was disconsolate. He had scored 0–11, ten from frees, but the joke among the Dubs was that Wally (Ciarán Walsh) held him to just a point from play. We don't make too much out of fact that Wally gave away about ten of those frees by fouling him!

Jody Gormley got their other score and we hung on to win by a solitary point, 1–10 to 0–12.

Our backs were thumped as we held our hands aloft and 'Boom Boom Boom' rained down on us. The fans spilt out, the pitch a heaving blur of beery bustle. A few of us were dragged over to do an interview under the Hogan Stand, where the Artane Boys Band used to come out and close to where the old GAA headquarters used to be. There was a fountain there too and beside it Dessie, Keith and I were interviewed. That's when Keith came out with the classic line that the win was a 'donkey off our back'. Typical Keith! After the interview they threw me into the fountain. I think that might have been my first ice-bath!

Finally I got back into the dressing room and that's where it hit me – the wonder of the whole thing. All along I had been dealing with the fuss, the scrutiny, the media, the attention, and I had coped reasonably well. But forty minutes after the final whistle I went to my spot in the dressing room, sat down, lowered my head into my hands and the tears started to flow. I knew how privileged I was to have been a part of something special but I also knew the scrutiny I was under and I was proud that I had contributed in the game. I had given every ounce that I had, in the second half especially. It was a release, the realization of what we had just done. It all came out. I took a few minutes and drained myself of the raw emotion before gathering myself and rejoining the hullabaloo. We peeled off our sweaty armour, the spoils of victory sprayed all over it, showered and made our way to Jurys Hotel for the post-match banquet.

We were sent to an upstairs function room for a private party for players, management, wives and girlfriends. Downstairs the masses piled into the main function room. A few hours into those celebrations I sat down in the hotel's Dubliner Bar for a serious chat with Kevin Moran, and if ever there was a sliding-door moment in my life, that was it.

'What do you want to do?' Kevin asked, referring to the constant speculation that I was set for a cross-Channel soccer career.

'I want to enjoy this,' I replied.

I don't do all this 'could've been a contender' stuff. But if the end result of that chat with Kevin had been him saying, 'Well done today, but for the betterment of your career I'm putting you on a flight to Liverpool tomorrow, good luck!' would I have gone?

In hindsight that was the only week to do it, to make the move.

At that moment in time, however, I didn't realize any of this. I was only nineteen and could sense no urgency. I made no decision, bar to see what would happen next. For the next two years I had to listen to the stories that Liverpool wanted me, but the window had closed by then because my life and career in Ireland simply exploded after the All-Ireland final.

But did Liverpool really want me? There was never any concrete dealing, but Roy Evans had spoken to me about it directly and given quotes to the press on a number of occasions. At the start of the 1995–96 Premiership, Roy told a reporter from the *Sunday World*:

> We played against the UCD team at the end of last season and I was very impressed with Jason. He might not be the biggest striker around but he is very quick indeed. I said at the time I would consider offering him a chance and within the next fortnight I hope to get him over to see how he shapes up. Just because we are a big club doesn't mean that we are not interested in seeing if we can develop players like Jason. It has to be in our interests – especially when you consider the crazy prices which are now being quoted for players in England.

Unfortunately or otherwise, 'the next fortnight' coincided with Dublin winning the All-Ireland title. And assuming the inevitability of things eventually just falling into place on the soccer front, and wanting to enjoy the fruits and spin-offs of my labour with the Dubs, I stayed put and celebrated.

If I was going to choose the cross-Channel route and avail of the technical coaching involved, I probably needed to build there and then on the momentum with Roy, but it wasn't even on my radar after the four months I had just had with Dublin. I told Kevin I'd hang around at home for a while longer. I wanted to enjoy the win with the lads and I think that was understandable too. There was no sense of urgency.

Little did I know that the rise and rise of 'Jayo' on the sports field was about to come to a sudden jolt, never again reaching the heights of that summer of 1995.

11

Jayomania

Every time the current Dublin football team go out to play a knockout championship game they are reminded that as a group they may never share a dressing room again.

Once you have played a game, conquered an ambition, won or lost a big final, things start to change. Sometimes quickly.

For the 1995 team that's kind of what happened. The dismantling process didn't take long. Lads started to drift, or were cast, away. Myself? For the next two years I scarcely had time to draw breath. It was chaos. In some ways it opened doors that would have otherwise remained shut and it presented me with massive opportunities and a high profile. In other ways it tested me and my family.

When we got back to the dressing room after beating Tyrone, someone mentioned that we should soak it all up because once we left Croke Park things would never be the same again. That wise head knew more than we did. From that day forward many factors conspired to ensure we would never replicate what we had achieved. You could say that life just got in the way.

Some lads hung on to the tailcoats of the panel only to be

jettisoned as a succession of managers came and went. Others left of their own accord.

I want to tell my story honestly and give a flavour of what life was like for me post-1995. It seemed I was at the hub of countless different scenarios in those next few years – some fun, some bizarre, some dark. I suspect I am perceived in a certain way for stuff that happened in those years but all I can say is that my reality changed around that time. It didn't last forever but for a while there was mostly just madness. The following anecdotes are intended as just a snapshot of how surreal it all was.

*

On the Monday night after the All-Ireland we took to a specially built stage outside the Central Bank, where 30,000 supporters were assembled. The city streets were thronged, a blanket of light blue.

After we were introduced to the crowd on stage we got on the bus to parade up O'Connell Street. The parade ended at the top of the street and then headed around the Rotunda and across to Gardiner Street to bring us back to Jury's Hotel. Slowly, the masses thinned out and we were suddenly celebrating almost on our own. Where had the craic and crowds disappeared to?

At the end of the street we stalled at traffic lights, with no one for company except a young lad who had cycled up from the Sheriff Street direction. There were forty or fifty of us, players and wives and girlfriends, and when one or two waved down to him I wondered briefly would he remember for the rest of his life getting a salute from the Dublin footballers on their victory parade?

But he just looked up with a blank expression. It was almost dark, and I'd say the young lad hadn't a clue who we were. As the lights went green, he looked up again, this time shaking his head in pure disdain. 'Fucking gobshites,' he said, as he rode off into the sunset.

Classic Dublin! From the high of 30,000 screaming fans trying to get a piece of you to the low of turning the corner and a lone kid on a deserted side street offering nothing but contempt. I loved that!

After we got back to the hotel we made for Hanlon's pub, which was run by the McCormack family, who welcomed many Dublin players in over the years. Spirits in the pub were high, with most being there celebrating from early in the day. A one-man band from Tipperary, Gerry Doyle, who was a friend of the McCormacks, was providing musical entertainment and after a while the crowd chanted for Keith, Mick, Jim Gavin and myself to get up and sing a song.

Whatever about the lads, I didn't have a note in my head, but we were more or less pushed and shoved through the crush towards the little makeshift stage in the corner. It was getting hairy and when the crowd surged forward, Jim, ever the voice of reason, turned around and shouted, 'If ye don't move back we're not sing-ing!' That sparked a minor panic. Some old lads took charge of the situation and started pushing everyone back for fear the Dubs' performance would be aborted. We were pop stars now as well!

*

Maybe I should have pursued that angle, because one day a showbiz reporter phoned me at 8 a.m. Mam got me out of bed to take the call.

'Jason,' said the voice, 'Louis Walsh is interested in putting you into one of his boy bands, what do you think?'

I replied that since I couldn't sing there might be a problem. To my amazement the journo told me he doubted that would be an issue!

Years later I was with my daughter Caoimhe at a Westlife concert in Croke Park and met Louis. Caoimhe was then at the stage all teenagers go through of being mortified at her old man and she got some shock when Louis gushed, 'Oh, Jason, you still look well! I could have put you in a boy band, you know.'

As Louis walked off, I gave Caoimhe a smile but got only a grimace in response. She must have been truly horrified at the idea of her da as a teenage heart-throb!

*

On the Wednesday after the All-Ireland final we played the GOAL match against the Rest of Ireland. Mick Galvin and I had lunch in Hanlon's until the weariness finally got the better of me. Exhausted, I decided to go home for a few hours' kip until Mick arrived to bring me to the match.

When I awoke I felt lifeless. How was I going to face another game?

For the game we came up with an idea for our forwards to play as backs and our backs to go up front. And so I ended up at full-back, marking Peter Canavan in front of the Hill. After a few minutes, with a rush of energy coming from somewhere, I tore upfield, got on the end of a move and scored a goal at the Canal End. Pretty sure I was the only man to score a goal off Peter the Great at Croke Park, I whipped the jersey off and twirled it overhead as I raced back downfield to resume my defensive duties, although, typically, as a forward it took me a lot longer to get there! No one was taking the game too seriously.

At half-time I signed a few autographs and with the ball about to be thrown in rejoined the match. As I did, two kids ran on to the field behind me. Two then became twenty and soon twenty became a mob, all demanding an autograph. Amid the chaos they had no option but to abandon the match!

It was colourful back then. Maybe a moment in time. Instant popularity from nowhere and sure you had to go with the flow. Since then, the player who's come closest to that pop-star adulation is Shane O'Donnell, when Clare won the 2013 All-Ireland hurling final.

I loved when Shane scored three goals in that final, but I also foresaw the challenges he might face. He wouldn't have seen what was ahead because he had come from nowhere, getting an unexpected start in that replay, and then exploding.

Eighteen years after me, Shane was the one being linked with Louis Walsh. So his scenario is probably the closest to mine in modern times. I hope Shane goes on to achieve all his goals. When you win an All-Ireland there are lots of things to contend with: external factors, internal factors, team factors. You can be rocked back on your heels in quick time.

Anyway, the GOAL game was abandoned but the madness raged on.

One big call to make was whether to do *The Late Late Show* or Pat Kenny's *Kenny Live!* as rival RTÉ producers battled to get a piece of me. I felt that Kenny would relate to me better than Uncle Gaybo, so I chose him and appeared on his show a few weeks after the final.

A few weeks later, as Christmas loomed, I went on *The Late Late Toy Show*. Earlier that day a front-page headline broke the news I had been voted 'Irish Gay Icon of the Year'. A few hours after that revelation I had a league game for UCD against Shels and as I arrived on to the field my teammates greeted me with catcalls and wolf whistles. Not to disappoint them, I camped it up as best I could. And once that match was over, RTÉ sent a car to whisk me to Donnybrook for the toy show.

Media proposals came flying in left, right and centre. The *New York Times* sent a reporter to interview me and the *International Herald Tribune* came over too. My life story was relayed all over the world. While all this was going on I leaned heavily on Kevin Moran. At that time the GAA lacked the structures and expertise to advise someone in my situation. Kevin created opportunities and tried to maximize the deals. The problem was there was still no order to my days. His arrival meant that, for a while at least, I more or less did what I was told on the commercial front. He made the big calls. I accepted deals with Pepsi, Penneys and Avonmore. I also wrote a newspaper column, which when you think about it was madness. No player should be writing columns before he retires, and especially not at the start of his career.

That was the commercial side. It's only in hindsight that I realize I lost focus on my ambitions in sport. I needed to have more than one eye on those sporting targets while the other one was on business deals. But Kevin was not a life coach, his job was simply to do his best for me in the commercial sense.

Generally I was left to my own devices way too much. The fact that I had neglected my studies in school was a big factor as I wasn't in a full-time college course and had too much free time. The Sam Maguire was doing the rounds all over Dublin and kids wanted to see me with the cup. Whatever player was picked to tour the county would invariably ask me to join him. I had no issue doing that because I could recall Barney Rock visiting my school and remember what his few words and seeing Sam had meant to me. But if it happened today, with proper structures in place, it would be different, the load would be shared equally among the squad.

Earlier that year the GAA president, Jack Boothman, had spoken of me veering towards professionalism, which is totally at odds with the association's ethos, and his words were seized by the media, igniting fevered debate. The whole thing turned into a 'Jayo versus the GAA' saga and there was a perception within the GAA that I wasn't on the same page, that I was flouting their amateur values. Some officials saw me as an agitator and I became the focus of countless articles and arguments.

Each time a GAA official commented on my business affairs the press reaped serious mileage. That all took place in a context where there were no structures to help inter-county players with off-the-field activities. What happened to me raised important issues and anomalies and paved the way for change, but at the time I was viewed as trouble.

Like most things at that time I tried not to let it faze me. I was actually invited to present medals at Jack's club in Blessington and I recall two club members collecting me one afternoon in UCD after a soccer game to bring me down. I did it without a second thought.

Kevin had never had a GAA man on the books at Proactive until myself and DJ Carey joined him, so he too was in pastures new. But having followed professional basketball and seen how MJ and his fellow superstars had built their brand and seen what Sky Sports was doing for English soccer, I was at least somewhat tuned in to hard realities. I found it hard to accept that after performing in front of 60,000 paying punters the players wouldn't get a penny. I mentioned that now and again to Bill Kelly, an executive at Arnotts. Bill, in fairness, knew the attention I was getting and he looked after me here and there, but at the same time he was always crystal clear in his mind that the Arnotts deal was with the Dublin county board and not with the players.

Before the arrival of the GPA, players were still trying to make sense of that whole commercial area. I became a focus for that curiosity. The reality was that as soon as you started losing on the field the deals would dry up. I knew I had a worth and was happy for Kevin to act on that as much as he could.

The downside was that my sporting ambitions took a back seat from 1995 until 1998. Businesses lined up to get involved

In my favourite colour – sky blue! Me and my mam, Alice. I was born on 10 January 1976, and it wasn't long before Mam had me in the Dublin colours.

Post All-Ireland win, 1983. Wearing my Communion suit and sitting with the Sam Maguire Cup at a Dublin Supporters' Club function.

I met all the Dublin players at that Supporters' Club function and one of those was Kevin Moran, who was then with Manchester United following his time playing for Dublin. Little did I know that years later our paths would cross again.

Where it all began. Here I am, far right in the front row, with the St Vincent's Primary School team.

Rivermount Boys were my first soccer club and joining them at the age of eight was my first foray into organized sport.

International duty first beckoned for me with the Ireland under-15 basketball team. Here we are after beating England on a famous night in Castlebar. My best friend, Gareth Winders, and my mentor, Joey Boylan, are to my right, the first boys team ever to beat an English team.

Hurleys and hoops. I discovered a lot about myself and the beauty of Gaelic Games during my summers in the parish Ballyhea. I also learned to play hurling down there and went on to win various different championships with the club.

Myself and Louise are pictured here after Dublin's 2015 All-Ireland final win. She has always been there to support me.

The Sherlocks. Martin, Eddie, Brian, Nanny (who passed away aged 101) and Mam all played a huge part in making me who I am. Also in this picture are Martin's children, Andrew and Christine, and Brian's daughter, Angela.

Not appreciating the full value of a third-level education was something that I always regretted, and I was fortunate enough to get the opportunity to pursue an MBA at Dublin City University. Graduating was a very proud day for me and for Mam.

With Josh and Caoimhe after the 2016 All-Ireland final replay win over Mayo, another proud day for the family. It meant the world to me to share that moment with those closest to me.

Here I am up against Phil Babb during UCD's friendly with Liverpool in 1995. I nutmegged him as well, which I don't think Phil was too happy about!

Playing for Shamrock Rovers and up against one of the best League of Ireland players, Paul Osam. Despite only being there for a brief spell, it was was great to play for one of the country's most historic clubs, Shamrock Rovers.

This 1995 Leinster Championship goal against Laois was an iconic moment in my sporting career and catapulted me into the public domain.

With Mick Galvin and Charlie Redmond in a pre-match parade for the 1995 All-Ireland semi-final. As a kid, it was so novel and so exciting to be in a parade in Croke Park with the team that I always wanted to play for. With the innocence of youth I was very relaxed and made sure I had fun.

For me, getting to the ball first before Seamus McCallan and getting a touch on it to put it past Finbarr McConnell was the most significant contribution that I made in 1995.

Sam is back. A precious moment. Most of the lads on the team had soldiered a long time to get the cup back.

Playing Meath was never easy. Mark O'Reilly is keeping close tabs on me in our 1996 Leinster SFC clash. Here, Meath got their revenge for '95 and it took seven years before we beat them again.

Like Meath, Kildare also got the upper hand on us around that time. They beat us here in the 1998 Leinster SFC and again in 2000.

Fending off Éamonn Fitzmaurice, current Kerry manager, in the epic 2001 All-Ireland quarter-final replay. Playing in front of 40,000 people at Semple Stadium was a great experience and an historic occasion but unfortunately it was another big game we lost.

After Alan Brogan hits the net and we both punch the air on the way to beating Kildare by two points in the 2002 Leinster final – it was our first provincial title in seven years.

Five Leinsters in a row! Josh in my arms and Caoimhe underneath me as I raise the Delaney Cup with Ciarán Whelan and his son, Jamie. It was nice to share our Leinster success with such an iconic Dublin figure and our children.

The game was tight when I came on and I was delighted to send a goal past Wexford goalkeeper John Cooper in the 2005 Leinster SFC semi-final. We went on to beat Laois by a point in the final.

Me and Brogie after we beat Roscommon in the 2004 SFC qualifiers. Alan was one of the best I played with; one of the finest teammates I had the pleasure of playing with.

Scoring a goal against Kildare in the 2009 Leinster final. Little did I know this would be my last for Dublin.

Sealed with a kiss. Blowing a kiss to the family after another Leinster title with a young Bernard Brogan beside me. During the week of that game I had to get stitches after a stud from Collie Moran's boot sliced me open in our last training session.

The men of '95. The All-Ireland winning team of 1995. These men had worked so hard to win Sam and they fully deserved this success.

Watching Tiger Woods practise ahead of the 2006 Ryder Cup at K Club. I have always been a student of sport and am always interested to learn more.

With a close friend of mine and a massive Dublin supporter, former WBA and European Super Bantamweight champion Bernard Dunne. This was my first day on the job in the Dublin management set-up. It's New Year's Day, 2015, at the Blue Stars challenge but my nerves were eased with such a good friend beside me.

Operating as *maor foirne* for Dublin in our 2017 NFL meeting with Monaghan.

Deep in discussion with Jim Gavin during the 2017 Leinster final. I have learned an awful lot from Jim and the culture he has created for the Dublin players.

Arm in arm with Jim after the 2016 All-Ireland final replay win over Mayo. When Jim and I first chatted, I mentioned to him that if I was getting involved, back-to-back titles was my first goal.

and I was seizing the moment. But was I in the GAA for money? No. I knew my value, but had I wanted money I would have chased harder for a full-time soccer career. But did I appreciate I was in demand? I did.

For all that, the only significant deal I had was for two years with the retail store Penneys. That guaranteed me a few bob every week to effectively live on. The Pepsi deal was for only one marketing campaign. The column with the *News of the World* wasn't the right fit and didn't last long.

There would be no retirement fund from my exploits, but I learned a lot. There were some shenanigans. One retailer came up with a Jayo T-shirt with my image centre stage and my signature scrawled beneath – without consulting me!

Vinnie Murphy arrived into the Jury's on the night of the All-Ireland final sucking the life out of a cigarette and wearing a big straw hat and the offending T-shirt. Soon after Mam arrived home from work with one!

But not everyone embraced Jayomania. In 1995, the All Stars were picked for the first time by players instead of journalists, and I suppose their selection demonstrated the range of opinion out there. Some people reckoned I should have won an All Star but clearly others didn't! Look, the important thing was that I had an All-Ireland medal and I am proud of my contribution in earning it. The All Star would have been nice but that was outside my control. The whole thing offered a fair snapshot of how I was perceived within the game. I certainly wasn't everyone's blue-eyed boy – there were other opinions out there.

For the most part, though, I was accepted and that was brilliant. All the time I was out and about at events or corporate gigs I was representing the Dublin footballers and I was conscious of that too. I tried to be polite and approachable. There were times when I struggled to deal with the attention and that happened when, for some reason, the vibe turned unfriendly or hostile. On those occasions I would use alcohol to blot out the negativity.

It's true, too, that when the shield came up I could be dismissive or show a sense of entitlement. I'm not proud of all my actions around that time and for any youngster reading this book I would hope there is a life lesson here: you should always try to act with dignity and humility regardless of what comes your way.

I was out three and four nights a week reaping the rewards of my new-found fame. I seemed to spend half my life in Peg Woffington's bar and on those nights out you could get punters coming over singing 'Boom Boom Boom' and happily embracing 'Jayo' or just as easily hear some fella calling me a 'wanker' or a 'Chinese prick'. As much as many people liked me I was fair game for the begrudgers too.

Certain situations made me feel detached or rejected, the polar opposite of what I had wanted as a kid – acceptance. And as the months passed it was evident that some people saw me as more of a celebrity or novelty than an athlete. Again, the opposite to what I had striven for all my life. I was fair game for anything: lavish praise or dog's abuse. It all became a little claustrophobic and maybe that's why I gravitated to Peg Woffington's, where the bouncers always had my back.

With the 1996 soccer and Gaelic football seasons underway, I did go back training with UCD but couldn't do myself justice because I was all over the country handing out medals, opening envelopes and doing photo shoots. The focus had gone off sport in the aftermath of the big win as I drifted downriver with the flow.

Instead of playing with the college in the early rounds of the 1996 FAI Cup, when we were beaten by Kilkenny City, I went with the Dublin team to San Diego for the craic and the sun. I missed a few league games with UCD too. It just shows the mindset. A year earlier I had made an impression throughout the country with a man-of-the-match performance for UCD against Cork City in the first round of the FAI Cup. But for the first round in 1996 I went to San Diego.

*

In fairness, some of the stuff that happened to me during this time was brilliant. Bizarre at times. Not the gigs you got every day.

I made my 'acting' debut in the RTÉ sitcom *Upwardly Mobile*, playing the role of a team coach. They had created a cameo for me that literally involved me opening a door, standing there awkwardly and waving before closing the door again. That was it.

Before that came the appearance on *Kenny Live!* Replaying the video of that interview I counted that I said the word 'like' forty-seven times. Cringe!

Pat cued me up to thank Arnotts for the suit Bill Kelly had arranged for me, but oblivious to the protocol, and thinking on my feet, I quipped that since I didn't earn the big money Pat enjoyed, the suit I had on would have to do!

Father Michael Cleary was also on the show that night and he had been our parish priest in Rivermount. Father Cleary presented me with my first trophy, which was for an under-8 tennis tournament in Erin's Isle Tennis Club. I was also mad into tennis when I was a kid. As I've said, I'd play any sport that involved a ball!

The really mad thing was I was top of Kenny's bill that night. Father Cleary was first; then George Best and his new squeeze, Alex; and then me! Months later I was back in RTÉ for another gig when the driver who collected me told how he had driven George the night we were both on. The driver said Alex had wanted to hit the town as soon as the interview was over but George had insisted on staying to watch my segment. That was nice to hear.

A while after appearing on the show, I played a charity soccer match for the Luke Kelly Festival and George was there again. Alex Ferguson was the manager over a team of well-known ex-pros such as Mick McCarthy, Phil Thompson and Mark Lawrenson. And me! Alex was giving the half-time team talk when the door burst open and there was Steve Collins, reigning WBO super-middleweight champion, looking mad, bad and dangerous. It seemed he was unhappy over a nutmeg I had pulled on him: 'Sherlock! Don't ever take the fucking ball off me like that again!' he roared in mock rage. To me it was like a dream or some movie scene. In front of all these superstars, household names, a world champion boxer crashing in and threatening this skinny little fella in the corner. And Fergie trying to give his team talk and wondering what the hell was going on.

In April 1996, I went over to Old Trafford with some pals to see Manchester United play Leeds United. Kevin Moran got me tickets for the game along with a couple for the players' lounge afterwards. Roy Keane got the winner that night with a low drive.

On our way to the players' lounge we saw Fergie being interviewed in the tunnel. I went to say hello and Alex smiled and shook my hand. Above in the players' lounge I stood beside Roy, with whom I had shared an Ireland dressing room a year earlier, but he had his back to me and I didn't bother him.

As we headed for home, I found myself in the wrong part of Manchester Airport – the section for domestic flights. Trying to get back on track I headed up an escalator and bumped into Robbie Fowler and Steve McManaman and mentioned I had played against them a year earlier for UCD. 'Jason, isn't it?'

said Robbie. A lad like him remembering me! Alex Ferguson shaking your hand! As I say, there was a bit of validation in all that. Meeting those great people and having them remember me. And for a young kid who for so long had craved acceptance that was no bad feeling.

I went on Gerry Ryan's midweek TV show, *Gerry Ryan Tonight*, and was a guest alongside Mr Pussy. When I look back on it, I cringe once more. I was twenty years of age and I was on these shows sounding off about this and that and not knowing my arse from my elbow.

The madness raged on over the next few years. In 1998, I was invited to attend the Planet Hollywood restaurant opening up by St Stephen's Green and thinking it was just a normal opening night I accepted. I went with a friend, Joe Dunne, both of us in good spirits after a few drinks earlier that day. We hailed a taxi but the driver said he could bring us only so far, that there was something big on in town. Grand, get us as close as you can! He dropped us, by now the worse for wear, at the top of Harcourt Street and we wobbled down a lane restricted by a line of barriers.

There were guards and I wondered would we be stopped, but they just waved us through, really friendly, and so we walked on for about six or seven steps before we twigged that we were on the red carpet for an event thronged with over 10,000 people. I had no idea the size of the gig!

We took a few more speed-wobbles negotiating the red carpet, in front of which seemed like every photographer in Ireland. And there at the end of the carpet were Arnie Schwarzenegger, Sly Stallone and Wesley Snipes pressing the flesh. This was huge!

The following day's papers reckoned that not since the arrival of Bill Clinton had there been such scenes in Dublin. All the great, the good and the ugly were there – and Joe and myself!

Arnie was chewing a huge Cuban cigar, Sly was talking over-time and Snipes was shaking hands with screaming admirers. And a 22-year-old from Finglas and his buddy rubbing shoulders with them. I was far from reality.

We weren't long in the official function room upstairs when nature called. On my way down to the jacks I saw Snipes taking a moment to himself, sitting there quietly in a cordoned-off VIP area. I'd say he was withered from it all. *White Men Can't Jump* was a few years old at that stage but he was in loads of movies around that time. Being hugely interested in basketball I watched *White Men Can't Jump* over and over again and with the few pints in me I wondered should I go over and say something profound to him. Having been on the receiving end of a thousand 'Boom Booms' and 'Up de Dubs' I should have ignored the voice in my head. But I didn't. I went to the jacks, composed myself and headed back out to Snipesy.

'Wesley!' I said.

He looked at me like a man hoping the ground would open up.

'White men can't jump!' I shouted, like it was the funniest line in comic history. I may even have given him the thumbs up for good measure.

He looked at me as if to say: 'You are a complete tool.'

I walked or staggered back up the stairs, cringing. Jesus, why did I say that?

Later I spotted Paul McGinley talking to Albert Sharp, who knew my friend Joe from Finglas. Albert came over to us and I told him I would love to meet Paul, who had just won the World Cup with Pádraig Harrington. Without hesitating, Albert went over to Paul, who was now chatting to Stallone.

'Paul, I have someone who'd love to meet you.'

Paul shot Albert a 'Can you not see who I'm talking to here?' kind of look and indicated he would be over in a minute.

According to Albert, Paul then asked who was wanting to say hello.

'Jason Sherlock,' Albert replied.

'Jason Sherlock?' McGinley repeated, and with that he shook Sly's hand – 'Sylvester, have a great night!' – and came to chat with us!

All of this was dreamworld stuff to me but in this circle I was 'someone'. That same year I opened Virgin cinemas in town with Boyzone and Richard Branson and we did a signing in the O'Connell Street cineplex.

The offers kept rolling. Through the Penneys connection I was at events all the time, meeting soccer stars, shaking hands and chatting with the likes of Paul McGrath and Mick McCarthy. The soccer lads, Branson, Boyzone – all these guys knew my story and maybe everyone just assumed there was more of the same to follow.

Sadly, there wasn't.

From a Dublin perspective the next couple of years post-1995 were all about failure. The life I was now leading made it hard to play to my potential and I still struggle to reflect positively on the next few seasons. In fact, over the next twelve years all people wanted to do was reflect on 1995 in a positive light whereas I didn't want to think about it. All the stuff that happened after the All-Ireland win seriously damaged my per-formances on the field. The legend of 1995 lingered so long simply because we won nothing for ages after it.

It took time for me to be able to look back on this period in my life with some fondness and focus on the good times.

12

No Country for Old Men

A month after leading us to the promised land, Pat O'Neill summoned us to a meeting at Parnell Park, thanked us for our efforts and along with his management team strode off into the sunset. My recollection of that night is that there was never a sense of us, the players, saying to management, 'Hang on now, yiz can't do that!'

I was only a backbencher at that meeting, going with the flow. Just nineteen, All-Ireland medal in the arse pocket. I felt there was more to follow so why not just get on with it? In my mind there was no sense of Pat's leaving being a disaster. But history shows that it was.

Some of the lads felt they had been stifled a little by Pat and even saw his departure as a positive, thinking we would move onwards and upwards. Other lads reckoned now that the management team had finally found the winning formula it was a disaster that they were moving on.

Either way that All-Ireland win merely pre-empted a shocking decline. We failed to win a Leinster Championship for the next seven years.

Should the panel have fought harder to keep Pat? Well,

maybe we should have had the cop-on to realize that here was a man who had finally concocted a recipe for success, who knew the raw materials he had and could get the perfect mix. No matter who came in next, he wouldn't have that knowledge. It was a big decision for the boys, but it was all new territory for me. I just presumed the Dublin show would keep on rolling no matter who was in charge.

When the hunt for a successor began, Mickey Whelan's name wasn't jumping out but he got the job. And what I can say with absolute certainty, again, with the benefit of hindsight, is that Mickey was the right man at the wrong time.

Mickey had won the 1963 All-Ireland at centre-forward with Dublin before heading for the US to study PE. He spent six years there and returned home as one of the first qualified PE teachers in the land. He had coaching experience, but mostly in soccer. In fact, the gig he had just before taking the Dublin job was coaching the Dundalk side that won the 1994–95 League of Ireland title.

He was his own man, with an American twang and distinctive ways and ideas. He took over, looked at the winning template created by Dr Pat and, in the manner of other managers, decided on a different approach. He had a load of sayings that he garnered from his time in the US but I'm not sure the lads grasped the full meaning of them all at the time.

When he eventually stepped away from the job, he reckoned we didn't buy into his system and he is probably right. But he was twenty years ahead of his time and it's hardly surprising that the lads didn't see the bigger picture.

Mickey felt the panel had been lucky in 1995 and he could make us a better team. No harm in that, it was just the way he went about it. The first thing he did was change our training regime.

The innovative ideas he had gleaned abroad ran counter to

the GAA philosophy of coaching, which maintained you hadn't really trained hard unless you ended up bent over and puking. Mickey was big into sports science long before the GAA was ready for it.

For some of the lads, Mickey was charismatic and confident. For others he was abrupt and blunt with his opinions. Some guys disliked or couldn't handle that.

Under Mickey, our preseason regime started with the panel running up the stairs of the DIT Bolton Street when the students were on holiday. My soccer season with UCD was already underway and so it clashed with his early sessions and I missed a lot of them. But I do remember a few runs up those stairs and some of the lads taking a break on the third and fourth floors.

The squad was now skipping to an altogether new rhythm. No more of the never-ending, mind-numbing cross-country, we became 'less is more' advocates. All of Mickey's training was based around the football. He wasn't developing athletes, but unfortunately that was an approach that had never sat well with inter-county teams of old.

In the previous regime we would have an 800-metre run after a warm-up. Next up were two 400-metre shuttles, five 200-metre sprints, five 100-metre sprints and five 50-metre sprints. Our times and data were recorded and put on a wall in Santry Avenue for all the world to see. Mickey had seen a copy of the data himself and I don't think he was too impressed. When he took over he just concentrated on working us with the ball.

There was a drill in which we formed a 20-metre box and we would solo from one corner to another. The lads wanted to know why all this short, sharp stuff with the ball? It's called games-based training these days, but back then we wondered where was all the flogging an inter-county player was supposed to get. It was never a slog and that seemed unusual. Mickey would bellow 'Money in the bank, fellas' although some lads were questioning whether we were putting enough cash away to prepare us for the intense battles ahead during the Leinster Championship.

While I missed much of that training, I would say some of the panel struggled with Mickey's tone and methods over his two years in charge. Take the 1996 Leinster final. On the preceding Tuesday he picked the team and told the lads who weren't togging out that they didn't need to show up for the final training session on the Saturday. That upset some of those who had missed the cut and it created a strange atmosphere for our last session as we were without the guys we had been used to all year.

Mickey didn't quite see the impact it had on us not having those guys around. He was borrowing a practice that had been widely used in soccer: only the starting eleven would take part in the final session before a game. But GAA players were not ready for such a revolution.

Mickey's ideas about strength and conditioning are now the norm and it's obvious he was a pioneer. But back in 1996 the Dublin team was an ageing unit and some of the senior players were probably too set in their ways to depart from a tried-and-trusted route mapped and paved through years of persistence.

Again with the benefit of hindsight, I would say there was also a lack of focus and fitness in the squad. Certainly that applies to me. I regret that I never had the opportunity to win a second All-Ireland. The one positive I take from my experiences post-2015 is that I can identify the pitfalls that winning players are faced with and now as a coach with the Dublin team I can pass these lessons on.

For Mickey's first championship game as manager, against a Westmeath team managed by Barney Rock, I lost the number

15 shirt to Damian O'Brien of Lucan Sarsfields. Niall Guiden and Joe McNally were Mickey's preferred attackers. They were not in with us in 1995 but had been involved before that. People just assumed the new boss had a problem with me because I had started the year on the bench. But I wasn't playing well, my preparation was poor and I wasn't fully fit. When you're unfit you pick up injuries and I had pulled a hammer in training which meant that I chased fitness ahead of our next game with Louth and got on for the last ten minutes but I wasn't right at all.

With journalists wanting to know what was going on with me, Mickey had spent much of his early days in the job answering questions about my schedule and how he would manage my parallel involvement with UCD. I felt that was unfair on him.

We had no issues at all and I got back in the team for the Leinster final. I was still way below par, but the team was as well. We barely beat Louth in the semi-final and were lucky that Cathal O'Hanlon missed what looked to be an open goal for them near the end of that game. In the final Darren Fay marked the shite out of me and we lost to a Meath team we'd beaten by ten points the year before. They won by two points on a slippery, scuttery day and went on to win the All-Ireland.

Meath were back on top when we met them again in the 1997 Leinster quarter-final, a grand collision of the two previous All-Ireland champions. They tore away early on and led 1–10 to 0–4 at one stage but we rallied before the break with 1–2 of our own and only trailed narrowly with ten minutes left and were awarded a penalty at the Canal End. It was the final kick of the game and a goal would draw the match. Up stepped Bealo and if you don't know what happened next you could maybe hazard a guess. And you'd be right!

Rasper. Off the crossbar. Game over. Back in the dressing room there was a bit of a dust-up when one of the lads asked

Bealo 'how the fuck' he missed the penalty. I just felt fair play to him, at least he had the balls to step up and take it.

Eamon Heery, or Yozzer as we called him, actually thought I took it. He couldn't bear to watch the kick and so he turned to the Hill to see their reaction. After the game he came to commiserate with me!

Anyway, that kick determined our fate that summer.

*

Early into his third season as manager, following a league defeat to Offaly in November 1997, Mickey walked away. At the final whistle he had taken some abuse from a section of the crowd and decided enough was enough.

Mickey was hurt at the time but history would ultimately be kind to him. As a trainer he was less hills and drills and more about skills. He went on to give eighteen years training and coaching GAA teams and enjoyed huge success. He won an All-Ireland club title with St Vincent's in 2008 and played a vital role in Dublin's 2011 senior title as coach alongside Pat Gilroy. The reputation that took such a battering between 1995 and 1997 was thoroughly restored over time.

I met him years later at Clontarf Golf Club and I made it my business to get his attention: 'Mickey, about your time with us. Youth is wasted on the young.' By then I was at a stage in my early thirties when I was able to reflect on the challenges he faced post-1995.

'Are you trying to tell me I wasn't such a bad guy after all?'

We looked at each other and smiled. He was in fact one of the good guys. One of the great football men. It just took people a long time to get that.

Long afterwards, Dessie Farrell was getting ready for a club match with Na Fianna against St Vincent's and was going through a fancy warm-up routine when Mickey passed nearby, smiled and shouted over: 'Ye used to laugh at me when I did that!'

He had a point.

*

On the field, in the spotlight of the 1996 and 1997 championships, my career had stalled. Meanwhile, off the pitch, I found myself increasingly in the middle of a wave of what the GAA saw as the 'new breed of player', swimming against the tide of amateurism, the bedrock of the association.

I was a 'modern' player and felt that players who were seen by a paying public should be rewarded financially. But Jack Boothman had made his feelings clear. And Liam Mulvihill, then director general, argued in an interview that I shouldn't be playing soccer if I wanted to play GAA. The reality was that I had a scholarship and a soccer contract with UCD.

I can see both sides of the argument. I was leveraging my worth from being a GAA player and maybe they resented the fact I was a soccer player too. On reflection I can see it might have made some sense for the GAA to make me an employee of the association and use me in a strategic role, through coaching or marketing. Many people felt that might have solved the problem but I can see the association's dilemma. I was also a soccer player. True, I might have been a marketable GAA commodity but I was also playing soccer for UCD.

It wasn't an easy one for the GAA and various groups were being formed to cement the GAA's amateur ethos with proposals at Congress. A statement was released announcing all these sub-committees and cautioning players to 'resist any approaches from agents or companies that might endanger their amateur status'.

Perhaps this was an indirect message to me, I don't know, but the non-stop media circus didn't help. The stream of interviews and quotes just ran and ran. Maybe the most inflammatory move involved myself, DJ, Nicky English and my old pal Mark O'Connor turning up at a press conference for Proactive Sports Management. That rattled a few more cages and caused weeks of commotion.

The GAA felt the winds of change were blowing hard and my name was to the fore.

But what really occupied my headspace in 1997 was an altercation with a Dublin county board official at an under-21 championship match against Offaly in March. The match was fractious. A fight broke out and heavy suspensions followed, including the removal of Dublin from that year's under-21 championship and the banning of both counties from the 1998 championship. At one point a spectator climbed the wall and ran on to the field with a bottle before being waylaid.

Davy Billings was in charge of the Dublin under-21s but because of my soccer scholarship with UCD I wasn't always available to him. I was selected for the team's first two matches, against Wexford and Offaly, but missed both because of UCD soccer matches. Nonetheless, I turned up on each occasion to support the lads and was on the sideline that afternoon against Offaly, as Davy was always keen to have me among the group.

I took my place in the dugout with the subs and the county board official in question was there too. He passed away late in 2015 and out of respect for his family I have no desire to revisit in great detail an incident between us. The key point I want to make is how the loyalty of two men in the wake of this incident has stayed with me for the rest of my life.

The board official was highly regarded within Dublin GAA and his club, but on a much wider level what happened showed how I was perceived by some people within the GAA family.

During the match passions ran high and I was hearing heavy criticism of the players. Eventually I went across to the official and the gist of what I said was, 'If you have nothing good to say, say nothing at all.'

Maybe that was, again, above my station, but I couldn't just stand there. The official didn't like what I said.

He spat at me.

Time stands still after something like that and I went into complete shock for the rest of the game. The next day I made a formal complaint to the county board and the incident played out in various committee rooms over the following weeks with several twists and turns. It was a stressful time for a lot of people.

But I found the whole incident exceptionally hard to deal with and my lack of self-worth came to the fore again. I wondered if I somehow deserved what had happened. Maybe I was to blame for the whole fiasco? I struggled to shake off the sense that it was all my fault. Why was I to blame?

I was this high-profile star and yet I wasn't even playing for the under-21 team that needed me. I had challenged the county-board man in the dugout when it could be argued that it wasn't my place to do so. Was I getting too big for my boots? Was I starting to become more trouble than I was worth?

The county board came close to splitting over the whole thing. During the investigative process it was even recommended that I should be banned for six months for refusing to play with the Dublin under-21s in the first place. Again, it just showed that not everyone was on my side. In fact, hearing that some people wanted to suspend me only raised the shrill of that inner voice in my ear: 'It's your fault, no one else's.'

When I look back now, there are only two things I take from that whole saga – Mickey Whelan's actions and John Costello's honour. People who struggle at times – through bullying, abuse in school, racial abuse, whatever – they all need to bear in mind that there are others who can help: peers, teachers, managers.

In my time of need I discovered that. My family and team-mates backed me to the hilt, took me off the floor and helped build me up again. Mickey Whelan was there with them.

On the way out of the game Mickey pulled the car up beside me to ask what I thought of the match. He saw I was badly rattled and I explained why. Mickey assured me it would be sorted out and meanwhile to call to his office at Bolton Street during the week.

During that meeting Mickey soared sky-high in my estimation, to stay there forever more. He offered to resign as Dublin manager if I felt it could help my case even in the slightest degree. I couldn't believe he would do that for me and I left his office with a wholly positive impression of the man.

As my complaint and the subsequent appeal hearings took their course John Costello, the Dublin secretary and now Dublin CEO, told one crucial meeting that he had witnessed what happened. Despite such tension around the whole affair and the huge pressure he must have come under to remain neutral, he backed up my version of events.

The actions of John and Mickey will live with me forever. And despite all the worry and my feelings of low self-esteem, when I replay that whole affair in my mind, admiration for their character and honour is what I remember most.

13

The Lost Years

It was late winter 1997, two years on from our All-Ireland success, and I was still looking for answers.

I wasn't sure what was next. I had started just two meaningful GAA games in two years and had nothing to show for them. We were beaten in both and from a sporting point of view that was just unacceptable.

Meanwhile, on the soccer front, the spoils of victory from that 1995 title win had stalled my progress. I still felt I could play both sports at elite level and would switch from one to the other in hope of finding some bit of spark. At the same time, I lacked clarity and fitness. I often wondered where I was going.

Before Jack Charlton and Maurice Setters moved away from the international set-up, Maurice, then Ireland's under-21 manager, had told journalists I was talented enough to go all the way to the top in England but that I had to choose one code: 'Part of Jason's problem in the past was that he never seemed sure which sport he wanted to play,' said Setters. 'But he appears to be ready to concentrate on soccer and if he does the sky's the limit. He's strong and he's pacy. And he has the intuitive skills of the striker in knowing where exactly the net is in every situation.'

Almost two seasons had slipped by since Maurice uttered those words and I still had no clear view of the road ahead. The only certainty was that my potential wasn't increasing. I wondered if there was a bigger picture out there.

During the summer of 1997, after we had been beaten by Meath in the Leinster Championship, I headed off to Boston with the intention of playing Gaelic football over there. I ended up getting a job in a bar and playing some social soccer with a team called Bohemians FC based in South Boston. I got a job in one of Joe Dunne's bars. Joe was a Finglas man and his cousin was married to one of the McCormacks who run Hanlons bar so that was the connection. He and his wife Gaye and their son Cillian looked after me so well for my stay and we had a great summer. To this day Joe commutes between Dublin and Boston. He has three bars over there and has built a great life for himself.

I loved the city and the craic and it was a few months that I wouldn't forget. But when I got home to Dublin and winter set in I found myself struggling. I went through some dark times. I didn't like what my life had become and I began looking for a way out.

I was all over the shop. I didn't have a normal day job, there was no progress with Dublin or UCD and I was nowhere near the levels I'd reached in 1995. And I had a lifestyle that wasn't conducive to ever getting back to those levels.

One night in January 1998 I was out drinking with a friend. I had been seeing Louise, my future wife, and like many young couples we had our ups and downs during those years. As my drinking buddy left to return home to his family I felt suddenly envious and rudderless. I had no such stability in my life. Nothing but chaos seemed to follow me. I had failed to take control of the change in circumstances that had taken me from being a largely unknown kid to a national figure who had daily media and commercial requests coming at him.

Late at night I phoned Joe Dunne in Boston and asked could he do me a favour. The previous summer in Boston, Joe and myself had met a guy who knew Brian O'Donovan, a Corkman and general manager of New England Revolution, a team in the Major League Soccer (MLS). I asked Joe if our mutual friend could get on to Brian and arrange a trial for me. Joe got on the case and sure enough it was arranged for me to go out there a month later. I was looking for a way out from what my reality had become.

After some initial reservations The Doc said he wouldn't stand in my way, so I flew to Boston.

When I stepped off the plane in Boston, I was thinking that we would pick up the partying from the summer before but Boston in February was a different place. The energy around the Irish bars, with all the J1 students together, was long gone. It seemed bleak. It was so cold; wintry and indifferent and not a bit like the previous summer. A day after I stepped off the plane, the squad flew to the Disney Sports Campus in Orlando for training. The ninety-minute flight from Boston to New York and the subsequent four-hour flight on to Florida didn't lift my mood. I immediately began to wonder if I would even cope with the logistics of the MLS season, with so many long journeys during a campaign. On a map, Boston to Orlando looked like a trip from Dublin to Wexford but after six hours' travelling I thought about what it would be like going from coast to coast.

I didn't take the trial as seriously as I should have. Another Dub, Paul Keegan, who forged a good career for himself, was out there too and went out of his way to help me. We had a few pints together.

Maybe sensing early on that I wouldn't settle, I saw the

experience as a novelty more than a contract opportunity. I did learn a lot though, especially in terms of sports science. They were streets ahead of what I was used to back home and I learned stuff that would stand to me for the rest of my career.

The club appointed a coach from the US Track & Field Academy to take recovery sessions in the swimming pool as well as core sessions and it was ultra-professional. We trained twice a day and with that work behind me I was set up nicely for the rest of the season, whether that would be in the MLS or back home in the League of Ireland.

Thomas Rongen, the Dutchman who would later become assistant coach to the US national team, was in charge of New England and had been asked by Brian O'Donovan to take a look at me. At the start of the week most of the squad were standoff-ish with me and I'm not sure if Thomas wanted me there either.

They played me at right full-back in my first trial game. But it was when I got game time at centre-forward, did well and had an assist for a goal that the boys who had earlier been a little hostile acknowledged me and began dishing out high fives.

As the days rolled by I started to yearn for home. I decided it wasn't for me. The country was too vast! And I thought of Louise and my family. I especially wanted to get back to Nanny, who was ill at the time. And, of course, the Dubs.

I called time on the experiment and sure it was no big deal to them. Some guys shook hands and wished me well. It was pleasing that those fellas who at the start would barely talk to me had now come round to treating me with a bit of respect. Maybe my intention was to run away but being so far removed from home reinforced how lucky I was and what was important in my life.

Overall it was a positive experience. I tried something new, got my fitness back and even bumped into Carlos Valderrama, the brilliant Colombian with the mad hair! He was playing with Tampa Bay Mutiny, who were also training at the Disney Sports Campus and staying in the same hotel. I passed him in the corridor and half saluted. He was on the phone but he nodded back all the same!

*

Home again, I had work ahead to get back to the desired level. By now Mick McCarthy had taken over the Republic of Ireland soccer team and his assistant Ian 'Taff' Evans was the new under-21 boss and a part of the Ireland B management team too. I was annoyed that my underage international career hadn't budged an inch but I can now see I had too much of a sense of entitlement. It was easier to blame others for my lack of progress than face reality.

Was I still believing the hype? Well it was hard to avoid because every time I took a taxi or a bus someone was telling me I was bound for Liverpool. That was constant for years. But the truth is that I just wasn't up to standard any more. Soon after the new Irish management were appointed, Ian arrived out to UCD to watch me and hadn't been all that impressed.

I really hadn't shown enough form to be picked at the highest level over the 1996 and 1997 seasons. I wasn't sufficiently fit. Nor was my lifestyle helping.

All the way along I had that insatiable desire to succeed. But I was missing that doggedness and focus that had driven my early success. One night in Peg Woffington's stands out. As a regular there I would often stay back until long after closing time drinking with the staff. One of the bouncers got talking to me about soccer and said: 'You'll never play in England. Sure you're in here more than we are!'

I laughed it off but it was true. And yet I kept thinking things would just continue to happen as they always did. It's quite easy to reflect and see how I strayed. Nowadays in Gaelic football, as well as soccer, everything is logged and recorded – training stats, physiological markers, hydration. An athlete's condition and lifestyle is tracked from day to day. Back then there was nothing like that and little to prevent me going out most nights, so I just cracked on, not fully committing to either code.

A few things happened to help me get back on track. I came back from New England fitter than I had been in a couple of years and I had a bit more about me. Not long after I returned, Louise and I got back together and later that year we found out we were expecting our first child, Caoimhe. That focused my mind.

My form lifted and the goals started to fly in again for UCD. Early in 1998 we played Derry City in the Brandywell and I scored a hat-trick. There were not many harder places to play at that time.

The next day I played with the Dubs against the reigning All-Ireland champions Kerry in the National League at Parnell Park. I scored three points from play and we won. Green shoots were again sprouting all over the place.

For the first time in a while my focus was on my sporting performance. I felt I had to look ahead.

I began to wonder how my GAA teammates saw me. Tom Carr was our new manager and would lead the Dubs in 1998. Going to and from Gaelic football, I wasn't quite one of the lads. I hadn't been giving 110 per cent to the cause and I wondered if they would see me as the county-board official who spat at me had seen me – above his station, too big for his boots, not worth the fuss.

My form improved throughout the 1997–98 season and that started to spark interest from a few potential suitors in League of Ireland circles.

As summer loomed Louise and I went for a break to Portugal

with Mick Galvin and his wife, Maura. We were in a bar watching Shelbourne play Rangers in a UEFA Cup game on a rainy night in Tranmere. It was an unreal match out of which Rangers scrambled a 5–3 win. For long stretches, though, Shels were by far the better team and played the more attractive football. As I sat there watching them I was thinking, 'Jesus, I'd love to have a go at that level!' I was curious to see if I would be up to that standard.

Shamrock Rovers came with an offer for me. I sat down with their manager, Mick Byrne, and chairman, Joe Colwell, and we spoke for an hour about where the club was going and where they saw me fitting in. They had just finished fourth the previous season in the Premier Division. I told them I wanted to play at a high level but also wanted to continue with Dublin, and they had no problem with that. Then they asked what fee I was looking for.

'To be honest I haven't even thought about money,' I said.

I met them on my own. Kevin had advised me in the aftermath of 1995, but the commercial stuff had dried up and I was now by myself.

'Well then, Jason, would you be happy with what you're on in UCD?' they asked.

'That's fine, whatever you think,' I replied.

It had been a good time with UCD – almost four years. We played in front of a few select and loyal supporters most weeks but I made 110 appearances, scored 31 goals and was grateful for the opportunity and the chance that The Doc took on me.

My last game was against Limerick FC in a relegation–promotion play-off in May, 1998. We were third from bottom in the top flight and Limerick were second in the First Division. We took a 2–1 lead with us from the first encounter and in the second leg down there I nabbed a nice goal when I spotted their keeper off his line and shot on the half-volley from near the halfway line and it went in. We won 3–1 and 5–2 on aggregate. I was happy to help UCD stay in the Premier Division.

I'm mostly proud of how we tried to play proper football at UCD, to keep the ball on the deck as much as we could. It was a challenge because other teams were set up to play a lot off the ground and murder you in the air. Playing surfaces were poor enough all over the country too – a lot of winter soccer. Opposition centre-halves were eager to flatten you, but our athleticism and resilience stood to us. We were only kids and we had a lot of fun. A lot of the lads, like Shay Kelly, Terry Palmer, Packie and Jody Lynch, Ciarán Kavanagh, James Keddy, Robbie Griffin, Mick O'Byrne and Jason Colwell went on to play for other teams

I'll always hold fond memories of the craic we had. Some guys were known for the sound of bottles clinking as we boarded the team bus heading to a match. They always made sure we were well provisioned in the liquid department for the journey home. Some wore their disco clothes underneath their UCD tracksuits for fear shirts and jeans would get creased if put into gearbags.

I had offers to go elsewhere – Jim McLaughlin and Tommy Heffernan wanted me at Dundalk. But even though I was a Northsider who had supported Bohemians until their fans abused me when I started playing for UCD, the notion of play-ing for a club with Rovers' history appealed.

With £120 a week – this time for fifty-two weeks and not just a season – in the jeans pocket and the use of a Mazda 121, I felt I had turned a page in my soccer career.

As with the Dubs post-95, however, there were challenges at Shamrock Rovers. Mick Byrne had recently been a Rovers player himself and the rapid adjustment from player to manager must have been difficult.

I don't know if we trained the hardest either. Mostly, I recall just having a training session on Monday nights on the

Astropark five-a-side and then another session on Fridays before a match. It was basic enough. We certainly trained much harder in the GAA but Rovers had some fine players: Marc Kenny, Derek Tracey, Tommy Dunne, Richie Purdy and Paul Whelan. Paul used to bring bin bags to wear in training to work up a sweat if he had enjoyed a 'good weekend'.

I don't think we ever came from behind to win a match because we just didn't have ninety minutes in us. The first league game I played was against Shels and we were 2–0 down. I got a late goal and we then nicked another to get out of there with a draw. The Rovers supporters are fickle enough but at least I was off to a good start. I nipped in for the goal, ran to the Rovers fans and clutched the crest on my jersey – as you do!

Still, it wasn't easy to steep myself in the history of a club evicted from its heartland, Milltown, who then played their 'home' games at Tolka Park. I don't know if I ever got the full sense of the tradition at Rovers.

A week after the Shels game Bray Wanderers, who had been in and around the bottom of the table, beat us a goal to nil. From there the arse fell out of our season.

I didn't help greatly, nor did I do myself justice. During the season I spent there I got eight goals in thirty-one appearances and scored most of those because Mark Kenny put the ball on my head from set pieces. Personally, I regret how I performed, but I would say the team in general under-performed for that season.

Mick moved on at the end of the season and Damien Richardson took the reins. He wasn't as sympathetic to me in relation to my GAA commitments and it was obvious this would create an issue. I would have been well within my rights to go through the motions and take my few pound at the end of each week but I told them I was happy to cancel my contract releasing some finance to invest on a new player. They went with that and signed Graham Lawlor, a centre-forward from Bohs.

Soon the slate would be clear again and I could give everything I had to Dublin football. I looked forward to it.

14

Finding the Footballer Again

Just one week before the 1999 Leinster final against Meath, I had been in New Zealand working on an RTÉ TV show called *Rapid*. I flew back into Dublin just a few days before the final and sure I can see now it was just not sustainable. But I was working and I had to go where work called.

The role on the show came to me through a proposal from an independent company, COCO TV. They were producing a new sports programme to replace *The Grip* – which had been presented on RTÉ by Ryle Nugent and Sarah O'Flaherty – and they wanted a well-known figure to co-present and comple-ment a little-known presenter called Kathryn Thomas.

Rapid was a magazine show following everything from minority sports to the cream of Irish and international sporting talent all over the world. The show ran for three seasons, from 1998 to 2000, got high ratings and we all worked well together. We were young and energetic and we clicked. Kathryn was great craic and did most of the dynamic, mad stuff like bungee jumping. I did most of the interviews with sports personalities.

It was a great opportunity because I loved sport and the show brought me from Cape Town, where I interviewed Springbok rugby stars such as Percy Montgomery, Robbie Fleck and head coach, Alan Solomons (who would later coach Ulster), to Manchester United, where I met Denis Irwin for a skills challenge and even coaxed Roy Keane into doing an interview. Another trip I enjoyed was to New England where I interviewed Revolution owner Robert Kraft and the Super Bowl-winning kicker Adam Vinatieri. During those three years I also interviewed Bernard Dunne, Darren Sutherland and a young Rory McIlroy.

On pitches and courts all around the world I was talking with these fellas and feeling I knew what they were about. The job was a perfect fit. But I was also playing at a high level with both Dublin and Shamrock Rovers. It was a demanding schedule. Whenever I was in filming, the production company would dictate where I had to be on any given day. And there was no way I could give all three disciplines 100 per cent. Again, with the energy and abandon of youth, I tried to defy logic.

A few weeks before the Leinster final in 1999 we had been on the brink of elimination against Laois in the semi-final when, with time running out, I got the nod to come off the bench. I went on, intercepted a ball in their full-back line and sent it across to Robbo at full-forward. The opposition said that Robbo looked to have picked the ball clean off the ground before fisting an equalizer in the last minute, but in his post-match interview he said there was a divot on the pitch and the ball had bobbled up to him!

I started the replay, which we won by two points and that night I flew from Dublin Airport heading south. It took five flights and thirty hours to get to Queenstown on the South Island in New Zealand for the shoot for *Rapid*. I got back home the Monday before we played Meath. The replay meant that instead of having two weeks to prepare for the Leinster final I now had less than one.

It was work and it paid the bills but after that Leinster final I decided there was no way the production company could dictate my schedule. I would never again put myself in a situation where I had to travel a full circle of the globe shortly before playing a big game. The show could justifiably have run for another season but I was happy enough that it was finishing after three. I felt I could always revisit the possibility of sports presenting in the future, whereas I would have only a few more years playing elite sport. The show ended on a high, with preview segments for the Sydney 2000 Olympics in the can.

*

When Tom Carr took over as manager he brought with him an obvious passion to succeed. You could see the hold Dublin football had on him, the love for the team etched in each line of his face. Tom had been a key player for Dublin in his time. His career ended in a type of understudy role in 1994 but, before that, he was used to being a leading man. He lit up when he spoke about football.

Army man and all that, Tom was also a disciplinarian and it was no massive shock to any of us when we started training at Cathal Brugha Barracks. It was a basic, no-frills regime and the barracks played host to a lot of hard graft in the winter of 1998, some of the hardest training a Dublin team ever underwent.

We were now a younger and fitter group but it was all to no avail. We lost a replay to Kildare by a point in the 1998 Leinster Championship, our first loss to Kildare since 1972. They subsequently proved to be a decent team, reaching the All-Ireland final that year, but that was no solace to us.

As for that 1999 campaign, despite coming good in the replay against Laois, we relied way too much on Declan Darcy and

Jim Gavin for our scores and were soundly beaten by Meath in the aforementioned Leinster final. It was a huge disappointment considering the campaign had started so well.

That's why I was so frustrated after that Leinster final defeat to Meath. We had worked so hard to get there, and trying to keep the head down and combine it all with my TV work had been tough. As I walked off towards the Cusack Stand I felt totally drained. Not the usual weariness I felt after games, this lethargy was of a different kind.

My daughter, Caoimhe, had arrived in December 1998 and that brought new responsibilities. Maybe there was a realization that I was no longer a happy-go-lucky teenager and the years were starting to fly by. Only now were Robbo and Mick O'Keefe, teammates from my minor days, coming on to the senior team, whereas I was now nearly a veteran and possibly on the way out of the team because my form had dipped.

The loss was doubly frustrating because I had a renewed hunger to win. Some years later I sat down for a questions-and-answers interview with a former inter-county player for his newspaper column. He asked me to rank health, wealth, family and success in order of importance and I chose winning an All-Ireland above all of the rest! I may have lacked perspective but that's just how obsessed I was. The seeds for all that were sewn once *Rapid* and my soccer commitments were out of the way. I wasn't concerned about wealth. And the health thing, well, I reckoned even if I lost an arm I'd still be happy once I had another All-Ireland medal.

My renewed focus was tested, however, when I was sent off three times in relatively quick succession. The first incident was in the 1999 League final in May when I reacted to being pinched and was booked. I then had an incident with Anthony Lynch and was shown a red card. On 31 October of that year I saw red again in a League match on our first ever visit to Healy

Park. Tyrone played virtually all the football and being a man down we were helpless to stop them.

Around the quarter-hour mark the ball broke in the square and my instinct was to volley it but instead I hit their keeper who hit the ground. It was a pure accident but I felt that he milked it and in such a hostile atmosphere up there that I knew straight away I was a goner. I looked over and Peter Canavan was in the ear of referee Brian Crowe. I was disappointed with that but sure I might have done the same myself. I'll never forget the abuse I got walking off. Jesus, the venom pouring out of the supporters' mouths! There was obviously still a lot of residual bile from 1995.

In 2001, I saw red against Roscommon in another league game. On this occasion Clifford McDonald was marking me when the ball broke around midfield. I went to chase after the break but Clifford grabbed my boot as he fell and he wasn't letting me go. I tried frantically to free my leg from his clutches and it may have looked like I was going to stamp on him, but I didn't and eventually wriggled free. That was grand. On went the play until an umpire put his hand up and the two of us were called to order.

'What's this about?' Clifford asked as we trotted up.

Ger Lynch from Fermanagh didn't answer. He just showed me a red card and then said I had stamped on Clifford.

'He didn't stamp on me,' Clifford insisted, to his great credit.

It was all the one. I was off. Suspended for three months.

I appealed and Clifford wrote a letter in my defence as he couldn't make it to Dublin on the night of my hearing with the Games Administration Committee (GAC). Paraic Duffy, who was Chairman of that committee, had been at the match and addressed me directly at the hearing. He felt I did stamp on Clifford and the ban stood. Maybe that was how it looked but I was sour enough and couldn't help wondering if some of the stuff happening to me was the result of bias. And maybe I was making a few excuses for myself too.

We went out for few pints after the hearing and I continued to bitch about the decision. Dessie Farrell turned to me and said, 'But that's three times you've been sent off now, Jason.'

'Jaysus, Dessie, I didn't do anything to warrant any of them!'

Dessie looked at me and in his methodical, low-key and direct style asked, 'But when are you going to do something about it? When are you going to take responsibility for your own actions?'

Just like Charlie Redmond's advice never to show you are hurt, Dessie's few words stuck with me. In a sporting sense it was almost an intervention and, as he would subsequently demonstrate, Dessie was never afraid to say what needed to be said.

That was Dessie. He wasn't afraid of confrontation with any of us; he cared too much about the team. His advice was a key point in my development and a big part of my renewed focus as a footballer. I never got another red card for Dublin. I started to take control of my actions.

Dessie was also a key player in the rich vein of form we had with Na Fianna around that time. We won three county titles in a row between 1999 and 2001 and a Leinster Championship in 1999. That success with the club and a more focused approach to discipline on the field definitely helped me.

In early 2000 I took off with the Dubs to Torremolinos for preseason training. The trip went well. On arrival we twigged that the hotel was geared less towards high-performance sport and more towards sun, sea, sand and relaxing with drinks by the pool. But that was no bad thing – we could cut our cloth to measure.

We did get the use of a soccer pitch to train on. Tom had us jog there each day for seven-a-side GAA games with goals only, all played out under a warm sun. By night we'd have the few pints. The only hard and fast rule was that the entire panel had to be present for team bonding and social engagements such as golf. Tom insisted on that.

I roomed with Brendan O'Brien from Trinity Gaels, a good Donaghmede lad. Coming from the same club as Vinnie Murphy he had a lot to live up to. Brendsy was quiet enough at the start but we got more out of him as he got to know us. Up in the room I unpacked all my training gear for the week, laying it out day by day on my bed. Next thing Brendsy dragged his bed towards mine.

'What are you at, Brendsy?' I asked.

'Ah Jay, come on. Sure I can't sleep on me own!'

Brendsy must have found it hard to sleep with the light off! When he finished moving the bed across the room, Brendsy started hanging up his disco shirts in the wardrobe. It was that kind of a week. We worked hard, trained hard and enjoyed the nights out good and hard.

One night on arriving back to our room I reminded Brendsy to set the alarm for the next morning's golf because the whole team had to be there. He set it alright – to be a half hour late! When I woke up with the sun streaming in and asked the time, Brendsy mumbled 'Nine thirty'. Panic! I dressed quickly and hurried to reception.

The whole team had taken off for the links. Or so it seemed. But then a few more Dublin heads appeared and it emerged eight of us had missed the bus. We had to make the best of it, so we took off to the pool for a while and then headed up town to watch the Old Firm derby between Celtic and Rangers followed by Paolo Di Canio's wonder-goal volley in the West Ham and Wimbledon clash.

When the lads returned from golf that evening we offered grovelling apologies to Tom. While he wasn't over the moon, he wasn't too bad either. It was the next day at training that the eight of us felt the pain. That was when we did our penance.

We put down a good week and on one of the last nights there Tom told us to be home by midnight, but with curfew approaching we said we'd chance a nightclub. We justified it because Dessie was going too. Dessie was our captain and if he was there, sure that was good enough for us. At one stage Dessie went towards the exit and about ten of us followed suit. If he was going home so were we. Before the door, however, Dessie pulled a hard left and went into the jacks. The rest of us were hot on his heels and we ended up in there as well!

We suffered again the next day when Tom found out we had broken the curfew. We were put through a 'screw session' – an hour of pure torture as Tom went around the lads one by one reminding them what time they had returned at. All of this – the penance, the endurance, the nights out – brought us closer together. Our character and spirit grew, and coming home we knew that.

Whether by accident or design, my style changed and the 2000 Leinster final was the first time I played at centre-forward. I worked hard on the technical side of my game and started to look at my overall role within the Dublin team. Was there more I could offer rather than non-stop movement and opportunist goals? I knew there was. I worked hard on reading the runs of teammates and how I could play them in. I ended up being able to more easily pick a fella out with a pass. I could see what was happening around me, two steps ahead, and had a picture in my head of where space was or might soon be.

I dedicated myself to improving; I wanted to become a better footballer. It took all those losses for the penny to eventually drop. The game was starting to go down the road of heavy weight training, putting on bulk, and that was never going to suit me. Whether it was because I wasn't strong enough to get past corner-backs any more or because I could get more space farther out and knew what type of ball was needed inside, I started to become an option out the field.

For the start of Tom's third season, we looked re-energized. Meath were reigning All-Ireland champions but they were knocked out of the championship by Offaly in the first week of June – before half the country even realized the competition had started.

We beat Wexford and I picked off three points. I managed 1–2 as we beat Westmeath to reach the Leinster final against Kildare. I wasn't as effective as I would have liked in the first half of that final and I was switched to centre-forward in the second half and put on Glenn Ryan. I finally clicked there and got three points, all from long range.

Glenn was very brave, a strong guy and a traditional centre-back who liked to hold his ground. But I roamed about the field, dragged him over and back and had the legs on him. Suddenly you want every ball played into you. You're floating. All is well with the world!

Then Kildare made a change, moving Glenn and putting another defender on me. That freed Glenn up and they surged back into the game. We had a free to win it near the end, out about 23 yards on the left, into the Canal End. It wasn't a particularly easy one and we already had a few different free-takers that day. With the vein of form I was in could I have taken it? I don't think you can just step up out of nowhere and start kicking frees, it's a really particular skill. Brian Stynes was the one brave enough to win the free and with our regular free-taker, Declan Darcy, injured, Brian stepped up, but kicked it wide. Back for a replay.

Missing penalties had been the scourge of Dublin football, but we also struggled for consistent, quality free-taking. We found it tough that day too. There's no point in me having a moan about any of that because, technically, I wouldn't have been good enough to have a go. Free-taking is a highly specialized skill and one that I struggled with.

In Dean Rock, the current Dublin team boasts one of the most reliable free-takers we've ever seen, but for a long time, with the exception of Mossy Quinn and Stephen Cluxton, Dublin didn't have a regular sharpshooter of any great longevity and that wounded our chances countless times.

Early in the replay we seized control all over again and led by six points up at half-time.

Aside from a few more missed frees, we rued a gilt-edged chance early on when Ciarán Whelan was bearing down on goal only for his run to go unnoticed by Stynesy. One deft pass, a sure-thing score and we might have been home because we had a nice lead built up at that stage.

Kildare came out and got two goals, Dermot Earley firing one into the Hill end to silence our supporters. Tadhg Fennin grabbed the other.

Had we started thinking of the final whistle and lost focus? It's possible. In the 1995 final the lads definitely struggled with a bit of paralysis as the game neared its end. I was young and carefree then but in 2000 I too had a bit of baggage and maybe we all froze slightly with the goal in sight.

We showed a lack of know-how at crucial stages. Nowadays teams are prepped for every scenario, but that day we didn't know how to react to losing a six-point lead. We hadn't prepared for it.

I looked around and lads were doing things they hadn't done all year long, reverting to panic stations, making silly mistakes. Self-destruction. A general malaise set in. We had improved our character but lacked in the tactical department.

With about ten minutes left Curraner got the ball on the Hogan Stand side and soloed up the sideline. You could see him getting frustrated with every step of his run because there was just no movement ahead of him. We were equally puzzled watching him coming on the attack because we didn't have a clue what he was doing or where he was going. There was no cohesion.

Kildare saw all that and belief coursed through their veins. Mick O'Dwyer was wired on the sideline after they got their goals and I can't blame him because they were such a momentum changer. They came back from the dead, we rolled over and they beat us 2–11 to 0–12. It's amazing now that we have won twelve Leinster titles since 2002, eleven since 2005, because back then we were five years without one.

Later that evening we walked through the crowd and up to the Sunnybank Bar for a few pints and dissected the whole thing. The following day we all met up at Harry Byrne's in Clontarf and the post-mortem continued. We were still devastated but we had started to regroup. There was a mix of banter and deathly silences as we recounted the game.

During one lull, Jim Gavin, who had been flying in the forwards that season, interjected: 'Where did it all go wrong, lads? Was it the backs or midfielders?'

When it registered with everyone what Jim had said – and that he was trying to absolve the forwards of all blame – we all started laughing. What else could you do?

15

Running to a Standstill

As I've already briefly mentioned, Na Fianna experienced something of a coincided glory era, winning three Dublin Championships in a row between 1999 and 2001. We had been out of the loop in Dublin football circles for almost twenty years before that, so it was satisfying.

Na Fianna attempted to grow their club from the top down. We had Dessie, Paul 'Pillar' Caffrey and Mick Galvin as leading lights. Pillar was our manager and he had a group of seriously strong characters who came together and wanted to win things. Mick and Senan Connell joined from Oliver Plunkett's, Mick later coaching Na Fianna before he went back to Plunkett's. Senan is still a Na Fianna man through and through.

Losing the 2000 All-Ireland final to Crossmaglen Rangers was tough. Coming back to Mobhi Road that evening after the final defeat and seeing everyone out to welcome us home was heartwarming and crushing at the same time. It was crushing mostly because we hadn't reached second gear in that final; we didn't even turn up. My regret is that we never got back to that level again to give the club's supporters what they deserved.

There is no hiding the fact that playing for Na Fianna

helped my Dublin career, but before the breakthrough there was heartbreak. We were beaten in the 1998 Dublin Senior Championship final. I found the build-up tough going. I was spreading myself too thin in the matches leading up to that.

For instance, on the day we played our county semi-final against Erin's Isle I was also playing with Shamrock Rovers at Tolka Park. I went straight from Tolka Park up to Parnell Park and came on as a sub for Na Fianna late in the game. The logistics were a lot more complicated on county final day; I played the game and then drove to Vincent's, where a helicopter with a reporter and photographer on board waited to fly me to Finn Park in Donegal for Shamrock Rovers against Finn Harps. I look back on all that now and wince. I wasn't doing either team any favours.

One highlight from that time was getting to meet and play with Kieran McGeeney, who arrived at Na Fianna in 1999 along with another Armagh player, Des Mackin.

The story goes that Dessie Farrell met Kieran in Coppers one night and McGeeney hinted he might be willing to transfer to a club in Dublin from Mullaghbawn. Before 'Amhrán na bhFiann' had struck up in the nightclub, Geezer was one of us!

It was no surprise to me that the year McGeeney arrived we won the Dublin Championship and beat St Brigid's in the final.

We proceeded into the Leinster Championship, a great novelty. I was suspended following that red card in the league against Tyrone so I missed out on our game with Rathnew in Aughrim. We got over that, then played against the Kildare champions Sarsfields in the final; beat Crossmolina in the All-Ireland semi-final at Pearse Park, Longford, in the muck and slurry; and met Crossmaglen in the All-Ireland final.

We just never got going that day. Experience should have stood to us since so many of our team had often played in Croke Park, but Cross were so prepared and so single-minded. They ran riot. They were in our faces from the start and we failed to come to terms with their physical stuff and verbals. They were a lot more streetwise than us and made the most of their experience on the big days.

Someone got injured and during the break in play big Joe Kernan came running on, a gentleman off the field but now in my face roaring and shouting. One of their players wore an Armagh jersey under his club shirt, and while I don't doubt the patriotism for his county, that was largely for the benefit of McGeeney, reminding him he had left Mullaghbawn, Cross's biggest rivals in Armagh. They were trying to get into his head.

Mick Galvin was about the only player who did the business for us that day. He was thirty-five but played out of his skin while the rest of us went missing. Mick scored an unreal point from the corner of the Canal End and Cusack Stand that afternoon.

We never really regrouped to push on and eventually win an All-Ireland Championship even though on paper we may have looked good enough. The following year we put back-to-back Dublin titles together but were beaten by O'Hanrahans of Carlow in the Leinster final. The disappointment was put into stark context, however, with the devastating loss of Louise's sister, Paula, who was killed tragically in a traffic accident when travelling home through Thailand after a holiday in Australia.

Two days before Christmas 2001, we played Rathnew in the Leinster final replay – our third straight year getting to a provincial final. Dessie was sent off early on but we thought we were over the line until Tommy Gill pointed for Rathnew thirty seconds into injury time to force two extra periods of fifteen minutes. We were a tired and bedraggled team by the second half of extra time and they even managed a bit of showboating, going on to beat us by nine points.

It wasn't the most pleasant build-up to the festive season! And that was the peak of my success with Na Fianna. In the years to come we were beaten in Dublin semi-finals and a county final but never got back to Leinster or All-Ireland Championship level again.

*

Instead the 2001 season will be forever associated with our clash with Kerry in Thurles.

Before we headed to Tipperary to play that game, however, there was another grindingly familiar three-point loss to Meath in the Leinster final on 15 July. At least this time we had the winding road of the qualifiers to get us back to the main thoroughfare and we showed serious character to find our way.

Back in the dressing room after the Meath defeat Dessie said we weren't done yet. I sat down wishing he would stop talking nonsense, but after a minute or so it dawned on me that we did still have a shout. We could get back. A new qualifier system had been introduced to the Senior Football Championship, so for the first time in history, defeated teams would have a possible back-door route to the business end of the season.

Dessie had the foresight and presence of mind to get us thinking like that moments after one of the most disappointing defeats of our career, even though the defeat was especially upsetting for him. As captain he would have loved to climb the steps of the Hogan Stand.

We were out again seven days later, on 22 July, against a good Sligo side. We scored 3–17 – Dessie got 1–4 – and that was fair going for a side beaten in a final just a week earlier. In later years it was extremely rare that any beaten provincial finalists got straight back on the horse. I played at number 11 against Sligo and was selected there again to face Kerry in the All-Ireland quarter-final in Thurles.

The night before that Kerry game we stayed in the Horse and Jockey Hotel and went to Mass in Holycross Abbey the next morning. The Mass was celebrated by a staunch GAA man, Father Eoin Thynne. Father Eoin was head chaplain of the Defence Forces for twenty-five years, he later became a monsignor, and he declared that morning that in sporting terms playing this match was like going to war. His words set the tone!

From there it was hugely exciting going into Thurles, like being in the square on Munster hurling final day. The atmosphere sizzled and everyone knew something special lay ahead. The roar we got when the Dublin fans saw our bus crawling through the town, the welcome we received – some of the lads had tears in their eyes as they processed it. Most of us didn't have much experience of playing big championship games around the country as the only times we had played outside of Croker were in 1995 and 1996. The lads were genuinely struck by the roar when the supporters caught sight of us. Travelling Dubs said it reminded them of Páirc Uí Chaoimh in 1983 when we played Cork in the All-Ireland semi-final replay. The M People song 'Search for the Hero' was played on our bus on the way into the square and that song still gives me shivers when I hear it.

As for the game, 51,000 punters paid in and Kerry were the better team for long spells. With Johnny Crowley and Mike Frank Russell bang in form they went six points up. Again we showed fortitude to come back when we could have dropped the heads. We started to regain ground and stayed in the hunt by nabbing two goals. The first came when I got on the ball and gave it to Vinnie. He had a lot of work to do but finished brilliantly to the corner. Then Wayne McCarthy stepped up for a 45 but left it 5 metres short and as it dropped Darren Homan rose and fisted it to the net. We led by a point with time almost up.

Then came the famous equalizer. All I can say about Tom

Carr on that occasion is it showed what Dublin and the job meant to him. Earlier in the game he had run to referee Mick Curley and roared, 'Mick, you're riding us today!' The passion for Dublin coursed through every vein.

As Maurice Fitzgerald stepped up to shoot an equalizer from the sideline Tom tried to put him off by shouting in his ear. He might as well have tried to rile the Dalai Lama. The sheer class of the man shone through as he curled an impeccable point that swung out to the left before being almost magnetically sucked to the right and over the bar.

We still got one more chance to seal a famous win when Kerry conceded a 45 but Wayne dropped it short.

Wayne was only twenty and a couple of pounds over 10 stone when he was handed the responsibility of taking frees, so I know the pressure he was under having to kick into a strong breeze and having missed one earlier. If he were still there kicking that free he wouldn't convert it. The prospect of asking a goal-keeper, in our case, Davy Byrne, to take it wouldn't even have been considered back then. Ten years later, mind you, Stephen Cluxton won the 2011 All-Ireland final with his last-minute kick!

We walked off in two minds, happy with the draw and yet gutted not to win. For all our heart we couldn't close the deal. I swapped shirts with Séamus Moynihan, a player I would have huge respect for, a true footballer. We applauded the crowd as we walked off – especially the Dubs down the Killanan End – showing we appreciated their support.

You could see what it meant to everyone. We were crying out for a return to the glory days and the draw was almost like a victory. It can best be described as the biggest game we hadn't lost after six years of bitter failure. Bertie Ahern was waiting for us in the dressing room and the place buzzed with a hint of the big time once more.

On the following Monday we went to Parnell Park for training and the Dublin chairman John Bailey spoke to the players: 'Lads, next match, win or lose, we are backing this man [pointing to Tom Carr]. If ye show the spirit he showed last Saturday we won't be far off it. Good luck, lads, but we will back this man regardless of what happens.'

Talk about the dreaded vote of confidence!

The replay will be remembered on our side for the chances we didn't take. We started the game with four natural midfielders and maybe lacked balance. When Tomás Ó Sé was sent off early in the game we should have taken advantage but, again, we struggled tactically. We didn't know how to max the opportunity. Curraner roved as the extra man, but maybe Senan Connell should have taken that role because he had the athleticism and passing skills to make it count. We lacked cuteness and didn't know how to give ourselves the best chance to beat them.

The replay was perhaps the more accurate reflection of the difference between the teams and Johnny Crowley's goals ended our dreams for another year. And while we did feel we were getting there, the county board felt otherwise.

Once the dust settled, rumours re-emerged that Tom was for the chop despite Bailey's recent endorsement. And sure enough it came to pass that at a board meeting the eject button was pushed on Tom's reign.

Outside the meeting some of our players had waited in the car park, canvassing incoming delegates in support of Tom. The vote was split down the middle – forty-six for his removal and forty-six for his retention. John had the casting vote and opted for change.

It all threatened to split the county because many players were aghast at Tom's treatment. Dessie had made an impassioned, but ultimately futile, plea prior to the crucial vote. He said the players were fully behind Tom but rejected allegations of a cosy cartel between players and manager. He argued that we were on the brink of something special and said he had never been involved with a more passionate group.

All to no avail. Tom had taken the team at a time when football in the capital had reached a low point and now, despite progress, he was gone. A storm brewed. Disgruntled players threatened to walk away while officials tried to move on. Sensing a split, Tom went public and urged everyone to get behind the new man.

He meant that too. Deep down Tom cared about Dublin more than anything else.

16

Arseboxing

In early November 2001, Tommy Lyons was appointed the new Dublin manager and within six weeks had put his stamp on the team. Players such as Wayne McCarthy lost out while in came young colts the likes of Barry Cahill, Alan Brogan and Paul Casey.

I was lucky not to get the chop because it was clear his perception of me was a negative one. You tend to take stock of your own situation any time there is change and I wondered where did Tommy see me in his plans. In those early days I think I was more outside his plans than part of them. I certainly wasn't high up the pecking order.

He was highly critical of what had gone on in the years beforehand and it quickly became apparent that I would struggle to get game time. In fairness to Tommy, he gave it straight to me – and he was probably one of the first managers to challenge me in what I was doing.

'In ninety-five you always got on the ball and went at players,' he told me. 'But you have stopped doing that.'

On reflection he was right.

Tommy was just as open – and even a little more

charming – with the media. In hindsight, he was too open and too charming.

For the hungry press he was a one-man show. He was full of colour. He used memorable terms such as 'arseboxing' and even compared the Dublin gig to managing Manchester United. The arseboxing reference was in the context of inter-county players having to sell tickets to fund team holidays, so his intentions were honourable. He reckoned the Leinster Council should fund post-season squad breaks.

Tommy was the complete opposite to Jim Gavin, who is very precise and succinct in what messages get out to the media. The press saw Tommy as pure box office and he frequently lived up to that billing. But, as I found out, the media is fickle. Tommy led us to a Leinster title in his first year, but it didn't get much better for us after that. After we won in Leinster, we beat Donegal in a replayed All-Ireland quarter-final before we lost to Armagh in the semi-final. In the following year, we lost to Laois in Leinster and Armagh again in the All–Ireland, this time in the qualifiers. By the time Tommy's third season came around, we were falling further off the pace. We lost to Westmeath in Leinster but did manage to reach the All-Ireland quarter-final where Kerry beat us. Along the way Tommy went from being a celebrated character to a media villain who just wasn't getting Dublin over the line.

I've met him in recent years and recognize that he has many qualities. He's a character but also a highly successful business-man. In 2002 he gave us our first provincial title in seven years but perhaps the biggest achievement of his time in office was to put the 2003 Dublin under-21 All-Ireland-winning manage-ment team in place that included Jim Gavin and Declan Darcy. The two lads had finished up as players with Tommy's squad but he asked them to stay on and lead the under-21s. He took a bit of credit for that win but, in fairness, that move to appoint the two lads has had a very positive impact on the future of Dublin football.

The hype started to build around us but I had planned on running a hundred miles in the opposite direction from any sort of fuss. I had had enough of all that. I turned more towards the 'internal' side of things, desperately seeking anything that could help me gain an edge. The external stuff wasn't going to help us win an All-Ireland. I knew that better than anyone.

We were not a million miles away but I think we would have preferred to go about our business less noisily, whereas Tommy was more inclined to shout from the rooftops about what we had to offer. It was against such a backdrop that we went to work.

He came into the job with some different thoughts and ideas on the back of the Offaly job after leading them to a league title and Leinster Championship. Would the same concepts apply to Dublin?

Whether I agreed or disagreed with him, I knew where I stood. In 2001 I had held my own against players like Séamus Moynihan and Éamonn Fitzmaurice, and felt I deserved to start games. Tommy felt otherwise.

I warmed the bench for our first championship game against Wexford in Carlow in the summer of 2002 and looked destined to be there all season. Early that morning Ireland played Cameroon in the group stages of the World Cup and by the time our game threw in there was a carnival atmosphere about. The supporters had been enjoying themselves all day and there were five streakers at Dr Cullen Park during the half-time break. It even struck me the streakers were getting more of a run-out than myself!

It was only when we failed to put Wexford away that I got on near the end. They pushed us all the way and when I eventually got on I scored two points and we won by two thanks to a goal-line block by Paul Casey!

I thought I might have started to win Tommy over and hoped to start the next game but I was wrong on both counts. At the end of that 2002 season Tommy thought that my attitude changed for the worse after the Wexford game because, 'You thought you were going to start every game after that!'

I don't know about that! Yes, I was left off the starting fifteen for the entire season but I came on in all of the matches, including the Leinster semi-final against Meath and the final against Kildare. I think I was in a positive frame of mind and made an impact in those games. The main thing was we felt the team could win an All-Ireland and I was desperate to contribute because I thought we could get there.

Maybe a little shortcut I took at Leopardstown in training one night gave Tommy more ammunition not to start me. He brought us to the racetrack for a running session and it gave us a chance to appreciate the nice little incline that faced us as we negotiated 100-metre and 200-metre sprints around one of the bends. Off like greyhounds tore the likes of Alan, Barry and Paul Casey while myself and a few of the older lads scouted around for a more laid-back, shall we say, energy-conserving group to link up with.

But it was a sign that I was pushing on because finding a bunch of like-minded spirits was no longer easy with all these young colts bulling for road. The going was tough that evening but we got through it and at the end Tommy told us to warm down with a lap of the track, which was about 2 miles long! Some warm-down. With that he said he'd see us the following Thursday, hopped into his car and drove off.

We trudged off to complete the session but halfway around the lap Curraner, Johnny Magee and I decided we'd had enough. We cut across the track, past the driving range, and into the warm confines of the winners' enclosure. As we rambled across the racecourse, delighted to have finished the session early, a group of people spotted us from the West Wood gym and tennis club and it turned out they were friends of Tommy's. They snitched on us and the next night at training Tommy made us pay. So maybe that was another factor in his decision not to start me!

Come the Leinster final I was on the pitch for the final whistle and dived in for a breaking ball and had it in my paws when that shrill whistle sounded. That title meant so much to me. In anyone's language seven years was a long time to go without a bit of tin.

It helped calm the ripples of frustration. I was twenty-six and from a long way back had felt I would reach the peak of my playing powers at twenty-seven. Uncle Brian had always maintained twenty-seven was the optimum age for an athlete. I was only a year off that landmark and had grown increasingly anxious to be at my maximum when I got there. Being on the bench wasn't part of the plan!

Tommy took ill for the All-Ireland quarter-final against Donegal and, with his selector Pillar Caffrey in charge, we drew with them. I came on in the game and made a goal for Cossie with a left-handed pass. Dessie set up him for another one and almost got his face rearranged in the process after shipping a heavy tackle!

Between that drawn game and the replay, Ray Cosgrove assumed centre stage, scoring 3–5 in two outings. Cossie was also our free-taker having taken on that job from the start of the 2002 season.

We ran out comfortable winners in the replay and at the end we did a lap of honour for our supporters. Croke Park was 90 per cent Dublin fans that day and it felt like our stadium. We gave the supporters a wave that was innocent in our eyes, but I later heard back that the Armagh boys knew they had us in the semi if this was how we were celebrating winning a quarter-final.

Once again I didn't start that semi-final. Tommy, now back to full health, went with Dessie and Shane Ryan ahead of me in the half-forward line, which was tough to take. But not long before the throw-in Tommy called me over as I warmed up with the team.

'Good stuff!' I thought. 'He's going to gee me up and encourage me. He'll tell me I'm the first sub in!'

Eh, not so much.

'Your on the half-time gig,' he said.

'Huh?'

'You're doing the RTÉ interview at half-time. Someone has to.'

'What?!!!'

I don't think there was any malice intended but, Jesus, there are things you say to a player on match days and this wasn't one of them. Being told you're doing a half-time interview might suggest you are not really in the frame. I thought I would be getting some positive reinforcement but now I had to be ready to talk to RTÉ and was questioning if I was even being considered to play.

I just wanted some assurance that I was an important part of his plans, but that was Tommy. The media stuff was all too prominent for him. The gas thing is he did actually intend to use me.

I came on as blood-sub early in the game, still not sure what to be thinking. Emotionally, I was all over the shop and I tried to rough up Kieran McGeeney, which clearly shows I wasn't in my right mind! In fairness there was some method in my madness — I was trying to bully the bully, trying to distract their alpha male.

And there was some context to that. In the days leading up to that game I was a bit perplexed because I knew at first-hand the work McGeeney, Armagh's main man, had put in. I knew how much he wanted Armagh to win, how ferociously he prepared, and I actually found it hard to see how we deserved to win more than he did. I rang Mick Galvin to talk it over because I needed to verbalize what was going through my head. I wanted some reassurance as well.

'Mick, I just can't see how we deserve this game more than McGeeney,' I said, as we got into the detail.

'What do you mean?' Mick enquired, puzzled.

'I've really got to know McGeeney and I know how much he wants this, how far he's gone to ensure they win. I just can't see how we deserve to win this game more than them. Just look at his desire and work ethic.'

'Jesus, Jason, you'd want to knock that out of your mind straight away!'

But I knew what was coming, both from McGeeney and his team. I knew he would lay his body on the line because I'd seen him do it, even in training and challenge matches when the rest of us might be holding something back. Armagh were going to come at us with ferocious intensity.

We had our own intense guys in the Dublin camp but I'd seen this fella empty himself on the fields and he had totally changed my way of preparing for games, especially in terms of strength and conditioning. So I was right to be worried. Here was the ultimate competitor coming to get us; a guy who maxed himself as a player, who drew the last drop out of himself. He stood between us and an All-Ireland final appearance.

That's why I tried to distract him. Think Frankie Dettori squaring up to Paul O'Connell! I should possibly have taken a different tack – running him about the place rather than squaring up – but mentally I was agitated at not starting the game and then being lined up for a half-time radio interview.

Late in the game we were a point down when Cossie stepped up to address a tricky free just inside the sideline on the Hogan

Stand side, facing into the Hill. As Wayne Mac had been cut from the panel early doors in Tommy's regime, the merry-go-round of Dublin free-takers had taken another whirl as the manager sought a marksman who would convert nine out of ten shots. They don't grow on trees, though, and Tommy did all he could to solve that problem, even organizing a couple of sessions for the squad with Dave Alred, the kicking coach who helped put the wind behind Jonny Wilkinson's sail.

And wouldn't you know it? Our season came down to that last-minute kick against Armagh. Declan Darcy was the senior free-taker on the field but he was only just on. He hadn't seen any action that year and may not have been expecting to get on the pitch but Tommy made the call to introduce him. That call came totally out of the blue and when Tommy told Dec to come down to the sideline his bootlaces were still undone. He was pretty much rushed onto the pitch and people could argue that, mentally, he was in no position to kick anything. Ray, in contrast, was on fire all year, both from open play and from placed balls. He stepped up again. His shot looked good but it breezed off the post and another season died. We lost by a point.

At the final whistle some of the Armagh fellas were celebrating and jumped right into me. I swung a petulant leg at one of them. They hadn't done it deliberately and I should have been more restrained. My frustration was not with them, it was with my own contribution on and off the field and that's why I lashed out.

I sought McGeeney out at the final whistle.

'Yiz have been here before,' I said. 'There's no point just beating us. Go on and win it now.'

He was the man with the ball in his hand when full-time was blown in the final and it was better still to see the emotion he showed up in the Hogan Stand. I have no problem admitting

I was delighted Geezer won an All-Ireland. Likewise when Tyrone finally broke through and Chris Lawn got his medal, I was just as happy for him. I knew what both men had suffered to reach the summit.

After the semi-final defeat we went to the Burlington Hotel for a meal. I wasn't in a good place and hadn't liked how events had transpired. I was frustrated and wasn't shy about voicing my concerns to anyone willing to listen.

Outside the camp there were rumblings too. Certainly from within my own circle I got a disturbing sense that even those who were in my corner all the way up, those closest to me, almost resented what the team had become. Through our media appearances they felt there was an aloofness, a cockiness, and they felt that Dublin football had become all about one man. They weren't too bothered that we had lost. Seeing those people turn away from us was an eye-opener.

*

In 2003 the team never settled at all. There were changes the whole time. We beat Louth well in the Leinster quarter-finals but ahead of the Laois semi-final game Tommy gave three players their debut – even though we'd hammered Louth. The lads who were dropped were surprised. There was no indication of any changes until the team was named on Tuesday and it created a massive contrast in mood within the camp. Some guys were very happy while others were shocked and distraught.

Laois had Mick O'Dwyer with them at that stage and they smelled blood and got it. The wagons circled after that defeat.

We got Derry in the qualifiers and in the lead-up I played an A v B game at Clones, where that qualifier would be held. I did well and maintained that form for the next internal game, though I was again named on the B team. When we eventually did play Derry, I came off the bench and got 1–3 and once more it was Dessie who set me up for the goal.

Actually, when I played in Clones I couldn't believe how compact and narrow the pitch seemed. Once you were within the opposition 45 you sensed there was a definite scoring opportunity, which wasn't always the case in Croke Park. From then on I always watched Ulster Championship games in a different light, maybe not getting as excited about some of those masterful long-range scores I once raved about.

The cameo against Derry at least reminded me – and everyone else – that I could do a job. On the way home that afternoon I got a lovely phone call from the former GAA president Joe McDonagh, who was a director of the 2003 Special Olympics World Summer Games. Joe wanted me to introduce an act in front of 80,000 people at the closing ceremony celebrations the following day at Croke Park.

I was to bring the family with me, so we all went up to a corporate box near the Canal End. There I waited for word of who Dublin had drawn next in the qualifiers. When the text came through it was Armagh again. In those days the draws were pre-recorded and later shown on *The Sunday Game* as if they were live. Very few knew that, though, and the whole pretence was that it was a live draw.

I walked around towards the back of the stage and met the two MCs, Nicky Byrne and Ian Dempsey, who congratulated me on the win over Derry and wondered aloud who we would get next.

'Armagh,' I said. 'The draw has just been made.'

I went up on stage to present the act and before I left Nicky went, 'Well done yesterday, and I believe ye will be back here next week, Jason?'

'Yeah, we're playing Armagh, so I hope all the Dubs that are here today will be back in the audience cheering us on next weekend.'

A big roar. I walked off the stage and cue holy war. My phone hopped.

'Armagh? How do you know that?'

'Is that draw not live?'

I had unwittingly let the cat out of the bag. Back up to the corporate box I went, oblivious to the ramifications that sharing the news with 80,000 people and a live radio audience would have!

So there was one thing I changed in the history of Gaelic football – the draw format. They went properly live after my revelation.

I was finally back in vogue with Tommy and started the next match against Armagh, who were definitely there for the taking this time. I did okay, got two points, but our chances were hurt when Clucko (Stephen Cluxton) was sent off for an incident with Stevie McDonnell. The management reacted by taking off our centre-back, Johnny Magee, to cope with the extra man. That was a strange move – when do you ever see a centre-back being taken off to compensate for losing a player to a red card?

The consequences were stark and immediate. We were a man down and in those days we didn't have retreating forwards rushing back to offer support in defence. Armagh saw gaps and pierced them ruthlessly. They beat us and went all the way to the final again.

The fallout was considerable. Tommy reacted by blaming Clucko, who was hung out to dry, and it didn't come across well at all. The worm had turned. Tommy and Dublin were once box office but now the whole thing had turned into a horror show.

The irony in all this was that I felt I had become a better player under Tommy. Maybe I was reaching my natural peak anyway, and being on the bench a lot I was definitely more focused than in previous years. But Tommy challenged me and brought something out of me that others didn't.

He gave me some good counsel away from football too, pointing me in the direction of a career in sales. Tommy has proven an accomplished businessman and still plays a role for the Dublin senior football team in that area. He signposted a route for me and I picked up a sales role with a company and stayed in that industry from then until this year. Sales was a role that allowed me to leverage my profile and, more importantly, it was flexible and conducive to letting me devote every other hour to Gaelic football – and to Louise and Caoimhe. Nothing else bothered me.

The rumblings of discontent continued at Dubs at the end of that season when a few player meetings were held, the gist being 'Have we the best chance of winning an All-Ireland with him in charge?'

It all got quite political within the squad and we had key players on different sides. Some of the guys wanted a change while others, including the young guys who had just come in and done well, wanted Tommy to stay. That was fair enough too. There was no unanimity either way.

It was messy, our meetings became public knowledge and there was a bit of a split in the camp. Dessie was even more desperate than I was to get another medal because he sensed his time was running out and there was a feeling we wouldn't get there with Tommy. But there was no consensus to be rid of him and he stayed for one more season.

The quest continued, flinging us frantically from high to low and back again. We lost to Westmeath in the Leinster quarters in the summer of 2004 and as he left the pitch Tommy had to dodge the spittle of his own fans. That is sad in so many ways. No one should ever have to encounter that.

We blew another second-half lead that day, but by then it

was an open secret that any team that stayed with us early on could take us coming down the home straight.

Every critic had a cut. Former Dublin players wrote that they had stayed away from the game because they had lost faith in us. We were flailing in the wind, going backwards.

The thing is we had the talent to do much better. Bryan Cullen had slotted in well at centre-back. Coman Goggins and Paul Griffin were rock solid in defence too. Senan was moved back out to the half-forward line. We had Dessie, Conal Keaney all in there too and we should have done much better. David Henry and Shane Ryan were pushing hard. Whelo was prolific at the time and in Alan Brogan we had a legitimate star.

I was doing well enough myself. Against Westmeath I had four points in the first half, Alan had three and we were motoring. In the second half I had a left-footed shot for goal saved by Gary Connaughton and had that gone in, who knows? They came back at us and their manager, Páidí Ó Sé, was punching the air at the end.

Earlier that season we played Westmeath in his first game as manager, a challenge at St Jude's. Afterwards Darren Homan and I hopped into a car and Páidí shouted over, asking where was The Three Sisters pub.

'Hop in, Páidí, we'll drop you down!'

Páidí was no sooner in the car than he offloaded: 'Jesus Christ, lads, what have I done? This crowd are useless, up to nothing. I've made an awful mistake. They're brutal!'

We were sympathetic. And then we took our turn to offload: 'Páidí, if you think you're bad, we have our own shite here.'

We informed him of the weekly soap opera running under Tommy and Páidí soaked it all up. The cute Kerry hoor had thrown down the bait and we innocent Dubs fell for it hook, line and sinker. Páidí had us in his cross hairs all along. He listened intently as we spewed out how bad things were. When

I saw him celebrating it was clear as day he had gathered his intelligence and then they came out and beat us in the championship. Classic Páidí!

Shortly before his death in December 2012, Páidí met me and asked if I would come down and play in his football tournament, Comórtas Peile Páidí Ó Sé. The following February I went down and I felt the best way that we – at this stage I was playing my club football with St Oliver Plunkett Eoghan Ruadh – could honour his memory was to win the tournament, which we did, beating An Ghaeltacht in the final. It was my last honour as a player.

On the day after that Westmeath quarter-final loss, Tommy rang and we spoke for a half hour; it was the first time he had ever come to me for feedback.

We were fortunate enough with the qualifier draw – we got the three Ls: London, Leitrim and Longford. We got back to Croke Park to play a Tommy Carr-managed Roscommon side. I scored 1–4, helping us to overcome them and to meet Kerry in the All-Ireland quarter-final.

Tommy had a habit of bringing people in to chat to us before games and the week before we played Kerry it was Brian Mullins. It's fair to say that Brian is quite pragmatic and called it as he saw it, but if the aim was to motivate us it didn't work. We came out of his motivational talk with heads down. 'Jesus, if we're as bad as he says we're in trouble!' one of the boys remarked on the way out.

Unfortunately, Brian's fears for us and the flaws he had highlighted proved well founded. Kerry got off to a good start and stayed well ahead. I managed a goal but it was damage limitation. I had another effort saved and then felt I was fouled for what I thought was a stonewall penalty but it wasn't given. This time we left the field not to jeers, boos, whistles or spitting but to an eerie silence. It was just an acceptance of where we were at.

Tommy moved on soon after and I reflect on his tenure through the calming prism of time. One summer he brought us to Kenmare for a training camp. We met Bertie Ahern down there on his summer holidays and Bertie offered Tommy a lift back to Dublin in his state car. Tommy offered a big cheery wave as he hopped into Bertie's limo – 'See yiz, lads!' – and left us. Maybe it was a hard offer to turn down! The squad stayed in Kenmare that night and although there was a drinking ban in place some of the boys vowed to go for pints that night just for that wave alone!

Then there was a preseason camp in Tenerife and, following a week of pestering, Tommy let us have a few pints in a self-service bar at the end of the hotel. When we ran those taps dry, a few of us decided to head into town – against orders. We got back early in the morning and we were ratted out. We became known as the 'Tenerife Six'.

Tommy was well within his rights to eliminate the Tenerife Six from his plans but he chose to overlook our indiscretion. He was fair like that and I felt he was always open to a chat with the senior players as well. It probably helped that two of the six scored a goal each in our first league game back from that trip!

Under the glare of an unrelenting media, the man who walked on water only two summers earlier was ultimately left to find his own way back to shore.

The rest of us? We were farther adrift than ever.

17

Obsessed

It's a horrible thing to live your life with a cloud of failure hanging over you but as I got out of bed each day that was becoming the overriding emotion. I was becoming obsessive, more determined and focused than I had ever been to do what I could to make success happen. It became so personal.

When I was younger I had dreams about everything – basketball, hurling, Liverpool. But all I wanted now was another Blue September. The dream was starting to turn into a nightmare, though, and a recurring one at that. I was twenty-nine and it was no longer just about winning. I looked back on the last ten years and saw nothing but a decade of failure. There was a stigma attached to that and that's why I carried it every day, far away from the fields and the gym. It seeped into my daily routine, chipped away at my self-esteem. I had become fixated on the whole thing.

If I'm being totally honest there were no trumpets blaring when word came through that Paul 'Pillar' Caffrey was to replace Tommy. This was nothing against Pillar – he was a solid fella and had done a great job when in charge of Na Fianna. But he had been a part of the previous regime. We were damaged goods and Pillar had as many scars as the rest of us. It took courage for him to go forward and try to heal those wounds, but ideally we had been looking for a new general with fresh battle plans.

As a player you are thinking, 'Will this guy help get us there? Will he get us over the line?' You make your mind up pretty quickly and if the answer is 'no' then another season or two is wasted. And Dessie, myself and Whelo, in particular, couldn't afford to lose more time.

Here we were needing to build bridges and reconnect with supporters with a new manager who had been part of the previous set-up. There was definitely a sense of 'guilty by association' at the start. And a sense the Dublin players wanted something different too. That was the daunting challenge facing Pillar. We had lost faith. We felt we needed a new rainmaker.

Mick O'Dwyer was heavily linked with the job at the time but I remember chatting on the phone with Brian Mullins a few times in the period between Tommy's resignation and Pillar's appointment and I felt Brian would be a good fit for the job because he was so straight to the point. No frills. No hype. A Dublin legend. Exactly what we needed. It didn't materialize and I don't know why.

Right from the first meeting we held at DCU in late 2004, Pillar could see we were low on belief. That meeting took place on the same night as the All Stars function and while I was the only Dublin player to get a nomination that season and was entitled to go to the Citywest Hotel, in my head, the team meeting was a hell of a lot more important than an awards ceremony. I wasn't looking for a personal accolade when the team had failed.

Like the two Tommys before him, Pillar was up for the job. He had buckets of passion and a boundless work ethic to win for Dublin. And as time went on he would build and cultivate an impressive back-room team, a trusted army of lieutenants.

By the time he finished up he had fourteen support staff in the 'inner circle' as he called it, all striving to help us break through. To empower such large numbers nowadays is nothing ground-breaking, but Pillar was ahead of the posse in that regard when he took charge in 2004.

That helped get us on board early. Apart from the three selectors there from the start, Pillar would later bring in specialist forward, midfield, defensive and strength-and-conditioning coaches, a mental-preparation expert and a goalkeeping coach, as well as the usuals – kit men and statisticians. This approach was in stark contrast to Tommy Lyons, who had tried to do everything himself.

Our first target was a very tangible one with no razzmatazz – we simply wanted to become a more workmanlike team, to achieve solidity.

Paul Clarke came in as our coach and front-line messenger on match days. Clarkey had knowledge and enthusiasm in spades, but he married that raw passion with forward thinking and developed a fitness strategy in tandem with DCU sports-science experts. Fast forward to the start of 2017, with the elite Dublin squad on holidays, and Clarkey was once again at the helm when he temporarily stepped in and led a shadow team to an O'Byrne Cup title. The point is, he could relate well to any generation of player.

Brian Talty was brought in to work with the midfielders and scour the county for talent.

On paper, Stephen 'Ski' Wade was improving defence but he was responsible for an awful lot more. Ski had a massive influence on me and challenged us more than anyone else had done. To gain his respect was a battle in itself but we had ferocious regard for him. He would be the Declan Darcy equivalent of Jim Gavin's current regime.

Ski was a hands-on coach and one of those fellas you wanted

to do well for. He was quite stand-offish, with a bit of a rough exterior, but he had a massive love for Dublin football. He wasn't one to put the arm around you, and yet once you saw what he was about you knew he had your back. I had seen him in action when he worked with us at Na Fianna and his philosophy was that a team that made six blocks in a game would win. He cultivated a new work ethic for us and we maybe mirrored some of his no-nonsense, hard-edged ways, in direct contrast to the colour and hype of the previous seasons.

Dave Billings, with his in-depth knowledge and huge array of contacts, would study our opposition devoutly. Davy always had a twinkle in his eye and knew how you were feeling just by looking at you. I played for him when he was our under-21 manager and when I wasn't available because of soccer commitments he always understood and still wanted me there even if I was just in the dugout. Davy always saw the best in people and had huge faith in me.

Kieran Duff was a hero of mine, a Dublin icon, and he worked with the forwards. Dully had been there and earned the T-shirt. We listened to everything he said.

Dave Whelan, a 1984 Dublin All-Ireland minor winner, came in during Pillar's time too and he looked after mental preparation and sports psychology.

The elite 400-metre runner Daniel Tobin was part of the set-up before leaving to take a job with Leinster Rugby and later Gloucester Rugby. I always felt Dublin missed a trick by not appointing him to a permanent role in his specialized field and I continued working with him one-to-one after he left us.

So the back room was as solid as it could be. I was so obsessed with winning, however, that I formed my own support structure outside of all that. I contacted Dr Liam Hennessy, then of the IRFU and now of Setanta College, and he met me in the grounds of Old Wesley RFC to work on speed and agility.

I had met Liam Griffin when he spoke to Na Fianna some years earlier and everything he said that day struck a chord. So I sought him out for advice and whenever I was in Wexford I would look him up for a chat.

Mick Spillane was a physio I started using after the 1999 Leinster final and he kept me in good shape. For nearly a decade I went to him before every game and found him top-class. Mentally he would give you a lift too, as would the 'Great AK' – Alan Kelly – who would go to work on your body but also your mind while treating you. AK was such a tonic.

So it wasn't just a case of turning up and training with Pillar and his back room. Far from it. Outside of the camp I had just as much going on. I was doing everything possible to be the best player I could be. There had been a time when I put my sporting career on the back-burner but that was all in the past. I developed tunnel vision. I spoke to few and trusted even fewer. I went from media saturation and wall-to-wall coverage to declining almost every interview request that came my way. If something was not going to benefit my football, why do it? I shared some of my previous experiences with teammates. What would be accomplished by being so public? Where would be the benefit?

I had plenty of chats with Pillar too. I was a senior figure and delighted there was collaboration between the manager and myself and other experienced lads such as Whelo, Paddy Christie and Goggsy (Coman Goggins). At times I overthink things; I have a methodical way of working through stuff; I like a kind of systems check before I go to do anything. If all the boxes are ticked then the performance should run smoothly. It was great that Pillar was willing to listen to my take on things. Again, this was the opposite of Tommy, who had placed his trust in younger cubs like Barry and Alan. I had always been willing to speak up and make suggestions – it was great that Pillar would actually listen.

Three immediate goals: the first thing was to tighten the threads between us, the players. We had talented individuals in various positions but seemed to lack ball-playing defenders and physically robust forwards, so we needed to be the hardest-working team in Ireland to get to where we wanted. We needed to close out games going down the home straight. And we needed to reconnect the team to its supporters.

Free-taking was another issue and Pillar looked at Mossy Quinn and Mark Vaughan to try and solve that one. Mossy became a very capable inter-county free-taker.

Vaughan was some character. He had immense talent and on his day could kick a dead ball over the bar from the next parish. And, even if he was more of a Leinster rugby head than your typical GAA fella, he was good to have around.

One day on the way up north to play a league match in Fermanagh we stopped off for a meal at the Lakeside Manor Hotel. As the name suggests, the hotel had a lake, and Whelo bet Vaughan 20 euro that Mark wouldn't wade out to a water bollard in the distance. This was February, mind, and it was bloody arctic! Off went his Dublin tracksuit and out swam Vaughany down to his boxers, wading through the freezing waters. Just hours before a league game! He touched the bollard and, now exhausted, somehow managed to scramble back. We were pissing ourselves laughing, looking at this shock of peroxide-white hair bobbing up and down. The poor lad even thought Whelo would fork out the 20 euro!

Pillar and I met for coffee a bit, and as he was going after every incremental gain that might get us over the line I suggested a nice way to unite the team would be to bring everyone, including the subs, into our pre-match pictures. At that time, for championship games at Croke Park, only the first fifteen used to line up. The suggestion was taken on board and the practice remains the norm to this day.

I also felt we needed to renew the bond between the players and the Hill. In our last championship match, against Kerry, the silence that greeted the final whistle reflected a damning acceptance that Dublin were just not competitive at that stage of the season. It possibly also reflected the scarring defeats suffered in previous seasons. But that sense of resignation wasn't good for anyone involved in Dublin football. Nor was the fact Tommy had been spat at the year before.

I thought we needed to rouse the Hill again, show them we cared and that we needed them. It was just one of plenty of ideas I had – ultimately it was up to Pillar whether he used them or not. I suggested that after the pre-match team photo shoot we walk slowly down to the Hill and acknowledge them. This was our spiritual patch and we needed to feed off the fans.

That was the seed of the idea. We did it for a while and we did feel a reconnection until the whole thing turned into a bit of a sideshow. Detractors used it as ammunition to fire at us when we lost games.

We won a Leinster title in Pillar's first year, 2005, beating a good Laois team by a point in the final. While we later lost to Tyrone in the All-Ireland quarter-final after a replay there was a definite feeling we were going somewhere again. We were on a journey that might eventually bring us to where we wanted to go.

The year went okay for me, even though I was taken off against Meath and was surprised to be. So much so that I said to Clarkey, 'Listen, I'm still in this game and I'm ready to go back on if needs be.' With five minutes left they did send me back on, which shows how I was managing to stay mentally tuned in.

Against Wexford, I was on the bench from the start so there was an element of thickness when they brought me on and I got a goal. I got the nod for that narrow Leinster final win over

Laois and hit two points, but the key that day was Mossy scoring two late placed balls under pressure to get us over the line.

I thought we had Tyrone in the All-Ireland quarter-final. We were five points up at half-time and they seemed out of ideas. We were dominant at midfield and Alan Brogan was running the show at centre-forward, but the interval came at the wrong time for us, when we were dominating.

Tyrone, in desperate trouble, made several switches to try and get things going. I was being marked by Ryan McMenamin (Ricey), whom we had identified as their stopper-in-chief, the Tyrone player most likely to break up an opposition attack. I dragged him out to the sideline in a bid to nullify him and kept him there but still managed to whip over a couple of points.

Mickey Harte changed it all up though. He put Philly Jordan on to me and moved Ricey back into the main thoroughfare, one of many positional switches. They started to win all the breaking ball around midfield and found their groove. The TV archives will forever replay that special goal Owen Mulligan got, where he cut through our defence, weaving, dummying and slaloming, before unleashing a rocket past Clucko. It goes down as one of the great Croke Park goals but our defence was torn apart too easily.

Tyrone edged in front but at least we fought back near the end, showing a bit of heart, and once more Mossy posted a couple of late pressure frees to earn the draw, 1–14 apiece.

Before the replay Pillar called me aside and told me that Paddy Christie, our captain, wouldn't be starting and I would lead the team out. It was overwhelming and it definitely affected me. I was sorry Paddy had lost out but when I was given the captaincy the tears rolled down my cheeks. It was a massive honour and I struggled to stay focused. To be leading the team around a packed Croke Park, behind the Artane Band, with my family looking on – I just found the whole thing hard to handle.

We were well off the pace in the first half but took off the shackles in the second and hit five points in a row. A comeback looked on and momentum was with us. The noise from 78,000 spectators was so deafening that we struggled to communicate on the field. It was the noisiest atmosphere that I ever experienced.

And then, just as the atmosphere reached fever pitch, Mulligan scored another goal and popped our balloon. He walked slowly to the Hill and we knew the game was up. We showed honesty and character and hit 1–14 again that day, but this time they scored 2–18 and beat us well.

Taking down a hardened Ulster side would have been a huge boost, but clearly we were still short of the mark. Overall, though, 2005 was a decent first year for Pillar and in the dressing room afterwards that much was acknowledged. There were plenty of positives we could take away – and that was a welcome change from the recent past.

18

Game of Inches

When the dust settled we realized we needed to keep improving. We stayed hunting for every available edge that was going. That's when the Blue Book came in.

The journey Pillar brought us on was one of a constant search for inches. One day we sat down to watch a documentary on how England won the 2003 Rugby World Cup and learned of a little black book Clive Woodward had given all his squad players.

Part of Pillar's strategy was to compile our own bible. We brought the Blue Book into the set-up from 2006 onwards. We wanted to be All-Ireland champions and so we listed stuff that was important to us, that reinforced our values. We logged everything for the year ahead and used it as a kind of creed. There was a bit of a siege mentality – the catchphrase 'Thirty-one versus one' was repeated throughout the book.

We focused on what other successful teams were doing and we introduced elements of the England rugby set-up. We looked at Tyrone's penchant for dishing out the 'verbals' and tried to develop a harder edge.

Early in the 2006 league we decided we weren't taking a

backward step. It was a case of one in, all in. We played Tyrone on 5 February – a first-round rematch between the All-Ireland champions and the side they beat in a replayed quarter-final. A melee broke out in the fourth minute and was followed by two second-half all-in skirmishes, one of which spilled over on to the sideline. I happened to be warming up in the far corner when things really erupted and I deemed it wiser for me to stay on the periphery!

There was another league game soon after against our main rivals, Meath, in Parnell Park. I captained the team that day and after an early altercation we had three players sent off to their one. Despite only having twelve players for the remainder of the game we displayed grit and determination to overcome them. The rivalry hasn't been the same since.

We wanted to lower our public profile too and keep things in-house. The book contained quotes from the likes of Confucius, Isaac Newton, Muhammad Ali, Bruce Lee and Vince Lombardi; it was nothing more than sports psychology. Still, when the contents of the book eventually got into the public domain – after someone leaked a copy from the printing press – we were ridiculed, especially for the cover slogan 'Dublin – All-Ireland Champions'.

I would say every inter-county player in the land has his own Blue Book in some shape or form or colour. It was just that we were the Dubs and, as with the march to the Hill, fair game for the begrudgers. Had we won an All-Ireland, every team and county would have copied us, but that's the way it is in sport!

I didn't live religiously by the Blue Book, but it was a diary that helped me record my moods, training and thoughts on games ahead. Alan Brogan and I met for a chat near the end of Pillar's tenure and I gave him my book and asked him to have a look at it. Every page had an entry. I told Alan I wasn't giving it to him in order to show anyone up – I just wanted to demonstrate what the whole thing meant to me. Alan in his sleep could give an eight-out-of-ten display every day of the championship, but I challenged him to help his teammates go from five or six up to eight. Could he help make them eight-out-of-ten players? That was what the Blue Book was for – to help us and help us encourage teammates.

We strove for a harder approach on the field and we looked at Tyrone as a template. They played the game to win regardless of what happened; they didn't seem to care about their legacy or what was said about them after the battle. They just did what they had to do.

It was felt that we were too nice. That was the feedback from year one. It was something our players were asked to focus on and it led eventually to a couple of ugly incidents after we scored. It also led to some bizarre stuff, like Vaughany doing the Texas Longhorn salute after he got a goal. That had the rest of us scratching our heads, never mind the opposition!

We started to use sledging. It was meant to help us become a more resilient, steely team, but in hindsight it didn't work for us. We tried it, we didn't get anywhere with it, and it was ultimately a distraction. But in the process we learned that whenever you change or tweak your systems you have to stay true to your values and culture. Realizing that it wasn't a good fit was all part of the journey.

We were tight, though, and you could see that when a TV documentary crew followed us throughout 2006 to make *The Dubs: Story of a Season*. Before every championship match we would meet at St David's, where after light training the producer Dave Berry would make a video for each game with his footage. I had shivers running down my spine as I watched, you can see in the documentary that we were very united.

It's just a pity we never got over the line during Pillar's tenure. His record in Leinster reads like that of a world boxing champion – thirteen fights, thirteen KOs, four titles – and up till then nobody, not even Kevin Heffernan, had such success. We were peerless in the Pale; we could just never get a real foothold in the All-Ireland series.

For me, that drawn Tyrone game in 2005 is the one that really got away. Mind you, the 2006 All-Ireland semi-final loss to Mayo also ranks as one of our lowest days.

Before big championship matches I had this routine whereby with Louise and the kids – by now little Joshua had arrived – I would head down to Screen, County Wexford, and from there we'd pop out to Ballinesker Beach. Louise's parents have a house in the area and a visit down there helped clear the head before games.

It was always great to get into the sea, maybe go to the Shelmaliers pitch to kick a few balls over the bar and then seek out Liam Griffin, who had a couple of hotels thereabouts. I knew Liam did a gym session at his Ferrycarrig Hotel each morning and I would try to synchronize my training with his, hoping to meet him there. He was and still is a busy man but he always took time to chat.

'Feedback,' he would remind me, 'is the breakfast of champions.'

Liam led Wexford to the 1996 All-Ireland hurling title and mental preparation was a huge part of that win. I always left him feeling positive about my own game.

I might walk up to Freddie's Bar in Screen with Caoimhe and Joshua for a pint of Guinness and a chat. I felt when I was there something of the connection I had with Ballyhea – and right at ease as big days loomed.

Before we ran out to play Mayo we got word from Davy Billings that they had gone down to the Hill to warm up. We got quite emotional in the dressing room upon hearing that and it was decided that we wouldn't yield an inch. The subs would infiltrate the Mayo warm-up, do their best to disrupt it, and any stray Mayo footballs that whizzed by were to be booted on to the Hill.

Out we ran, some of the lads charged to the gills, got our picture taken, and down to the Hill, side by side and jostling Mayo fellas out of our way. Chaos reigned for five minutes as bodies and balls flew everywhere. The Mill by the Hill.

Alan Brogan and I tried to stay out of it. We passed balls to each other on the fringes of the madness. A lady in the Mayo back-room team was hit accidentally by a ball and it was just complete mayhem. After that things calmed down. Ever since, Alan has always tried to blame me for his stray pass!

But when order was eventually restored and the match started it looked like the chaos had done us no harm at all because we took control. We opened up a seven-point lead and with just twenty minutes to go we were still six points up. It was then, I think, that the reality of what was about to happen hit us – reaching an All-Ireland final. Maybe we let our minds drift. As for Mayo, they just fought back and started to play with abandon, maybe feeling there was little at stake any more.

Ciarán McDonald dropped back and pulled all the strings. He was blessed with fantastic talent and, unfortunately for us, his genius shone through that day. Andy Moran came on and his class and mobility were evident as well. Gradually they reeled us in and pipped us at the death. Devastation is not the word.

Of course, in the post-mortem it was suggested we had lost the moment we reacted to Mayo trying to seize the Hill. I can't go along with that. Yeah, a lot of emotional energy was spent before the ball even threw in, and maybe that did catch up with us near the end. Either way Mayo earned the right to play Kerry in the All-Ireland final, a game that became a non-event after ten minutes or so.

Would it happen nowadays, Mayo going to the Hill end?

Absolutely not. All that is taken care of by match protocol. Ultimately you are guided by your management team on how to react and if it did happen I have a feeling Jim Gavin might take a different approach.

After I lost games I had a routine too. Usually that meant flying out of Dublin Airport a few days later. But that Mayo defeat took a particular toll. I entered a dark space.

Truthfully, all of those losses, to Mayo, Tyrone, Kerry and Armagh, they just took away little pieces of me. Like so many other players I was never really taught how to deal with the aftermath of losing, and I would go on a binge for a few days just to dull the pain. It was only when the dust eventually settled that you could face going into work in the hope people wouldn't still be talking about it.

Mentally, you would withdraw into a darkened cave to get by those few months in early autumn. Then you would reach the stage where the championship draw was being made for the following season and you could finally look ahead. That was my cycle for fourteen-odd years.

All of those games, the cumulative defeats of several seasons, they really took a toll.

*

It was an eventful time outside of the Dubs camp as well. Later in 2005, Na Fianna reached another county final but Kilmacud Crokes beat us comfortably enough. It was Mick Galvin's last year as our manager and most of the other lads I had known moved on.

Vincent's hammered us in the 2007 championship and a break-up of the team looked likely. There was nothing under-hand about my decision to move on. The 1983 All-Ireland winner John Caffrey's wife, Bernie, was chairperson at the time and I approached her about it, met the club executive too, telling them why I wanted to move on. I explained that I wasn't enjoying playing and that the motivation to win wasn't there as guys I had soldiered with had retired. I wouldn't have felt right winning without them. The fact that most of the underage talent in the club was focused on hurling meant that there was little opportunity to mentor players and help bring them through. When I explained all of this to them, I asked if they could give me a reason to play. I met Dessie and that was a hard one. He wasn't happy with my decision but he never held it against me.

I asked Pillar, a Na Fianna stalwart but my Dublin manager too, if a move would jeopardize my inter-county career and he assured me it wouldn't. So in 2007 I left Na Fianna after thirteen years, three Dublin Championships and one Leinster title. I had spent all those years with Na Fianna and they had been super to me.

I joined St Oliver Plunkett Eoghan Ruadh, who were newly promoted to Division One. I have a strong friendship with Alan Brogan and we always had a good understanding on the pitch with Dublin too. That was a big hook. We travelled together to matches with Bernard as well as Ross McConnell, another Plunkett's and Dublin player, and I actually spent more time with those lads than with the Na Fianna crew. Part of the appeal of joining them was the challenge of assisting them in becoming players for Dublin. That was a big part of my decision.

*

Back with Dublin, we beat Derry in the 2007 All-Ireland quarter-final only to lose to Kerry again, this time narrowly. We were only a point down with time up but they were playing keep-ball and knew how to close games out. We didn't. But at least we were pushing hard.

In 2008 we beat Louth, Westmeath and Wexford to win another Leinster. There were 70,000 at the final against Wexford and we were completely dominant. To be honest, right up until Pillar's last game, a heavy defeat to Tyrone, I felt we were on an upward curve. The real hard thing to accept was how it all ended, beaten 3-14 to 1-8 in that 2008 All-Ireland quarter-final. Hammered and embarrassed.

The day itself was shite: flooding along Jones's Road and little shelter from the on-pitch storm either. It was an afternoon game but the elements were so bad that the floodlights were switched on. Tyrone knew us better than we knew ourselves. We expected them to have done their homework but they went above and beyond. They were kicking balls into space without even looking, able to exploit us because they just knew our game plan and twigged where there would be no cover. They found our weakest points and pumped ball into those areas.

Supposedly, this was a Tyrone team on the decline and it was finally going to be our year. But this time there was no comeback. We knew it and Pillar knew it. He resigned after the game.

A big factor in this loss was the five-week break we had to endure after winning the Leinster final. We had to wait to see who we would play, contend with all the hype that was building around us and the perception that this was finally going to be Dublin's year. This is not the place to give my perspective on the GAA fixtures template but such a lengthy gap, especially when we had been so dominant, between games was too much.

In three of the four years Pillar was involved we were knocked out by the eventual All-Ireland champions and it was never going to be easy to break through because we came up against two of the greatest teams Gaelic football has seen – Mickey Harte's Tyrone and an all-star Kerry side. The learning and improving curve hit the buffers in that last game.

A lot was made of how much Pillar's group had socialized, the suggestion being that part of the reason we fell short was because we partied too much. But I think we were a good old group. The social stuff might involve a round of golf at Hollystown and a few pints on the Monday to celebrate some of those Leinster wins. And while some of the young lads might have partied hard at the start, the celebrations were always done and dusted by the Tuesday after a provincial championship match. And by 2008, following our fourth Leinster title on the spin, all of that was a thing of the past. In fact, the after-show party was so dull on the Monday evening that only a clutch of us were on Shay Wade's bus back from Hollystown.

Light was fading and the evening yawning into submission when Whelo sat down beside me in the front seat.

'Jesus, Whelo, isn't it bad form that the boys aren't even out tonight!'

'Shocking altogether,' he said.

'Wouldn't it be gas, Whelo, if we called to the homes of all the lads who said they'd be here for the golf?'

Derek Byrne from Ballymun was on the panel at the time and lived close by in Tyrrelstown. When we knocked, Derek got up from the dinner table and answered the door. His missus, still at table, asked him who was it – but she never got a reply. When Derek opened the door he was whooshed out and hauled on to the bus. He had no phone so his better half couldn't even ring him to find out what had happened. We allowed him one phone call after a while to explain himself.

Next up was Castleknock to look for Barry Cahill and Alan Brogan. Barry's mam said he was at the cinema and Alan was said to be at club training. We said we'd call back later.

For the next six hours or so we criss-crossed the city picking up targets. From Rathfarnham to Castleknock, from Portmarnock to Blanchardstown, from Northside to Southside.

To Plunkett's GAA club, then, on the hunch that Alan was down there. When we arrived we were told Alan had left but, not to leave empty-handed, we saw Gareth Smith – aka Nesty – emerge from club training. We knew Nesty from various Dublin underage teams before he went on to play for Cavan. We blocked his exit from the car park with traffic cones and bollards. He was still wearing a GAA jersey, togs, socks and football boots when we hauled him onto the bus and off we headed again.

Whelo turned to me and said, 'Jesus, Jay, we can't leave the lad like that.'

When I turned to check on Nesty's welfare, he was smiling like a Cheshire cat and availing of his one phone call!

'Ma, I'm not going to be home tonight,' he said to a huge roar.

We called back to the Brogans' later that night, our second visit. And while we got Bernard there was still no sign of Alan. As we waited for Bernard to join us, Derek Byrne did a runner. He leapt off the bus, darted over the green in front of the Brogans' house, sprinted across a field, jumped over a bridge and made good his escape. He waved down a taxi and jumped in. Breathless, he kept looking back for fear the Vengabus was following.

The taximan was concerned: 'Jesus, son, what are you after doing? Who are you running from?'

'You wouldn't believe me if I told you,' Derek gasped.

Senan was next. At the time Senan's girlfriend's sister was going out with Jonny Magee. We called around and dragged Senan on board – and next thing Johnny comes running out of the house: 'Will ye take me as well?'

We stopped at an off-licence for a few beers before Shay took us off to collect Cathal Jackson, the owner of Copper Face Jacks, at the Gravediggers pub, where he was having a drink with

Pillar. We got Cathal on board and Pillar waved us a hearty goodbye as he left to go home: 'See yiz tomorrow evening for training, lads!'

Back to Barry Cahill's again and this time he was home. The following morning a young neighbour of the Cahills was having breakfast when he said to his father, 'Da, a bus pulled into the estate last night and Jason Sherlock and Ciarán Whelan got out and the next thing I seen was Barry Cahill being dragged out in his pyjamas and on to the bus.'

'Ah will you stop rambling, lad. Cop on!' said the dad.

But that's what happened. We knocked on Barry's door and a bunch of us went up to his bedroom and dragged him from his bed, broke the banister as we rumbled him downstairs and out on to the Vengabus.

Between every stop we belted out the song of the same name.

Goggsy's house was next. And when his ma learned what we were about she wasn't best pleased and started going at us with a tea towel, telling us we weren't 'getting up them stairs'. But up them stairs we went and into Goggsy's room, about ten of us chanting: 'Goggsy is our leader, Goggsy is our leader, nah, nah, nah, nah – nah, nah, nah, nah.

Operation All Star took no prisoners either. A gentle knock on the door of Ray Cosgrove's house at first but no answer. Then a gentle bang to the window frame until the alarm went off. Ray simply had to answer the door then and when he did we forced entry and invaded Cossy's home. Two lads got inside. One grabbed him and hoisted him aboard the Vengabus. The other grabbed Cossy's All Star.

Up at Conal Keaney's his folks were not the happiest either. I can't blame them because I think they failed to recognize the first intruder and thought something sinister was afoot.

We called to Mossy Quinn's house in Portmarnock and

he was wearing one of those sleeveless Aussie Rules tops and pyjama bottoms. We took him as we found him.

Momentum was building nicely. Cathal Jackson, one of the most successful businessmen in the country, turned to me, beaming with excitement: 'Who are we getting next, Jayo?'

It was getting late. We'd been on the road a long time. We'd crossed and recrossed the city and made several abductions. Confidence was high and the dander was up. It was time for Operation Clucko.

'Lads, only the bravest of men need sign up for this one,' I warned. 'Some of you might not come back alive.'

But I got plenty of volunteers. We parked the bus a bit away from the Cluxton family home and plucked our target, much to the bemusement of the locals. No quick kick-out could save him this time. Up the road the boys returned with the prize possession hoisted high on their shoulders.

Around 1 a.m. the bus pulled up outside Coppers and in strolled the Dublin team and associates, dressed in football togs, pyjamas, Aussie Rules shirts, tracksuits, golf clobber and whatever had come to hand. It went down in our history as a legendary night. It was a one-off, a harmless bit of fun never to be forgotten by those lucky enough to be dragged on board.

Its legacy lived on, mind. Months later, during the winter, we were out having the few pints and we texted the other lads on the panel: 'The Vengabus is coming!'

Cully (Bryan Cullen) got the text at home in Skerries. Bricking it, he hopped out of bed, got fully dressed and climbed back into bed to await the inevitable extraction. This time it never happened.

It was a unique night, unforced, spontaneous and never to be repeated. And while we didn't get that All-Ireland we so eagerly craved, we at least forged memories that can never tarnish. You get solace from that as the years pass.

We gave it everything and despite history not looking favourably upon us, being naive and wrong with some of our decisions, there is pride in the effort we put in to achieve our goals.

19

The Long Goodbye

Deep in the winter of 2008 I got a phone call from Dublin's new manager, Pat Gilroy. I took the call with apprehension. Did I have the stomach for another year after the accumulated disappointment of the previous thirteen years? Did Pat even want me in his plans?

Sport constantly evolves. Your outlook should too; but my mood was darkening.

For all our failings, Dublin were still a top-eight team. Had we made the breakthrough under Pillar I think we would have been in the top two for quite a while because I could see the quality of players coming through the ranks, each one of them bringing new hope. If we could just once get over the line, I felt, we would tack on a few more and go on to dominate. Dermot Connolly, Alan, Barry, Flynner (Paul Flynn), Berno (Bernard Brogan), Clucko – these players were as good as any in Ireland. The margins were tight.

And yet for all the gradual progress, we were still vulnerable to a hiding in that period. My mind kept racing. I wondered if I should have done more in the Pillar years. Did I need to show more leadership? And then the prospect of all these guys coming through!

I decided if I was going back I was staying true to myself. Did I want to be Niall Quinn, a very good player who was liked by everyone, or Roy Keane, not liked by everyone but respected by all? I decided I wanted to be Keane. Not that Quinn wasn't a top player and a top guy. He was. But I was after a different mindset, a different approach to the top. It didn't matter a fuck any more whether people liked me. Most of my life I had been striving for acceptance but that quest had taken a back seat in favour of the chase for success. I intended to max every last drop by preparing the best I could.

Did that help others? Maybe not. In Pillar's time I probably didn't invest heavily in helping lads on the fringes, lads I felt weren't going to help us win an All-Ireland. Were they really going the extra mile to get us over the line? Would they have much input when push came to shove? I wasn't convinced. I put most of my focus on guys I thought could influence things on the pitch. I was selfish in my goals and consumed with winning, simple as that.

I could have the craic with the rest of the lads but I would call them out if I thought they were shirking. As a result I got to know the likes of Clucko much better and met him in the gym quite often. We struck up a relationship simply because he knew the work I was doing away from the set-up.

The daily mental grind of fretting about the whole thing wore me down. I had my demons, constantly dealing with being a failure. That emptiness rested in the pit of my stomach throughout the day and spread into my mind when I lay down at night; an inner voice that refused to let me settle. That feeling of not succeeding in life, lacking in self-esteem and letting others down in the process. It's nothing but a cross to carry.

When I was a kid I kept those thoughts to myself. I carried them for fourteen years as a player.

I had started a job as head of business development at the

Louis Fitzgerald Hotel and even in work that spectre of failure lurked. At my desk, in between meetings with clients and contacts, I would sit and replay games in my mind. Likewise on the drive home. I thought about everything and anything that had happened on the pitch the weekend before.

I was frequently under the public microscope for not doing the business on the big day, but I focused that lens on myself quicker than anyone. The most recent case against me was the Tyrone game. They had slaughtered us and I had barely made a mark. I had a great point chance at one stage, maybe 16 yards out from goal, and I set up for the shot as I always did – and somehow sliced it off my boot and wide. A shot I had hit thousands of times. How did that happen?

Such questions raced through my mind. I would jot things in my diary and the logical side of my mind emerged with certain realities. Being a forward, especially a small one, wasn't easy. And if there were better players out there where were they? It was 2008 and after thirteen years I was still an important cog in the machine. That's why I placed so much pressure on myself.

That was the backdrop to Pat calling. He asked me to meet him a few days later in a hotel in Airside and said he wanted me to be part of his plans for 2009. That was a big thing; I needed to hear from him that I had a serious role. I would go back only if I felt I could continue to improve as a player and help improve the team too.

After the annual Dubs Stars challenge we took off for a training camp at La Manga, ready to see if the new man could bring us forward. Mind you, we may have had a new manager but there were still disciplinary issues to be ironed out on that trip, which just shows that we players still had growing up to do. Overall, though, little shoots of promise grew from that camp and I was sucked in again.

Pat's early interaction with the squad convinced us that the right call had been made in appointing him. Firstly, he let us bring our families to La Manga, which showed he understood that families had to be looked out for too. And when we hit the training ground he did a good job there alongside Mickey Whelan.

Mickey had remained true to himself and his philosophies and that is the beauty of the man – he treats everyone the same. He had backed himself and from his ill-fated term as Dublin manager in 1996 and 1997 he had now become coach alongside Pat. That is some journey to take and I fully admired him for it. His reign had ended poorly a decade earlier, his stock seemed damaged, but with his qualifications, pedigree and enthusiasm he resisted the temptation to fade away. Among other achievements, he returned to lead St Vincent's, with Pat as an impact player, to an All-Ireland club title in 2008.

Now Mickey was Pat's trusted sideline ally. From the early days of that camp we all thought this template could work. Time had moved on and the rest of us had caught up with Mickey, who along his journey had learned even more from being with other teams. The Dublin team of 2009 was now more receptive to his progressive ideas.

The first session in La Manga lasted only thirty minutes but the two lads spoke to us about our defensive structure and explained in detail where they felt we went wrong against Tyrone the year before and how Mickey Harte had countered our game plan.

Our kick-out strategies, usually a collaboration between Clucko and Shane Ryan, had been nullified and the limitations of our shape had been exploited. During Pillar's tenure, for example, we became increasingly vulnerable under pressure at crucial stages because we still defended man on man.

The session was really positive in that it mapped out just how much improvement was needed. It would be a long road back, but players don't mind such feedback as long as it's constructive.

There would be a more defensive focus, almost a zonal marking philosophy. The approach was to shape up as a back four would in soccer – most of the boys would hold their positions in defence instead of going forward en masse at the hint of a counter-attack. Tyrone had shown that we were leaving too many gaps when counter-attacking. It was time to evolve.

The first step was not to be overly concerned with what our forwards were scoring, but to look more at what we were conceding. In the last game of 2008 we had conceded 3–14 to Tyrone; in our last game in 2007 Kerry took us for 1–15; in 2006 Mayo had scored 1–16 against us. Those were big scores. It wasn't so much how many scores we were getting at one end, it was more what we were leaking at the other.

Meanwhile it seemed Pat and Mickey still appreciated what I could do. For the start of the 2009 National League they picked me at full-forward for a game under lights against Tyrone to mark the launch of the GAA's 125th anniversary celebrations. All week leading up to the game it had been in the headlines after it emerged it was costing 500,000 euro to stage, complete with fireworks to finish.

But what an occasion! It was a sellout. Both teams wore retro, old-school jerseys for the pre-match presentation parade, and despite the fact it was a freezing January night it turned out to be a huge occasion. It boasted the biggest attendance at any sporting event in the world that weekend. To put that in perspective: there were 74,000 at the Super Bowl final between the Arizona Cardinals and the Pittsburgh Steelers, and Manchester United played in front of 75,000 earlier that day.

That was the backdrop. The game itself was notable for the fact that no defensive structure, no matter how tight, could have coped with the individual brilliance of Stephen O'Neill that night. He kicked ten points, some from impossible angles. My achievements were more modest – two points from full-forward – but though we lost by two points, it was a positive performance considering how they had walloped us the year before.

I showered, left the dressing room and took my place on the bench – with Josh on my lap and the two of us sitting beside Pat – for the fireworks display. I was so appreciative to be in that situation. I was thirty-three, still improving, still a Dub. That was so important to me.

This would be the year to bookend 1995. After so many seasons proving myself to various management teams, trying to make up for a lack of physicality, this would be the regime in which I shone again. Thrived even. Mickey and Pat favoured a brand of football that required quick interchange, passing and movement. And they wanted someone to direct traffic in the forwards. The job description could nearly have been written with me in mind.

In keeping with the roller-coaster trajectory of my career, however, the feel-good factor didn't last long.

We played Galway away in the next league game and faced into a first-half gale. With the tempest keeping the ball at the other end of the field, neither me nor my marker, Finian Hanley, saw much of the ball. But Berno had the better of his man beside me in the corner, so I got the nod from the line to drag Hanley out from full-back and make more space for Berno. I ran Finian out the field and at half-time I looked forward to getting a good run at him in the second half with the wind on our backs.

It didn't happen, because I was taken off at the break. One of the statisticians observed that I hadn't been in the game much, but that was hugely frustrating because I had been directed to take Finian out of it and I did my job. I held my counsel but wondered if Pat even knew of the instructions I had been given.

We played our third game against Donegal and won by two points. I came on early for Dermot Connolly as we won up in Ballyshannon. But in the next game against Roscommon I never got a sniff of game time and, again, I was frustrated. I was so sick of trying to prove myself to all the managers who had come and gone. It was mentally exhausting.

Word of my concern got back to the manager, via Whelo, and I got a speedy return of serve from Pat, who told me it was a crazy mindset. He said he was looking to unearth new players and didn't need to watch me because he knew better than anyone what I was capable of. He was giving others game time. When we met for a follow-up, we agreed I would train by myself for the rest of the league and link up again before the championship.

I was happy enough with that and hooked up with Will Heffernan, a strength-and-conditioning coach that I had worked with before, at his gym between Finglas and Cabra. That's where I prepared, fully convinced I would make the team tick better when I was playing. It was a positive for both parties; I could get myself ready for the championship and Pat could look at new players.

I returned to camp for the 2009 pre-championship challenge games against Louth at Carton House and Down. I did really well in that Down game, proving I had trained to a high level on my own.

Being away from the group hadn't affected my physical preparation one bit and I invested more and more time in my mental preparation as the years went by, trying to bleed every last drop of improvement from my game. But I just couldn't hack it when other guys slacked. There were a few flare-ups along the way because I was frustrated in training and maybe that's why Pat wanted me out of that environment.

Take Dermo. There has never been any question of his

incredible talent, but back then I felt there was a nonchalance about him that grated on me when we trained. There was friction between us at times back then and I have no doubt it came across in that period under Pat.

Yeah, I could rub people up the wrong way, but confrontation for its own sake wasn't my thing either. I wasn't calling people out for the craic. One evening we were playing As v Bs and I felt that Dermo wasn't fully tuned in. That was frustrating. So frustrating that I walked off the pitch. There was no point in being out there if Dermo was allowed to get away with that stuff. Where were the standards?

The physios hurried over to me because they thought I was injured. But I wasn't hurt – at least not physically. Afterwards I talked to Pat and Mickey about it. I can see now that maybe they felt they had to go through a certain process with Dermo to get the best out of him. But at the time I couldn't see it that way. I was raging.

Soon after we had another session at Carton House and I called Dermo out again. This time he was straight in my face.

'I heard you were at it in training the other night as well,' Dermo said, referring to an exchange I had with another of the lads. Obviously word had gone around that I was having a moan. My watchdog nature wasn't to everyone's liking.

Was I narky? Yeah. The problem was I cared too much. I was trying to drive the others on, guys who had years ahead of them. If they learned from the mistakes I had made maybe they would avoid the dark days I had experienced.

These days working with Dermo in the current Dublin set-up has been a privilege and I understand now that, no matter what my grievance was, I was wrong in how I dealt with my frustration. I see at first-hand now how much it means to Dermo – he just shows it in a different way to me. We had lunch together in the Friday before the 2016 All-Ireland final to put some finishing touches to his preparation and as we finished up I quipped that it was hard to believe he was there willing to listen to me! I have the upmost admiration for him.

Mark Davoren got in ahead of me for the 2009 Leinster Championship but, unfortunately, tore a cruciate late in that game and I got a run. In the semi-final against Westmeath I scored six points from play and got ready for Kildare, under my former teammate Kieran McGeeney, in the Leinster final. Those six points were huge for me; I was prospering again. The team and the forward line were in good shape, with Berno clearly coming of age.

In the Leinster final, Barry Cahill got a great goal early on but Ger Brennan was sent off and that left us vulnerable. Geezer, knowing my game inside out, put Emmet Bolton on me, and Emmet didn't once look at the ball – he just marked me face to face and toe to toe. It was a good tussle. I stood still to shake hands with him before the throw-in and then kept moving for the next fifty-five minutes.

I darted here and there, popped passes off, slipped into various channels and set about dragging him and the rest of the Kildare defence around the place. At one point I looked up to see Alan was on the ball at midfield. He floated a lovely pass in to me, over the top, diagonally. Emmet stayed looking at me, not the ball, so he didn't know where the pass was going to land. I didn't want to move too early, for fear he'd react and block my run, so I waited until the last second, jinked to one side, turned to the other, got a hand on the ball and struck it home with the left boot. We needed something to settle us and that helped.

We won another Leinster title – my seventh – but more than anything that game showed the importance of teamwork and joined-up thinking. I cannot emphasize enough how I was always at the mercy of the ball coming in. Without that precision pass from Alan, I wouldn't have had a chance to score.

We were on an upward curve heading to play Kerry in the All-Ireland quarter-final, and they looked in trouble after rumours of internal discontent and a less-than-convincing run through the qualifiers. We hadn't beaten them in the championship since the 1970s but this was our time. It was going to be our era to dominate! The build-up was similar to the 2008 scenario against Tyrone; the perception was our opponents were there for the taking and Dublin were the coming team.

It was over before it started. Gooch (Colm Cooper) had the ball in the net after thirty seconds and we soon fell asunder. We were rushing things, forcing shots. We should have sent one of the lads to the ground with an injury, or slowed things down, tapped over a few points to get back in the game.

I was substituted after twenty-four minutes. How low can this game make you feel?

I still remember coming off the field, with that horrible, dull emptiness. The embarrassment. The sensation your world has just been thrown upside down. Walking up the steps of the Hogan Stand, my head was bowed. I knew where my family sat on match days, close enough to the subs bench, and before every game I would try and spot them and make eye contact with Louise or the kids. Uncle Brian was sitting there too, they were literally to the side of me, but I felt I couldn't look at them because it was too embarrassing. I felt I had let them down.

But again I clung to my mindset: 'Jason, you have to stay in this game! Just in case the boys turn it around and you're asked to go back near the end.'

But we were being hammered. I had been called ashore before some lads even got their second wind. In reality there was no hope of me going back on. I sat there feeling humiliated. That inner voice again: 'All the doubters and critics were right after all – I am a failure!'

Afterwards Pat said any of us could have been taken off and

he did what he had to do. We were being taken apart and he had to change something.

When I did meet the family after the game, all they showed me was warmth. Caoimhe, Josh, they never cared if I won, lost or drew. My mam, Brian, Louise and her family, well, they had been there through everything. Seen it all. They didn't have anything but support. But still that churning, cutting feeling that I had let them down.

The squad went into town and, low as I was, I always felt it important to stay united as a group. Louise and I shared a taxi with Pat and his wife. We went into the Dandelion Bar and that night out was an insight as to where we were as a team. Within a couple of hours lads were dancing on tables with their tops off. Was it any wonder we were where we were? Or maybe I was just too old and bitter to understand.

I got out of there. Some of the lads stayed on the beer for a couple of days but I just kept the head down. On the Tuesday I got a call from Pat about how things needed to change. Pat was hurt and frustrated and said we couldn't go on with our naive way of playing the game. The number one target was now to keep the score down.

A new form of Gaelic football was being played and we had to adapt even further. I agreed wholeheartedly. The call lasted about ninety minutes and as with chats I'd had with Tommy Lyons near the end of his time and Pillar, I was happy with the collaborative tone of it. Things were going to change and I felt I would still be part of it. Pat had taken time to phone and talk it through, and that demonstrated that he respected me and cared.

When the storm passed we had a player review meeting with Pat and Mickey. Again the indications were positive. They reiterated that anyone could have been subbed against Kerry; they reiterated that my level of performance had been good in 2009.

They said they would look at me after the 2010 league, similar to the year before, and see how I went with the club.

That was fine, but the weeks and months moved on and I heard little or nothing. I made contact with Pat and he said we would meet after the first round of the Dublin Senior Fotball Championship. We played Fingal Ravens, I scored five points from play, and met Pat soon after in St Clare's. We chatted inside the bunker and moved out to finish the chat in his car. The news was not good.

'Jason, they will never be leaders while you are around,' Pat said. 'I ask a question in the dressing room and they all turn to you before they answer to see what you'll say.'

'What? Jesus.'

It was hard to process. Something you had been doing all your adult life was suddenly being taken from you. Tears flowed. I got very upset. Pat felt I was such an influence on the players it was starting to affect them. He said I had turned into a Roy Keane character around the camp. That was ironic! Over the years I had striven to become like Keane and now it was one of the reasons I was being dropped.

I reassured Pat I was willing and ready to accept any role to help Dublin. But I was devastated. I was the only one in the squad with an All-Ireland medal, so I saw it as natural to try and lead.

I emphasized that I didn't need to be a focal point but it didn't seem to matter. Much of that night was spent wiping tears away as I tried to get my head around what had happened. It wasn't much different for the next few days.

Eventually, I used the hurt to prod that resilient streak again. The one I have had since I was a kid. I had shown it the year before when I came into the championship team having scarcely featured in the league. That was a show of resolve in itself.

Now there was a new goal. In my eyes earning a recall into

the Dublin squad was not an outrageous proposition. I made a vow I would get back to Croke Park – either with my new club, St Oliver Plunkett, on St Patrick's Day, or with the Dubs.

David Henry was the new Dublin captain and I met him to explain that I hadn't given up on the team. He didn't know I had been dropped and said he would do all he could to help. I'm sure when he went back training he had lots of stuff going on as a new skipper but David definitely supported me and it meant a lot.

I took off on a journey of defiance, ambition and self-torture that would ultimately last three-and-a-half years. Throughout that time I remained highly motivated to play for Dublin again and I used the services of a sports psychologist, Caroline Currid, who was working with Pat and the team. I loved collaborating with anyone who could improve my performance and I knew she was in direct contact with Pat. I insisted I hadn't given up on making the squad again and I wanted her to relay that back to Pat. I had been written off before. This was just another test.

I threw myself into Plunkett's season, trained just as hard as I had with Dublin and played really good stuff with them. This was no ego trip; it was a battle to keep my identity. But more importantly I still had something to offer. I could make a difference.

But it was a strange time too. Having not been picked for the 2010 championship panel, I started getting calls from the media again, people wanting to talk about my career drawing to a close. A few days after news broke that I would not be in the Dublin championship panel, a producer from the *Marian Finucane Show* phoned to ask if I would come on and talk about my sporting life and times. I turned them down for four reasons: I hadn't given up on my career at all; my heart and loyalty were still with the team; I didn't want to say anything in public that could be construed as negativity towards the set-up; and, finally, I would have broken down in tears had I gone on air. They would have been looking for nostalgia, a fluffy segment, whereas all I was feeling was inner turmoil. It was horrible; people wanted to talk about my career but I wouldn't accept it was over.

Throughout that summer I kept my form up with the club and when Dublin were hammered by Meath I was still hoping I could get called in for the qualifiers. That didn't happen. Instead, the lads really bought into Pat's defensive focus and they rallied to beat Tipperary, Armagh and Tyrone. Then eight days before they played Cork in the All-Ireland semi-final I had a text from Pat looking to have a chat with me.

We met on the Monday before the Cork game and I won't lie to you, both my head and heart were racing with the possibilities of what this might mean. What could it be only something positive? In my mind, Pat had heard about me playing for the club and seeing that I was doing well. Maybe he was going to bring me back to the squad for the final if we beat Cork, just as Tyrone did with Stephen O'Neill in 2008. Now I was no Stephen O'Neill, but could I help finish the job off with twenty minutes to go in an All-Ireland final? Absolutely I could.

The actual conversation couldn't have been further removed from that.

Pat said that he had never really come back to me. He continued by saying he had sounded out some of the lads to see if they would like me back and they had said no.

I was seriously taken aback. Again. You're six days out from an All-Ireland semi-final and you're telling a former player this? Why invest your time in an exercise like that? It was surreal.

Long after the Cork game I phoned some of the lads on the team and none of those I spoke to had been approached. Of course, it is probable that the lads I was known to be friendly with were simply not approached and that it was most likely other guys who said they wanted to move on without me. Even if that was the case, it was unnecessary, I felt, for Pat to come out and tell me that with Dublin preparing for their first semi-final in fifteen years.

Despite a turbulent end to the season, I shared a few hours with the team after they lost that Cork game. On the Monday after that loss they went to the Strawberry Hall bar to get away from things. They had been five points up in the second half, with Down waiting in the All-Ireland final. The lads knew they had been close to a shot at a medal and there was serious disappointment. I wanted to be with them and I was confident that if there were some players in the squad that had issues with me they were in the minority. Also, I had plenty of experience of how lonely it can feel in the immediate aftermath of a big loss and I wanted to show them that I hadn't given up on them.

The dust settled and I still refused to give up. Ahead of the new season Pat and I met one more time.

'Jason, if you had another ten kilos on you, well, then it would be a different conversation because that's the way the game has gone,' he said.

Pat may have been putting the ball back in my court but my interpretation is that he was pushing the pen further down the road, because there was little or no chance of a whippet like me putting on that bulk, but I saw it as another carrot dangled in front of me and pledged to pack on the required muscle.

I rang Bernard Dunne, who had made some changes to his fitness programme before finally becoming world champion. Bernard switched away from more traditional boxing methods to focus heavily on strength and conditioning. I explained I needed to put on 10 kilos of muscle. He said what was ahead of me would be tough but it could definitely be done. That was all I needed to hear.

I also made contact with Will Heffernan again and threw

myself into the task at hand. In November 2010 I weighed just 70 kilos. For the next three months I changed my approach to life and training. My days were centred around dead lifts, pitch sessions, circuit training, bench presses, elevated split squats, sit-ups, leg raises, dips, medicine-ball slams and pull-ups. You name it. There wasn't a rep or a weight or a stretch that I missed.

I lifted way beyond my means and ate like an Olympic athlete. On extreme days the diet could be limited to eggs, low-fat cheese, chicken breast, tuna, green salad, steak and spinach. On 4 February 2011, just a few months after making that pledge, I tipped the scales at 80.2 kilos. I had piled on the extra muscle Pat was looking for.

I relayed my enhanced stats back to the management but there was radio silence. Serious sacrifices had been made to pile on that extra muscle – with no reward – and I began to suffer for my efforts. I hurt my back in January as a result of too much weight training and when Plunkett's played Dublin in a challenge I wasn't at full tilt. I shouldn't have played but I felt I had to if I wanted to make any impact. I didn't do much and, understandably, after that all talk of me being involved dried up.

I felt so strongly that I could help the team win. And aside from the disappointment of being jettisoned, which hung over me every day like a cloud, there was now the fear of what life would be like without football. Without my identity. How would I do without that competitive drive that had fuelled me all of my life?

At the start of my exile, I literally didn't speak to anyone about the situation.

In 2011, with the gaping, gradual realization that my days were numbered, I relented and started doing some media stuff. I loved the GAA, loved sport and wanted to share my thoughts from a player's perspective so I took on a newspaper column and did some pieces with RTÉ. But my emotions remained raw. Still, it was important to me never to say a bad word about Pat or any of the lads involved.

I bottled a lot of things up, still feeling I had let people down. Part of the reason I wanted to continue and win with Dublin was to thank the people who had invested so much in me. But there I was, sixteen years on from 1995 and still looking for that second fucking medal. A career of failure. I felt I'd let down Brian, the family, Joey and my other friends. I was embarrassed at how I had finished up.

Yet, I hadn't given up on my belief in the team. On the day Dublin won the 2011 All-Ireland final, I was able to suspend all those negative feelings. Despite internal torture it was one of my happiest days. You might find that hard to believe, but to see a group of lads I had so much faith in actually achieve what I knew they were capable of was fantastic! Yeah, there was a fierce longing to be there and to be part of it with them, but I was delighted for them too.

On the final whistle I punched the air. I looked down and Senan was on the pitch doing media work. I phoned him and pointed out where I was in the stand. Then I saw Berno and Flynner and asked Senan to get them to wave up to me. Senan called them aside and said, 'Lads, Jay is up there.' When they looked up and waved I just thumped my heart and waved back at them. It was a brilliant feeling.

That night I went to the team hotel. I felt it was important to embrace the likes of Mossy, Berno, Alan and Barry Cahill as All-Ireland winners. I met Pat too and congratulated him. He was gracious to me but at that stage his words felt quite empty.

I didn't stay long at the hotel but headed into Coppers, where we had the mother of all sessions, truly one of the great nights. Katherine Lynch, the TV personality, called on Damien Dempsey for a song and he gave an impromptu few bars. The goalscorer on the day, Kevin McManamon, also broke into song, and a sing-song really took off.

We went straight to an early house for another impromptu sing-song before moving on to the Quays where we were joined by some of the players. On Monday evening I finally drew a line under it all and went back home with Louise. That's when it all hit hard.

I sat on the couch, reflecting on how I had missed out on the glory, and the demons began circling. I was distraught and began to wonder if indeed I had been the reason we hadn't won an All-Ireland for so long. I questioned my worth again. It took a long time to shed those emotions. It was a dark time.

When I meet Pat now, I greet him with the respect he commands and deserves. He led Dublin to their first All-Ireland title in sixteen years and, as a supporter, I'm grateful for that. But such was my drive and ambition to win again that I wonder will that awkwardness ever go away. Our meetings are probably just as shitty for Pat because, as manager, he had a hard call to make and it involved casting an old teammate aside.

He won an All-Ireland, though. He was justified in all that he did.

20

The Road Ahead

Soon after my playing days ended, I was keeping myself to myself, walking down a street in Dublin, when a man coming the other way stopped me.

When I was out and about, I mostly kept my head down. Always scanning ahead to see who was coming. Avoiding eye contact, small talk, the possibility of being recognized and associated with 'Jayo' the Dublin footballer because, in my eyes, that meant a link to fourteen years of failure.

I wasn't on good terms with myself.

I was embarrassed to meet people.

The absolute frustration that lingered from the fallout of that Kerry game, three years on, still lingered and aside from keeping a low profile about town, I also avoided people I trusted and respected, people like Joey Boylan, who I felt I had let down.

Same with some of my family and friends. Kept my distance.

I felt I had let them all down.

So, when your man came right up to me on the street, I got a dull ache in the pit of my stomach. Another trip down memory lane. Another burst of nostalgia, 1995 and all that went with it. I didn't quite know how to react.

But I needn't have worried. He offered his hand. 'Thank you,' he said, shaking my hand firmly.

For what, I wondered? Sure most of the teams I played on lost out on the big day.

But this fella just looked me in the eye. 'Thanks for all your effort over the years,' he continued.

As he walked off I could see that, unlike me, he wasn't judging my career on whether I was a success or failure, he was just thanking me for my commitment. A little thing like that went a long way. Some people had actually appreciated what we had tried to do – even if we hadn't won. It was a small thing but it was a huge positive and maybe it broadened my horizons a little.

In 2012, Dessie mooted the idea of me applying for a GPA scholarship and studying for a Master of Business Administration (MBA) at DCU. I always respected and trusted Dessie's opinion and when he pointed out the value that an MBA would command in today's workplace, I listened. He said that it would be something that could help benefit me in the future. As you know, education and I had never been close allies and going down an academic route was not something that I was ever interested in as a kid. Foolish me. I had regretted it the odd time. Here was a chance to do something about it.

It took persuading to go back.

I don't know if my lack of self-worth reared its head again but I doubted if I was up to going to college and gaining a prestigious qualification like this one. Crucially, though, I allowed the idea to breathe, spoke to Bernadette McCulloch, the head of operations for DCU's Executive Programme, and she gave me some good advice and no little reassurance. I felt she was someone I could trust.

One of the main selling points of the programme was that it was centred on leadership, a subject I was fascinated by. It read: 'You want to develop your awareness of your leadership style and expand your leadership toolset?' That appealed to me more than anything else. I had always felt capable of leading but Pat Gilroy's words had made me question all that.

It was a very daunting prospect, heading back to college but, deep down, I knew what a massive opportunity it was and part of me wanted to give it a try. So I applied for the course, did an interview and was accepted for a place on the programme.

It was one the best things I ever did in my life.

I started the course in September 2012 and on the first day I looked around the classroom. Apart from Denis Bastick, my former Dublin teammate, and Michael Kennedy, who was involved in the Dublin back room around then, I knew no one. Like that first night in UCD when The Doc left me off outside the lecture hall, I was just as nervous taking my place in the class on the third floor of DCU's Business School but it was very reassuring to have Denis there. I had admired how he had progressed his Dublin career having been written off on numerous occasions for various reasons. In the early stages, we offered each other a bit of support.

The MBA contained a significant workload but, while it was daunting, I really got into it, principally because one of the first modules we took was Organizational Behaviour, which centred on teamwork, group leadership and individual leadership. Right from the start this module stood out for me. Like, how often do any of us take time out of our daily routine to reflect on how we got here and where we are going? It's very rare that happens. We don't get time, life gets in the way. This module allowed me to reflect on my personality and to examine my obsession with success from a healthy distance. It was like studying and actually figuring myself out at the same time.

I got to know the others in the class and felt more comfortable. One exercise on the first day helped us get an insight into each other. We were asked to talk to a classmate next to us, find out some information about them, their name, where they worked, their family and learn one thing about them that nobody else in the class would know. Then we had to present the person to the rest of the class.

I turned to the guy beside me and told him I wanted to play in Croke Park again. He looked at me and I'd just say he thought I was off my head! My mindset even at this stage was to play in Croker, that was my only goal.

In the class there were accountants, engineers, businesspeople. And there I was: Jason Sherlock, former Dublin footballer. What could I offer a classroom like that?

I started to reflect on what I had been through in the previous few years in sporting terms. I had been insular. I took things for granted from my sporting experience like teamwork, communication.

I began to appreciate that there were numerous traits that I had to offer that weren't restricted to the field of play. My identity had been forged there but as the weeks went on I sensed that there were other qualities that Jayo had to offer. During this time, I was able to see that I had defined my self-worth purely in terms of how I perceived my Dublin career and the lack of success that came with it.

It was time to adjust.

In lectures we looked at the structures of our workplaces and examined ways in which they could be improved. Issues such as workforce motivation, culture, team building and the actual working environments were all examined.

I was interested in all of that.

I soaked up the life experiences of all the others in the class – some of whom were leaders in their various fields – and I slowly realized that we were all on different paths and that I could offer them something from my experiences, mine just happened to be carved out via sport. Realizing that I could use the tools gained from my career – and still contribute in a non-sporting environment – was massive progress for me. Another part of my journey.

Before taking the course my self-value rested on the floor. I honestly questioned if I had wasted fourteen years of my life playing football just to fail season after season. Outside of the Dubs, I didn't really know what I could offer anyone. Genuinely. What set of skills did I really have outside of the playing field?

A big moment for me during the course was the realization that I did have something to offer away from the field of play because up until then I only focused on my objectives on the pitch.

Through the MBA, and that Organizational Behaviour module especially, I had a lot of time to reflect on where I had been and slowly started to become positive about my future, believing that I had plenty of value to offer. The coursework, the studying – and locking myself away from the world for almost two years – gave me a huge insight into my real self and restored some confidence in me about my worth.

One of my key lessons was the amount of things that we take for granted in a sporting environment. Stuff like setting goals and targets and devising strategies to achieve those goals. Demonstrating leadership, having to gel as a group, showing empathy, being a good communicator and having understanding.

Sporting groups are top of the tree when it comes to those disciplines and businesses and companies all over Ireland are extremely keen to develop these qualities within their workforce. They are proactively looking for people with those fundamental skills to build a business upon.

That knowledge ignited something inside me.

I had been known as a footballer with certain attributes on the field. But I began finding out that I could also apply the skills I had picked up along the way to a life outside of football. My experiences of resilience, adaptability and teamwork could all be useful elsewhere.

When that dawned on me and the message sunk in, I gave the course absolutely everything. It was hard to balance things at times and the workload was immense. Indeed, I rang Bernadette more than once protesting to her that, academically, I simply couldn't hack it, but she always encouraged me to hang on in there. All we need is someone to share our doubts with; a chat with someone who believes in you.

The coursework gave me something else to focus on and I began to see my past failures in a different light. Over the two years I studied at DCU I found that I could use the experience of that decade and a half to help lay a foundation for the future. Memories of hard times accrued through constant failure and frustration began to lose their sharp edge. Sometimes it was through a lecture, other times a case study on various business leaders, or a real-life example that a classmate came out with, but all the time I was discovering that I could contribute or add value in other ways outside of sport.

By doing the MBA I armed myself with some tools and developed an outlook that I can offer for the rest of my life. I looked at my Dublin journey and the facts were stark – post-1995 it took seven years to win a Leinster title again but then when Pillar came in we won four on the trot. Some of the group never got to win the All-Ireland title we all wanted but history will show that we came up against two of the greatest teams of that time in Kerry and Tyrone. Such is life.

There is a perception from the outside that the Pillar years, in particular, saw us come up short time and again. I am intrinsically associated with that, but there was much to be proud of too. We tried things and, yes, we failed over and over again but we never stopped trying. We were a tight squad with a great work ethic. We had resilience, a fair clutch of Leinster titles and a serious amount of players who later become involved in coaching with various Dublin teams.

Business can be like this too. Sometimes companies have to fail frequently before they succeed. Any business in Ireland will tell you they have endured hard times like those we experienced on the field.

The reality is that some people are not in a position to push on further with their lives and careers but I was lucky that the GPA gave me that shot. They want players to be their best on and off the field. I know they have been seriously criticized for the amount of funding they have secured here and abroad but they have changed so many players' lives for the better. In recent years they have shone a light on player welfare and mental-health issues but the greatest thing I can say about them is that they handed me a life path with the opportunity of that scholarship.

My identity had been slipping. Former footballer? They showed me that I could surely be more than that. The GPA has the potential to change lives and that's what they did for me. They allowed me to develop my story. They frequently warn about the fickleness of a player's identity and the perils that come with life outside the arena. What happens to a local hero when he steps off the stage and he's gone? Are they ready for a life after? With help from them, finally, I was.

I graduated in November 2014, with the family there to share the day. I was especially delighted for Mam and you could see she was proud of me. I only ever wanted to make her happy.

I came out of DCU a stronger man, and this time not in terms of muscle added, but in terms of perspective gained.

An example of that came towards the end of the Organizational Behaviour module. Around that time Lee Chin and Aaron Cunningham brought their racial abuse issues into the public domain and I appeared on *The Late Late Show* with Lee. Without the confidence and assurance that I had got from going back to college I don't know if I would have been up to coming out publicly and backing the lads in a clear and comprehensible manner. But I finally did that too. Another step.

On the day before *The Late Late Show* I even shared with the class that I was going on and outlined my reasons for doing so. I explained that I never would have done it before but such was the knowledge and confidence I had received from the class that I felt it was the correct thing to do.

Soon afterwards, a cousin of mine contacted me to see if I would get involved in the Cycle Against Suicide. I couldn't cycle with them on the day in question but they asked me to talk to a school that happened to be the first stop-off point on their journey.

It was a girls' school with over 400 students present and it was daunting; a huge challenge if I'm being honest. But while researching what areas I should talk about I came across the phrase 'It's okay not to feel okay', used by the charity Suicide or Survive, and that gave me a real focal point. I based my talk on my own story when I was younger, the slagging I received, how I bottled things up, how I was left frustrated because I couldn't see why people saw me as different. I worked my way through a few areas and spoke for fifteen or twenty minutes. I received a fantastic ovation when I finished and I headed down the side of the stage as the next speaker took the microphone. Two girls came towards me, one with her arm around the other. One of the girls was pretty upset and you could see that she had been affected by what I had said. The girl that spoke was Polish and she said she could relate to everything that I had said, that she understood how I felt, thanked me for sharing my story and she gave me a massive hug.

That was a powerful thing. I had walked into the room wondering how in the name of God I would be able to connect with a hall full of schoolgirls who hadn't the slightest clue that I used to play for the Dubs. But I left the school humbled at the prospect of making even the slightest little difference to just one person. That really ignited something within me and got me thinking about the next stage of my journey.

I had been working at the Louis Fitzgerald Hotel for nine years and I wanted a change of direction. After doing the MBA, and reflecting on my experiences working with the Dublin senior football back room and the Dublin development squads, I truly realized that the development of people was my passion. In the summer of 2017, I pursued this further by setting up JAYO Authentic Mentorship.

The concept of JAYO is in the title – authentic mentorship to assist with improving performance is what I feel I can offer. There are three areas I can give real-life mentorship in. I will speak about sport later but I also feel I can be of value in the education and business fields too, working with both individuals and groups.

You will have gleaned that, had I my time back again, I would place a massive focus on education and striking a balance in life. It was not in my thinking way back when I was a kid. However, I go into a class now well armed with such knowledge when I talk to pupils.

There were cool things I got to do by following my dreams and kids should have loads of dreams too. But no matter what those are they can also have a plan that involves education. It doesn't have to be one or the other. If their goal is to play GAA, the majority of Dublin players, for example, are either attending or have qualified from college so I tell the schoolkids if that's one of their dreams they have a better chance of realizing it if you go to college. That makes it real for them. That's what I want – to emphasize that education actually enhances a student's sports career if that's what they would like to pursue.

These kids must have something else in their lives, another purpose, some balance. It will make them more rounded, it will better prepare them for the future. Education will give them a platform for all the other things they pursue in life. We want our children to dream big and go after their dreams, but they can also ensure that education is a part of that.

Going into schools and classrooms, I can also reflect on the other experiences I had: racism, low self-esteem, keeping things to myself, a lack of understanding of how important education is and a lack of motivation to pursue an academic career. These are all live issues today.

I'm not going to force my story on anyone but if they listen they will understand why I felt the way I did and they can grasp themselves how important it is to share their worries. By sharing we gain more perspective. I kept things to myself and the frustration only grew. It wasn't the best policy.

When I speak in classes about some of the issues I had growing up a silence comes over the group. It's like they are not even breathing, they listen so attentively. It convinces me that they can relate my story to their own challenges.

I now believe that I can also be of value in the business sector where companies are looking more and more to the sporting world for examples of high performance. There are numerous traits that sport can bring to business, like strategy, teamwork, resilience, leadership, execution, dealing with failure and communication. Right now there is a strong appetite to avail of that knowledge and a renewed investment in the development of employees.

I have developed my own template to help achieve high performance. Through my experiences in a range of sports, both as a player and now as a coach, I believe I'm well placed to assist like-minded companies improve the performance of their team.

That attitude probably wasn't a priority for companies in the recession but in the last couple of years you see more wellness and development programmes being introduced for employees.

I am always curious about a company's 'mission statement'. It looks nice on the wall, but how many workers actually feel that they can connect with the values of the company? Is the mission statement real to the employee? Can an employee relate to it and align their actions to it as they go about their working day?

Not so long ago, I spoke at an IBEC wellness conference at Croke Park and based my presentation on effective performance. There were about 150 people in attendance from various business sectors and there was also another guest speaker from the UK who gave a presentation during my part of the conference. He had worked with various CEOs all over the world, he was very impressive and you could tell that he knew his stuff from the content of his presentation. His presentation went down very well but what struck me when it was opened to the floor for questions was that many of the queries were directed to me based on my sporting experiences. Again, it validated my belief that I can add value in the business sector based on my experiences and by working with companies I can improve the performance of their team, both individually and collectively.

The MBA awoke something inside of me. It challenged me and it gave me a wider understanding. I came to terms with my playing career. Of course I wanted to win more medals but I have learned to see the value of all those unsuccessful years with the Dubs. Maybe that was the process I had to go through to give me a foundation for my future.

Nowadays, when I walk down the street, I am fiercely proud to shake the hand of anyone who associates me with Dublin Football.

21

The Wheel Turns

On a wet, miserable November evening in 2012, I got home from work and went inside to my family. The sitting room was warm and inviting and the temptation was there to settle down for the evening with Louise and the kids.

Instead I went upstairs, threw on some training gear and went back out to pound the pavements around the neighbourhood. I was two months short of my thirty-seventh birthday and I still hadn't given up on my goal to play in Croke Park again.

As I ran, my mind wandered. No matter how slim the chance was, I wondered if Jim Gavin's appointment as Dublin manager would offer me a lifeline to return to the squad. As I ran against the driving rain, I used that possibility as my motivation to put one step ahead of the other as fast as I could.

I came back home, went upstairs to shower and I heard my phone ringing. The caller? Jim Gavin!

It turned out that Jim's reason for calling was to enquire about a hotel base for the team for the year ahead but I felt I had to seize the moment.

'I know this might sound crazy, Jim,' I said, 'but would you consider me as an option to get back in? I still feel I have something to offer.'

Without hesitation Jim responded: 'I'd have no problem with that,' he said. 'I'd look at any player.'

Now, Jim may have got off the phone and wondered what the hell I was on about, but he was as good as his word. He said he would take a look and, in many ways, he gave me a lift by not slamming the possibility of a recall.

He put me in touch with Fergus Connolly, a leading strength-and-conditioning coach. Fergus was from Monaghan and had a hugely impressive CV having worked with Liverpool, Bolton Wanderers, the Welsh rugby team, Munster Rugby, Harlequins, New York Knicks, Cleveland Browns, Northampton Saints and San Francisco 49ers. He is currently director of performance for University of Michigan Football.

From his time attending seminars at AC Milan, Fergus was able to give the example of experienced players like Maldini and Seedorf and cite how they were 'minded' by the club with specialized training programmes. He agreed to set out a similar route for myself, to proceed with some adjusted training, and then we would see how I was faring around April 2013.

I explained to Fergus that I was having issues with my back so he devised a programme to protect me in that regard and went through what I could and couldn't do. I set about the schedule and focused a lot on hill running and sprinting, the latter I did mostly at Magazine Fort in the Phoenix Park. I got to know that place well over that winter! I mainly trained on my own but sometimes invited Ross McConnell and Declan Lally along to gauge how I was doing. Then we progressed the programme to longer runs, to replicate what was required in Croke Park. I was really impressed with Fergus, he had a great way of connecting and passing on his expertise in a way that felt managable.

I rigorously put myself through this process for the next couple of months, between February and March, but Mother Nature intervened now and again and I started picking up little strains that would set me back along the way. The reality began to hit that the body just couldn't take the physical toll required any more and the realization that my inter-county days were over finally became a reality.

By May 2013 my chances of getting to Croke Park with the club were ended when Plunkett's were knocked out in the first round of the championship. In my time with Plunkett's I gave it everything. I hoped I could influence them in a positive way but we fell short of winning a championship. Still, I was very proud to see some of the players progress and I really appreciated the welcome I received in the club, particularly from the former club chairman, Pat Bugler, who unfortunately passed away in January 2017.

But knowing that my race was run, I called Jim: 'Jim, I appreciated the opportunity but, physically, I am not going to be where I need to be. Thank you for considering me and I wish you and the team all the very best.'

Jim thanked me for my effort to play for Dublin again and the phone call ended. I was calm, my mind and body finally at ease. There were tears, but this time tears of pride. I was satisfied that I had given everything for one last rodeo.

And there was the closure I needed – it came almost four years after I had been dropped.

The reason I tell this story is that people automatically think that I walked away after Kerry in 2009 and from the outside that may seem the case, but the truth is I trained my arse off over the next four years to get back to help the team win.

On Saturday, 1 June, the day before Dublin's first 2013 Leinster Championship match, through a GPA statement, I announced my full retirement – from club football as well. It might not have meant much to the outsider but to me it brought about closure. It gave me pride too.

> I would like to close a very important chapter in my life today by publicly announcing my retirement from Gaelic football.
>
> It isn't easy for any player to take the ultimate step, particularly from club football as well, but it is time for me to move on.
>
> As a child, my dream was to play for Dublin and to have represented my county for fifteen years was a privilege. It also provided me with some of my greatest memories and it was an honour to play alongside and against some wonderful footballers and people during that time.
>
> However, making the transition gives me an opportunity to publicly thank all those who have supported me throughout my playing career; family, teammates, management and supporters. No player can operate at the top level without a team of people helping him; I was fortunate to have great people behind me.
>
> While bringing closure to a very important part of my life, I look forward to the future opportunities that lie ahead for me and my family.

There was finally an acceptance that my playing commitments were over.

I now felt comfortable enough to go watch the Dubs play Westmeath in the first round of the Leinster Championship and actually enjoy the experience, rather than use it as two hours of self-torture. It was the first day since 2009 that I could go to a Dubs game and not have an itch to be out on the field. I was able to sit down, watch the game and feel at ease within.

For the best part of four years, far away from the thronged masses that fill Croke Park on championship Sundays, I put my body through hell and back, running up hills, pumping weights in gyms and eating like a professional. A million miles away from the drama, the hype and the Hill, I kept fighting to get back. I was willing to do whatever it took to represent Dublin again and help the team.

With closure now secured I started to look at how I could satisfy my fascination and love of sport in a non-playing capacity. Sport means so much to me, it has always played a pivotal role in my life and I wanted that to be the case with whatever steps I took next.

I represented my county, province and country in basketball and soccer. I represented my county and province in Gaelic football, won a county title and numerous North Cork titles in hurling. But I was never the biggest nor the strongest and my skill levels always had to be improved. So I have always been fascinated by how I gained this level of success. Ultimately, I believe it came down to what was going on between my ears. I always wanted to be the best and I never gave up. I knew what I wanted to achieve and how I was going to do it. The rest was down to great support and an aptitude to figure out what I needed to do to be the best that I could be.

I have always been a student of sport: American sports (I loved Channel 4's American football coverage every Sunday evening in the mid-1980s), golf, horse racing, soccer, Gaelic football, hurling, tennis, boxing. When I was a kid I would park myself in front of the TV and watch anything that moved.

My childhood memories are peppered with great moments like when Gerry 'Ginger' McLoughlin scored that iconic try against England in 1982. I used to move to the edge of the chair whenever the Irish rugby team got the ball to Simon Geoghegan on the wing. His tenacity, brilliance and flair!

Then there was Barry McGuigan beating Pedroza in Loftus Road with the engaging tones of Jimmy Magee commentating.

I was so engrossed in the fight it seemed like Jimmy was broadcasting just to me!

In horse racing I remember Jonjo O'Neill on Pinch Hitter, the horse I always looked out for, and Pat Eddery winning the Prix de l'Arc de Triomphe on Dancing Brave.

And of course, like so many other kids, I was fascinated by Diego Maradona and had a Mexico 86 wallchart up in my room.

There was Northern Ireland beating Spain in the 1982 World Cup, John Treacy taking silver in the LA Olympics in 1984, Stephen Roche chasing Pedro Delgado up the hill in the 1987 Tour de France, Ray Houghton putting the ball in the English net a year later and Eamon Darcy and Christy O'Connor Jnr representing our country to help win the 1989 Ryder Cup. I have fond thoughts, too, of Dennis Taylor winning the World Snooker Championship in the Crucible.

I want be a part of such sporting moments in the future in some capacity.

I am very lucky to have experienced some great moments with the current Dublin team over the last couple of years and feel privileged to have assisted them in some small way through my own experiences.

That process of learning started in earnest when I was a kid. I mentioned the great rivalry that St Vincent's had with Coláiste Éanna in schools and club basketball over the years. Our games were a big deal, the talk of the respective schools, and they were always billed as 'Joey Boylan's St Vincent's versus Gerry O'Brien's Coláiste Éanna/Notre Dame', which only upped the ante.

It was personal – we wanted to do it for Joey as well as ourselves. One under-13 game with them at Firhouse stands out. They were our big rivals and we badly wanted to take them down.

At that stage I had only been playing basketball for a few months but I was already fascinated with the inner workings of the game. We were well down by the interval and we decided we would play a half-court press from the third quarter onwards.

They had a little point guard called Clarkey and the press tactic put him under huge pressure. We trapped him at every opportunity and forced him to make passes he didn't want to make. I was at the back of the press and could read his passes, so we made a few steals and we got back into the game.

Gareth Winders was our shooter and in the last play of the game he hit a three-pointer, got us a 21–20 win, and the hooter blew almost immediately. We jumped all over Gar, he became my hero that day, we became best friends and we still are today.

That under-13 win resonates just as much with me as any of the All-Ireland finals I have been involved with Dublin in, either as a player or a coach.

Why?

Although it's nearly thirty years ago I can still remember the situation and how we tactically changed things to improve our performance. I have experienced so many scenarios like that where I have succeeded and failed throughout my career that I believe, as a coach, I can add value to sporting performance no matter what the discipline.

I always looked to other sports to assist my own performance. When I presented *Rapid*, I spoke to boxers, rowers, tennis players, hurlers and athletes and related to them all because we spoke the same language. Whatever sport I work in with my new business venture I feel I can add value. I have a desire to assist people in realizing their potential.

In basketball terms I was tiny but yet I had to go on court and get the better of some fella that was invariably taller than me. That can't happen by physically overpowering them or running them down – that has to be a mental battle. Such a situation focuses your attention and it's that purposeful attention that I believe I can develop in any sportsperson that wants to be the best they can be.

*

At the end of October 2013, Stephen O'Shaughnessy, the former Dublin corner-back and now head of the county's development programme, contacted me asking if I would be willing to head up a development squad for two age groups. Although there were more attractive enquiries from Dublin clubs and a senior inter-county team, I felt that the development squad would be the best option on my first step into a coaching career. There was an obvious connection with my own county and part of me wanted to demonstrate that I had Dublin's best intentions at heart.

Shocko explained what they do. The plan would be to bring the two age groups up from under-13 right through to their minor year. Once I agreed to take on the under-13s, it was a case of getting guys I had played with – lads with the character that I wanted involved in the set-up – to come in with me.

I undertook some research on talent development and sought out people that could assist with my strategy, applying some of my learning from the MBA. I looked at fellas who would be role models for those kids, people who wanted the best for Dublin like Paul Casey, Paul Griffin, Davy Henry, Brendan O'Brien and Declan Lally. We were also able to attract Ger Gleeson, Jim Lehane and Wally Durkin, all of whom had numerous years of coaching experience.

We do things in a fashion that is true to our environment, values and culture. We focus on winning the hearts and minds of as many players as we can. There have been days when we invited every club in Dublin to bring out ten players for a blitz.

Other times we might have 500 kids out for a coaching day. I can't emphasize enough the willingness of the mentors to be out coaching all day long. They understand why we are doing things the way we are. Without their commitment, Dublin football would lose out.

A big challenge for development squads is that players feel like they are on trial. We try to reduce this by operating with bigger panels, assessing them at club games and inviting players out from their clubs for open sessions on occasion.

We used a silent sideline in our blitz days to assist their development. We explained the concept to mentors first, we wanted them to have the time to observe their players and be able to praise them on certain things after the games ended. We make it clear to the lads that we won't be shouting instructions from the sideline, it is up to them to figure it out and it is very satisfying to see these young men working together as a team on the pitch. After one of the first days with the silent sideline we brought the players in and asked what they thought of it. 'It was great,' one fella said. We asked why. 'Because no one was shouting at us.'

Leading these development squads for the last four years has been a great opportunity and it has intrigued me. Leadership, to me, is fascinating.

I often thought about what good leadership looked like. From what I have learned and experienced over the years, I believe the most effective leaders are true to themselves and their beliefs. The sign of a great leader is if they can remove themselves from the group they are leading without having any impact and this is something that I have aspired to do.

We are now three years down the road with the current under-15 team and into our fourth year with the under-16s. Next year they will play in the first All-Ireland Under-17 Championship which will be a great developmental experience for the players involved.

Success, to us, will be seeing these players represent their clubs with pride and we hope to see some of them play for Dublin in the future.

When I was playing I learned from every manager and coach I had – both the successful ones and the ones who didn't win. Every day was and still is a learning day. Pádraig Harrington came in to give us a talk with Dublin some years ago and his message was that you never stay the same. You either get better or worse – but you never stay the same.

I will be learning for the rest of my life.

I love meeting people and drawing from their experiences. A guy I really liked to chat to was Billy Walsh, the former Irish boxing head coach. I sounded him out over the years to see if he could assist me with my performance. I listened to him talk about his coaching journey and philosophies and Billy passed on this piece advice he had received from his boxing coach Nicolas Cruz in relation to his own career: 'The medals you think should be around your neck will always be in your head.'

This has always resonated with me. My interpretation of that is that all those negative experiences in defeat will now assist me as a coach.

I am better prepared for the challenges that may come and, in a lot of ways, whether we win or lose is irrelevant, it's performing that I will focus on. The absence of the medals I think I should have earned as a player can be offset by knowing what to do as a coach.

When Jim Gavin asked me to join the Dublin set-up as Dublin offensive coach in the winter of 2014, I also saw it as an opportunity to learn from him and the rest of the lads. Jim is always looking to progress and I'm in a privileged position to be learning from him. He holds true to our values and culture, he reminds everyone that it's an honour to pull on the jersey and that we must try to one day hand it back in a better place.

For some reason, Jim took a chance on me and fast-tracked me to be involved with the seniors. I'll always be grateful to him for that. During my own playing career, he and his wife Jennifer always went out of their way to show me kindness and I never forgot that. After just my second game with Dublin, we went back to Delaney's bar in Smithfield and then on to the Cuckoo's Nest and they both made me feel so welcome.

The satisfaction that I have gained from playing a role and being part of an All-Ireland winning dressing room again has just been fantastic and I would like to think I have assisted in the success in some small way over the last three seasons.

It's no secret how Jim refers to his process but the broader message is not to become fixated on the outcome or result. If you start making your decisions based on the scoreboard in a game there is a risk of reacting too emotionally and that's not necessarily going to help the team.

I was never the biggest, strongest or fastest and so I needed my teammates to help me and that's a message I have brought to the Dublin senior team. There is a great culture and environment and not once have I felt inhibited, not by Jim, the other members of the management team or, more importantly, by the players. It is humbling to see just how willing they were to accept a guy coming from nowhere really, in coaching terms anyway, to help assist a team that had recently won an All-Ireland.

Striking up relationships with the players is a key aspect too. Again, Joey Boylan springs to mind – it's not what you say, it's how you make people feel. Joey inspired me and I never forgot that.

I've changed as a person as I have grown older and I have definitely tempered my approach to dealing with players. When I played, I may not have seen the value in players towards the fringe of the squad, but now I better appreciate that you are only as strong as your weakest link.

In the latter years of my playing career, the only goal was to get back to Croker and somehow that happened when I least expected it after I retired.

Since the All-Ireland final of 2016 I have been used in the role of *maor foirne*, which means I can run on to the pitch to communicate with our players during breaks in play. The good thing about that is these days I get to run around the pitch safe in the knowledge that I won't be milled out of it!

Being part of Jim's set-up is hugely enjoyable, but it also raises the question, one that has often been asked of me: 'What will you do when you have no role with Dublin?' It would have been a fair question to pose up till recently.

Throughout my own career, I sought out and listened to sportspeople from various codes. I have spoken to teams and individuals and I believe various aspects of high-performance coaching in sport are universal. My identity in coaching does not have to be restricted to Dublin GAA and I look forward to pursuing opportunities to work in sport through my business, JAYO. I'm excited to see what the new venture holds.

For much of my life I was best avoided when we lost a big match. I couldn't see anything but dark clouds and reacted in typical GAA fashion – by drowning my sorrows and getting away from everything.

Losing a game still brings massive disappointment but it doesn't have the hold on my personal or family life that it once did. Defeat simply can't consume you when there is a development squad to look after, or there's someone looking for help in education, sport or business. There is perspective.

I have learned the hard way – and it has taken some time – that success is only a very small part of what we are all about. It's more about the journey you take. I can thrive in a non-sporting environment now, something I never thought would be possible for long stages of my life.

Don't get me wrong, I'm far from perfect. Like us all, I have various challenges to deal with from time to time but I have made peace with myself, I have come to terms with Jayo. I am the driver of my own bus.

It was an honour to contribute to Dublin football and I have grown to be very appreciative of the experiences I have been given. Of course, I have worries and stresses and, yes, there can be tinges of regret from time to time but I can accept them and be satisfied that it was all part of my process to be able to embrace whatever lies ahead in the future.

Sometimes when I lay my head down at night, my mind drifts to a balmy championship Sunday at Croke Park. I see myself on the pitch with my arms around Caoimhe and Joshua, looking up to Louise and the family. The pitch is full of ticker tape that's reserved for when the All-Ireland winning captain has raised Sam. The captain is Stephen Cluxton, he is about to lead the players on a victory salute around Croke Park and they're heading straight for Hill 16.

Dublin can be heaven.

EPILOGUE

17 September, 7 pm, Croke Park
Dublin 1-17 – Mayo 1-16

The lads found a way to get over the line again. Somehow they found a way.

To be part of a team that wins three All-Ireland titles in a row is special. It's historic, too, because this is a win that will stand the test of time.

It was all quite surreal after the final whistle. The emotional part is looking up at Louise and Mam, getting Caoimhe and Josh on the pitch again, and knowing that I have been a part of this. There is a clinical side to it also. Delighted, but there is no mass elation because I'm a bit disappointed that we didn't perform to the level we are capable of. There is a bit of hurt for Mayo, too, to be honest; they have gone through an awful lot on their journey.

I stay on the periphery of the whole thing because, ultimately, it is the players who have won this game, but a key guy for me to turn to is Declan Darcy, a major cog in Jim's wheel. When I first came into the set-up, Dec accepted me and gave me a huge welcome. When the final whistle sounded earlier today, it was great to embrace him.

It all came down to the men on the field, however. Our guys

simply did what they had to do. The big thing for me is that they were going to find a way to win, no matter what. There's always a role in sport for that pure determination, that drive and desire to win, and I don't think it's any coincidence that we have won All-Irelands by a point two seasons in a row. As a coach, you want the lads to go out and perform as best as they can. I don't think that happened on this occasion, but they found a way to get the win and it's special to be a part of that.

We prepared as we always do, but some things are just outside of your control. Jack McCaffrey, for instance, going off injured so early in the game wasn't part of the plan. It was a serious blow for us and we seemed to get lost in the chaos of the first half.

Scoring a goal from our first attacking play was something unusual, too. For whatever reason, it didn't settle us down; in fact, it almost threw us out of kilter. I don't think we really regrouped fully until half time, but Dean Rock's kick just before the break was key. It left us only one point down and we went into the dressing room knowing that we hadn't fully performed in that first half. In the second half, things stayed frenetic and I have to admit there was something beautiful about standing on the sideline, looking out at all the chaos on the pitch and knowing that I was part of a back-room team attempting to solve the issues that they faced. On the field it was fiery and manic. On the line we had to try to bring some calm to things, make sense of it all.

Players like Dean set the tone on the pitch. Dean is one of those guys who has made so much progress over the past three years, one of those fellas who just wants to make their team mates better, and he's a joy to work with. After missing a kick late in this year's National Football League final against Kerry, it was fitting that the kick to win the All-Ireland came down to Dean succeeding at the time it was most needed. As he said himself, that match-winner was the best kick he had made all year, but it came from countless hours spent over the winter and summer months honing his craft.

*

Dean will continue to look for improvement and that development has been the strength of Jim's reign. He has never once taken anything for granted and he won't in the future either. Dublin will be looking to improve upon what we have done this year and that is Jim's philosophy: always keeping one foot just in front of the other. No doubt that will be the case next season, too.

At this moment in time, I don't know what role, if any, I will hold with Dublin football next year, but I do know that, no matter what happens, I am better prepared now than I was three years ago to accept whatever comes my way.

I am proud of the way I have evolved over the past few years. Whatever the outcome of this All-Ireland final was, I still knew there would be a tomorrow. The Mayo players will see that too as time passes. In the raw heat of losing, they will be absolutely devastated and they will wonder how they can get so close time and again without winning. But there will be a tomorrow for them also; there will be a next day.

Being involved with a successful team hasn't changed my life, but it has given me more contentment, and the coaching aspect has certainly helped me.

I would consider myself a student of sport. I am always looking to learn. In my first year involved with the Dublin Senior management, we reached the 2015 All-Ireland final. It was my first year as a coach of any description and we had made it to the point in the GAA calendar that had eluded me as a player ever since my first season as an innocent nineteen-year-old. I may have been forgiven for feeling overawed but, in the build-up to that game, I learned a lesson on how to deal with this massive sporting occasion in the unlikeliest of places.

In the final, we would face our biggest rivals Kerry, a team I had never beaten as a player. This was a whole new situation for me and I felt that there was so much at stake. We had found a way through the Leinster Championship pretty smoothly, and in our All-Ireland semi-final with Mayo we were six points up and on the verge of making the final.

With the finishing line in sight, we became edgy in our play. Mayo got a goal and it caused a bit of panic. You could sense that Mayo felt it was going to be their day and there was relief when the final whistle went and we would have to do it again. That draw gave us time to assess and see what we needed to improve. What had we done wrong? We were six points up but lost Diarmuid Connolly, who got a red card, and near the end Mayo hit 1-4 without reply. We had been on top as far as the third quarter, but the momentum shifted. We didn't close out that first game in the way we would have liked. It gave us a real opportunity to reflect and to refocus.

I had a ringside seat in that process and gained first-hand experience that, in sport, one of the biggest challenges is not to look ahead to the end destination or think of the final outcome. You just have to focus on what you are doing in the game, the systems you use, the plans you have worked on, to get you a consistent performance. From a Dublin perspective, this is simply what Jim refers to as the process.

We all reflected on how we could improve, but a big learning curve for me, as we beat Mayo 3-15 – 1-14 in the replay and I faced my first All-Ireland in twenty years, came from the most unusual source – a TV show I was involved in called *Ireland's Fittest Family*.

Early in 2014, the production company that created the show asked me to be a coach. They sent over a few links to episodes from the first season and as I sat down on the couch to watch them on the iPad, Josh sidled up beside me and asked: 'What are you watching, Dad?' He was nine at the time and there were not too many TV shows that we would both watch together. But as he sat down and watched the show, he really got into it. He loved those episodes and would watch them over and over again on his own. He became a big fan of the Davern family, the mixed martial artists from Tullamore! I thought to myself that it would be great to be part of something that Josh was interested in, that he could relate to. And that was the appeal of the show – people from all backgrounds and age groups could get into it.

As well as that, I also thought the show itself was excellent, so I agreed to do it. Josh accompanied me to some of the events over the course of the series and that was lovely, too. I came on board for year two of the series alongside Derval O'Rourke and we joined the other two coaches, Davy Fitzgerald and Kenny Egan. Seeing how those highly elite sports people worked was great learning in itself.

In my second year on the show, one of my families, the Farrens from Gortnaghey in Derry, reached the final race. We were up against Davy Fitzgerald and his family, the O'Brien Devines, who had Waterford senior hurler Tom Devine in their team.

The first event was a 'plane drain' in which families had to pull a Cesna plane 200 m along the runway of Shannon Airport, where the event was being held. The second event was the 'trolley dash' in which we had to fill airport trollies with 15 kg sandbags and pull them to the finishing line. The last event was a head-to-head battle in an endurance circuit and it went down to a nail-biting finish. I had been clear in my instructions and tactics all day, but it wasn't until we fell behind early in the final that I got caught up in the emotion of things and what was at stake for me and the Farrens.

At the end of it all, we were just a split second behind in making it to the top of the ramp and winning the competition.

Now, I know it's just a TV show but my family was beaten by only a second in the final, and in losing in such a heartbreaking fashion I learned an awful lot about the scenario I found myself in. I wanted the Farrens, Mickey and his three children, Micheala, Niall and Gabriel, to win so badly, but I felt I didn't help them during the final race. We had done our tactical preparation and strategy beforehand, but as the race started we fell behind and that's when I got caught up in the emotion of things, shouting for the sake of it and not providing clear, concise, motivational instructions. I should have communicated calmly and issued simple tips, but the excitement of being in the final took over.

I was roaring as they negotiated each circuit. I was too hyped-up. We got so close to winning. But maybe if I had advised the Farrens on their footwork, encouraged them to take a few deep breaths, or to use a different tack in going up that last ramp, we might have won.

I looked over at the O'Brien Devines and Davy. They were ecstatic. We were distraught. You get so wrapped up in any project that you are involved in, one that you are passionate about anyway, and I just wanted the best for the Farrens; I was so disappointed for them to lose by such a small margin.

Davy hadn't won the title before either and you could feel his competitive edge throughout but, had I been more specific with my instructions instead of shouting 'Get up there!', we might just have won.

I remember driving back to Dublin and replaying the whole course in my mind, going through what I did and what I would do differently. There is a time for emotion but there is always time for clarity. That was a great learning experience in my coaching career and, as I say, it came from an unlikely place.

The final of the show was held after the replay against Mayo, just two weeks before we played Kerry in the All-Ireland final.

It might also have been easy to get caught up in the build-up to my first All-Ireland final with Dublin since 1995, but after what I learned in the final of *Ireland's Fittest Family*, I felt I was in a clearer coaching mindset ahead of the final.

In the lead-up, I was only absorbed in the performance of the team. We beat Kerry 0-12 – 0-9 on a dirty old day, with my old teammate Alan Brogan coming on late in the game to kick our final score, I can remember the absolute satisfaction after the game of standing on the pitch in Croke Park having been involved in another Dublin All-Ireland winning team.

Aslan's 'Crazy World' boomed over the tannoy, a song that had often been played for victorious Dublin teams over the years. Looking down onto the pitch in 2011, hearing that song, that was when it really got to me that I wasn't involved any more. It was a theme song for Dublin teams throughout the noughties and I vividly remember travelling with Senan, Colly Moran, Darren Homan and Paul Curran to training and games with Christy's voice blaring, 'How can I protect you in this crazy world?'

Now, here I was a few years later in mid-September, absolutely overjoyed at being in the middle of it all again. Being accepted again. To finally grasp that it might not have been me who had been holding Dublin back all those years.

Here I was being part of something good once more.

Rightly or wrongly, that win changed my own impression of myself. Nowadays, I don't feel I have to justify myself or question everything that I have gone through. I stay true to myself. My career as a player for Dublin had finished earlier than I believed it should have, but, from a coaching point of view, I was part of a winning team again. I felt that the experiences from my playing career had led me to this point and, from a personal point of view too, that was a release for me.

Caoimhe and Josh got down to me on the pitch and that was the most special moment of all.

But, to be honest, there was no real dwelling on that success or satisfaction. One of the first things I had said to Jim when we met was, 'Jim, if I'm getting involved, the goal for me has to be back-to-back titles. You have already won an All-Ireland.'

Winning successive titles was in my head because one of the biggest regrets that I had as a player was that in 1996 – after winning in '95 – we didn't give ourselves a real chance to get back there again, both individually and collectively.

As much as winning in 2015 was great, this was my personal aim when I came on board. I knew what potential danger signs were out there and I knew the younger players, especially, would face challenges. From what I can see, the current Dublin team don't get too high or low when they win or lose, whereas in my day we did.

But after all is said and done, it is only a game. That is something I didn't grasp for many years. Moods were dictated by what happened on match days and the subsequent result. The final whistle determined my behaviour and actions as opposed to the understanding I now have that it's only a game. We do our best to win, but sometimes you lose, and it took me a while to figure that out. I wanted it so much for so long; I was caught up in it so badly.

The big challenge in 2016 was reaching our targeted performance levels again and we managed to retain the All-Ireland title. We beat Laois, Meath and Westmeath in Leinster, and once we got into the All-Ireland series the bar rose even higher.

Against Donegal in the All-Ireland quarter-final we had five points to spare in an intense game and we were tested hugely.

It was even tougher in the semi-final in which we beat Kerry 0-22 – 2-14, giving a fantastic second-half performance coming from five points down at half-time. We then drew with Mayo in the All-Ireland final, before winning the replay by a point, 1-15 – 1-14.

It was a serious test of the team's character along the way, and the end result meant we were champions again. When the elation dies down, you look back on the performances from a coaching perspective and the reality was that we did not perform at our best in either 2015 or 2016.

Yes, our All-Ireland final and replay against Mayo were two physical, intense and terse encounters and, on the second day, we did enough to get through, and, sure, it's great to win. But, through a coach's eye, part of me believes we didn't really perform as well as we could have. That's the oxygen to get us breathing even stronger in the future and it serves as part of the motivation going forward.

We won three All-Irelands in four years leading up to September 2017, but the reality is we are capable of improving our performance and, as coaches, that's what we are going after. The players, too. That's our motivation, that's the challenge ahead. It would be nice to get to the biggest stage and perform at the level we have set for ourselves.

Constant learning has helped me. The outcome of a match won't determine my mood any more. I realize also that the relationship between the player and the person they confide in is crucial, too – you always play harder for someone you know and understand. In sales, for instance, I always maintain that you won't buy something off a person you don't like. There must be a connection, a trust, and it's the same in sport. It took a TV show to tell me that if you tick the boxes, stick to the checklist and hit most of your targets, then you can take some satisfaction even if you don't succeed.

Going back to college to study for an MBA has also put me on a new and promising path. The challenge is to harness and utilize the qualification so that it helps me and my family, as well as helps others I come into contact with in the future, in business, education or the sporting world.

Being around the Dublin set-up and Jim has allowed me see traits and character that I admire and respect. There is loads of stuff I don't like about myself – I am impulsive, for instance, and I have been known to be quite stubborn too! There are also plenty of things I have said and done that I am not proud of. But I am learning to hone the better traits I have and apply them in my day-to-day life.

We all have our own challenges that we feel are unique to us. Mine was a different road taken, but the key is acceptance of our path and finding happiness along it.

I have been involved with Dublin football half my life and no matter what happens now I can walk away on very good terms. I wouldn't have been able to say that when my playing days ended.

I'm looking forward to seeing what the future holds.

ACKNOWLEDGEMENTS

I am blessed to be involved in sport.

It has given me great opportunities, from when I started playing soccer, basketball, hurling and Gaelic football right through to my present-day involvement with the Dublin development squads and senior football team.

And I am very fortunate to have people who supported me and guided me along the way because I came with my challenges. As much as I had talent, I was also confrontational, I brought anger and I lacked discipline at times. The teams I was involved in, the people who were coaching me, they would have had to deal with all of that, but it was never a case of 'We don't want him playing for us.'

Instead they stuck by me and helped to develop me and that's so important for any young boy or girl who wants to pursue sport. They need people with such guidance and patience.

So, I am very appreciative of anyone who coaches or volunteers in the sporting sector. They can have a profound effect on a young individual's life – I am proof of that.

I would also like to remember those people who helped me but have since passed away. My nanny, Kathleen, and my father, Dennis, are the first in mind. I would also like to remember Louise's sister and my daughter Caoimhe's godmother, Paula, who passed away far too young.

Family

Mam and my uncles Brian, Eddie and Martin all looked after me when I was brought home to Carrigallen Park. They shaped me, accepted everything about me, provided for me and supported me unequivocally.

Mam has always been there for me and worked so hard to ensure that I always got the best of everything. She brought me with her everywhere, from getting her hair done to going on holiday! I got every bit of sports gear that I looked for as a kid. I will never understand the challenges you faced and the sacrifices you had to make when I came into your life, Mam. Thanks so much for everything.

Nanny is my inspiration and I know I got my resilience from her. She defied everyone by staying in this world to reach 101 years of age. I always identified traits of her tenacity in myself.

Eddie later headed for Cork, Martin moved out to Cabra with his wife, Esther, and their children, Andrew and Christine. In recent years, Brian married his beautiful wife, Vanessa. Their daughter, one of my goddaughters, Angela, has been a blessing to all of our lives.

To Joshua and Caoimhe, to see how amazing you are as individuals is such a humbling thing. Without question, having you in my life is what I am most proud of.

I've always been struck by the beauty of my wife, Louise, both inside and out. I think anyone who comes across her is. I've put her through a lot but she has always been there for me. Her family, the McGreals, have also shown me so much love. I will be eternally grateful to them all.

Finglas

I am proud to be from Finglas. The perception of the place from the outside would certainly not tie in with the experience and upbringing that I had. I was very fortunate to live in a warm home on a great street in a fine estate with some unbelievable neighbours.

I went to school at St Oliver Plunketts NS and, later, St Vincent's NS, before I attended St Vincent's secondary school. All three were great learning environments for me. I am thankful for all of the guidance that we got in the classroom and on the sports fields – which was just as important to me!

Soccer

Rivermount Boys were my first team and joining them at the age of eight was my first foray into organized sports. I spent six years there and they provided a great outlet for all young boys in Finglas. I am indebted to all of the volunteers there who gave up their time to help us. I later moved on to St Kevin's Boys before joining UCD, where Dr Tony O'Neill was a great friend to me, before finishing my soccer career with Shamrock Rovers.

With all of those clubs I had some great teammates and managers and I never felt judged by them. In fact, I always felt supported by them in the challenges I faced from opponents. After Dublin's success in 1995, things changed dramatically for me, but UCD continued to treat me as I was – one of the lads.

Basketball

I started my basketball career in St Vincent's NS and it was there I met Joey Boylan – a man who would have a huge impact on my life. I got to play for Vincent's, represent and captain my country from under-15 to junior level. Our club and school teams won several national titles and I played for various Dublin and Leinster representative teams. The experiences I had from basketball and the friends I made along the way, including meeting my best man, Gareth Winders, and his family, will stay with me for ever.

Joey Boylan's dedication and devotion to St Vincent's basketball club has also made a huge impression on me. Joey trained us three to four times a week and coached us in games at weekends. His commitment and loyalty afforded us the chance to pick up great skills and life lessons. I'd also like to thank my teammates, other coaches and club members for their support over the years.

The GAA

The GAA has been a massive part of my life, right from when I was reportedly brought to Croke Park at just six months old! From the start, Eddie and Brian brought me to all the Dubs matches and I am grateful to everyone involved with Dublin GAA. I have always identified with Dublin football and it has given me so much.

As a boy I spent a bit of time going up to Erins Isle and then heading to Na Fianna for mini-leagues during the summer, but I don't think that my appreciation of the Association would be the same without the time I spent in Ballyhea.

It was in Ballyhea that I first fully became part of a GAA team and part of a parish. Being in a tightly knit club like theirs seemed unique to me but, through my time in Ballyhea, I grew to learn that such a culture was replicated in every parish and club in the land. I went to Ballyhea with my own challenges but they also accepted me, they were proud of me and I was proud to be one of them. Their sense of community and warmth gave me an insight into what makes the GAA so special.

Also, from the club point of view, I have rich memories with Na Fianna where I have some fine friends and teammates. We got to an All-Ireland club final, fell short, but it wasn't through lack of effort.

Towards the end of my career, I finished off my playing days with Oliver Plunketts, and the welcome I got there from the players and club members was very heartening. I was hopeful we would bring a Dublin senior title back to the club, but it was not to be during my time with them.

From a Dublin point of view, I am very thankful to Alan Larkin and his management team for taking a chance on a kid who didn't have a big playing background and for calling me up to the county minor team in 1994.

As much as I've shared some of the challenges that I faced from various Dublin managers, it's only as the years go by that I appreciate the faith they all placed in me. Dr Pat O'Neill was the first to show that trust by starting a nineteen-year-old on his team after they had been beaten in two of the previous three finals. I am appreciative of what Pat and his selectors did because I would say he came under massive pressure not to play me.

Through my current Dublin involvement I have experienced the commitment required for the job. You have some good days but there are a lot of bad days too and anyone who is willing to put the time in, and put themselves out there, has to be thanked. All of the Dublin managers I played under went into the job with the best of intentions. For the majority of my managers it didn't work out but it wasn't through lack of desire. I can only apologize to them that we weren't good enough and thank them for their efforts.

Acceptance was a massive part of my journey and it couldn't have been easy for the majority of my Dublin teammates to put up with what I brought to the fold – both on and off the field. Still, I'd like to think there are not many players I've fallen out with over the years and I'd hope that, to a man, I could shake any of their hands and thank them for putting up with me for whatever period of time they did!

I would like to thank Mick Galvin, in particular. He took me under his wing, and so did his wife, Maura. Mick had vast experience by the time I joined the Dublin panel and he went from being a hero of mine to a friend and mentor. He looked out for me and that was massive. I learned a lot from Mick and I try to help young players nowadays in their own development.

Gaelic Players Association

No one knows what the future holds for the GAA in terms of demands and structures. But I do know that the GPA has had a massive positive impact in the welfare of players and will continue to do so. I will be grateful and indebted to them for their support and for the opportunities they have afforded me and I hope I can assist them in shaping the future in some way.

Jim Gavin And The Current Dublin Senior Football Team

To be asked by Jim to get involved with the team was special enough – but for his management team to accept me, bearing in mind they had already won an All-Ireland title in 2013, was incredible. To welcome me the way they have says a lot about them and the environment that they've created. It has been a blessing to deal with the players and to also be accepted by them, and it is an honour to see what they do for their county and the way they represent Dublin. It has also been a privilege to be involved with the Dublin development squads for the past number of years. I would like to thank all the mentors and coaches for their efforts. Thanks also to the players who inspire me in every session by wanting to be the best that they can be – both on and off the field.

Bringing My Story To Book

Iain MacGregor and all of his team at Simon & Schuster UK helped me so much. Iain has been working with me a long time on this project and he has always been encouraging and patient. Thanks, too, to Ray McManus of Sportsfile for his cover image and pictures, which can be seen inside.

I would also like to thank Damian for all his help. Your commitment, positivity and energy have been above and beyond the call of duty. The landscape of sports journalism is changing and I can only commend your integrity and wish you and your family the best for the future.

Finally, I am so thankful to see how passionate and proud we are of sport in this country.

Sport is a game of opinions and, in Ireland, it assumes a high and lofty status. We should be very proud of our make-up and I love it when we are the underdog in international sporting competitions, always fighting above our weight. That underdog spirit is something I've always identified with.

I am so appreciative of all those who supported me during my career. I can go to any part of this island and have a conversation about sport, or the GAA, and I am also very thankful for that. I have been privileged in life so far and I hope that I will receive similar support in the future in whatever lies ahead.

Jason Sherlock, September 2017